a memoir

CELEBRATING THE COYOTE

BARBARA WATERS

a memoir

CELEBRATING THE COYOTE

DIVINA
DENVER

Acknowledgments are due and are gratefully made to the following:
Excerpts from *Women Who Run With the Wolves* by Clarissa Pinkola Estés, Ph.D., Copyright ©
1992, 1995. All rights including but not limited to performance, derivative, adaptation, musical,
audio and recording, illustrative, theatrical, film, pictorial, reprint and electronic are reserved.
Used by kind permission of the author, Dr. Estés, and Ballantine Books, a division of Random
House, Inc., Excerpt from "The Creative Fire," © by Clarissa Pinkola Estés, Ph.D., 1994.
(*Magical Blend*, Issue 43, July 1994.) Used by kind permission of Dr. Estés.
Jenna Paulden, for the poem "Sacred Oak."
Imogene L. Bolls, for the poem "The Walk to the Upper Pasture."
Ann E. Merrill, for her poem about a wounded horse in the pasture.
Oclides Tenorio, for the poem "Memories of our Father Jose Maria Quintana."
William Farr, for excerpts from his letter to Barbara Waters, June 1995.
Ronald L. Kampfe, for an adapted portion of the fifth setting in "On Being Open: Seven
Settings" about Frank Waters.
Diana Huntress, for the poem "She Is a Very Together Person."
Arleene M. Arnell, for the content of the correspondence written by her to Barbara and Frank
Waters about a happening in their home on 8/9/90.

Printed and bound in the United States of America

1   2   3   4   5   6   7   8   9   10

Library of Congress Cataloging-in-Publication Data
Waters, Barbara, 1929–
Celebrating the coyote / Barbara Waters.
p.   cm.
Includes bibliographical references.
ISBN 0-9659521-5-0 (hc)
0-9659521-4-2 (pb)
1. Grief.   2. Bereavement—Psychological aspects.   3. Loss
(Psychology)   4. Husbands—Death—Psychological aspects.   5. Waters,
Frank, 1902–   .   I. Title.
BF575.G7W37   1999
155.9'37—dc21   99-12655
                                                      CIP

Celebrating the Coyote cover design by Laurie Dolphin.
Cover photography by Robert Miller.
Photo on back flap by Lorraine Lener Ciancio.
The text was set in Janson by Chris Davis, Mulberry Tree Enterprises.

To our Oneness
—and our Otherness

Contents

Foreword

There are seasons in this book, precious and difficult as winter in the high cold country of northern New Mexico. In the springtime a late and sudden vitality rises while snow remains heavy in the mountains above the irrigated valleys. Summer is complicated by water wars, the brutal death of new lambs, an abrupt and wonderful fecundity. The lingering autumns can be too much of an ache to bear. Always the natural world and its metaphors abide.

Barbara Waters' *Celebrating the Coyote* is about grieving and the great natural seasons of loving and being together. It commemorates the wisdom and patience required to heal after a great loss on earth. The memoir begins on the day Barbara's husband, Frank, died in June of 1995. Early pages are rife with tears and the sorrow of parting with a beloved and famous man. Then she moves back and forth through time, building the history of their delightful and complicated relationship. Included is a straightforward memoir of life in Arroyo Seco, her adopted hometown north of Taos. Barbara and Frank also took grand trips through Mexico and Latin America, but the most wonderful journey occurred in their passionate interactions with each other.

Along the way we encounter spirits, ghosts, and witches, hexed
waterfalls, and much "ignorant superstition." Some of the more re-
splendent figures in Taos mythology come alive again, most no-
tably Dorothy Brett, Frieda Lawrence, and Mabel Dodge Luhan.
At the center is Frank Waters as Barbara perceived him, loved and
admired him, and cared for him on an equal footing that she fought
hard to establish and maintain. Living with Frank wasn't easy, but
they shaped a marvelous adventure together.

Barbara speaks forcefully of the energy involved in healing, and
for me her most simple observations contain her deepest insights
about how to get on with survival: honor wood; never harm a rattlesnake; respect the mountains; watch trout in a stream; love the
trees.

But this writer is a complex and introspective soul, and her
courageous story proceeds along many different levels at once.
Humorous and homey one moment, she will extol Jung and Joseph
Campbell the next. In the same breath we are likely to meet Crazy
Horse and Fools Crow and a twelfth-century nun, Hildegard of
Bingen, credited with being one of our planet's first great ecolo-
gists. Every page is erudite, intelligent, humming with information
and folklore. When Barbara's son miraculously survives a massacre
in Vietnam, there is a sense of awe and magic. A woman is speaking her heart, her fascinating mind, and also her richly imaginative
spirit.

Thank goodness there's plenty of titillating gossip for all us literary voyeurs and budding Frank Waters scholars. And enough
funky stories to jolt the chronicle back to a down-home flavor that
perfectly balances its sojourns in more ethereal realms. Frank
comes alive as a great artist and also a fallible human being his wife
called "Dr. No." In one bubbling chapter, two of Frank's wives and
a girlfriend sit down to lunch together and take off the emperor's
clothes. Yet always there's a veneration for the vagaries and accomplishments of the creative life.

The narrative carries us from Machu Picchu to Mt. Fuji to
beauty parlor *mitote* and an automobile engine fire that almost de-

stroyed an original Fechin painting of Frank. Barbara and her spouse are witty, cantankerous, playful, industrious, and imbued with fabulous curiosity. Although Frank was a magnificent dancer he couldn't drive a car worth a damn. At regular intervals Barbara's observations soar into heady intellectual realms, then bump to earth with neighborly squabbles over stolen water, murdered puppies, male chauvinism, and a mythical bottle of Scotch poured over her noted husband's head.

This is a poetic, informed, and spellbinding elegy for a man and a marriage, and for the wondrous complexity of all life. It is brimming over with brightly hued and important details. Barbara exults in panorama, describing not only the stimulating path that she and Frank followed arm-in-arm, but also how the universe moves through us all.

Her journey through grief and the past is full of insight and compassion. "To encounter death," writes Barbara, "is to wake up, to live more inwardly, to live more keenly." That's what this courageous book is all about, and it should be read with joy and gratitude for generations.

—*John Nichols*
Taos, September 18, 1998

1
Shards

The ambulance swerves, stops. A paramedic eases down from the passenger seat, walks back. He worked hardest. Felt worst when it all fell apart. "You can't drive this fast, ma'am," he says wearily. "You have to slow down. You can't follow us."

CPR makes your thighs stiff. Mine have begun to ache already. I know how his must feel. Or doesn't he notice his thighs? It seems unnatural to notice one's thighs right now. Almost obscene.

The emergency room nurse opens her arms and whispers, "In your heart, you knew already."

They must have told her I had been crying. Part of the time. The rest of the time I'd urged him to come back. A year ago he did. This time he squeezed my hand. Once. Before the line went dead. And straight.

To this day her six words make me cry. And her hug. When did hospitals start getting kind? Last July in the old hospital near here, I had to scrub Frank's floor myself. They had World War II furniture and hand-cranked beds like Model-T Fords and electric table fans as air conditioning. And a straggly string mop without a wringer. No one had answered his ring. So he'd thrown his tray full of food on the floor, deliberately. He had spirit, you know. And charisma. Nobody ever got mad at him.

I'll hate this new emergency room for the rest of my life. Windows trimmed in Taos Blue. Like Taos Pueblo doors. Stands for good luck, they say. Wards off evil. Ha. Emergency rooms should have black window trim and black windows and black doors and black shrouds around the beds, where you say good-bye. Alone.

During this first sleepless night I sort and put away high mounds of clothing brought from Tucson just yesterday. Did these cloth mountains frighten you when you lay on the floor below them? All alone. Never mind; don't think. Work. Everything looks beautiful again for your lingering spirit. Stay! Please. Smell the piñon perfume from last winter's fires? "Piñon is the best. Always buy piñon wood," you said.

When Crazy Horse was murdered, in his final moments he made his friend Touch-the-Clouds understand he wanted to be taken off a bed and placed on the floor, close to the earth. Your way.

Acute grief soon numbs the outside. Shattered inside, shattered to infinitely small, stabbing shards. Shattered beyond repair. But now most things are possible. Sleeping. Coping with relatives and friends and unending phone calls. No one sends food. Odd. One hears about food pouring in at times like this. Why? Who feels like eating? Cards and calls are enough. People care. A lot.

Hug the boys, so handsome and tall: six foot six and six foot eight. Can tall men over forty still be called boys? Terry carves Frank's initials somewhere up in the mountains. Bill remains silent, unnaturally silent, silenced by the unexpected beauty of northern New Mexico, perhaps. They lay down planks when Salomé's ditch overflows down our path to the oak tree, and they lean on the neighbor who shoots Trickster in the stomach the morning of Frank's service. "Your dog dies if my mother's dog dies!" Terry says. Luckily she lives. We don't need a civil war on our hands right now.

Mentally numb, physically cold—chilled to the bone. They put him in a freezer for three days. Not exactly a conversation piece. Visitors wonder how anyone can be so cold in June; no sense telling them how come. Sharing beyond limiting boundaries of time and place. Sharing many lifetimes. That's what soul mates do. On his memorial card I write that we are soul mates. One acquaintance says with caustic emphasis, "I'm not sure I understand exactly what *soul mates* are."

Once while sitting in our Tucson backyard before enlarging it and cutting back greasewood tall as trees, Frank said, "I feel like we've sat together before in a jungle clearing like this, in another lifetime. Probably in Mexico."

"Yes," I said. "Tall red poinsettia trees ran wild."

If you must have a definition, that's what soul mates are.

Arrange his memorial service in the Sacred Aspen Grove and in the pasture at his favorite oak tree, an upbeat Celebration of His Life, like Craig Vincent's "fiesta," where his widow sang and played her guitar. Iron the simple black dress trimmed with beige seeds worn three years ago at brunch with Wallgrens on Easter Sunday. Who wears black on the Day of Resurrection? Maybe dangling earrings will make it look more festive. Hayfoot. Strawfoot. One foot after the other through this morass.

Order food for a hundred. Arrange for ten persons to speak. Write my tribute, titled "His Way." Pick up his ashes. Pay. Numbed *anguish.* Can there be such a contradiction in terms? It tears at my heart and stomach, doubles me over, rocks me back and forth. Sets me howling like a coyote, howling. Howling for my mate. Howling to Mother Moon for help. Howling through the universe.

Gone. He is gone. He is *gone.*

Prepare his ceremonial altar. Indians have ceremonial altars in their kivas. Frank was part Cheyenne. They don't have kivas. Taos Indians and Hopis do. On Mabel Luhan's table Frank's faithful 1956 Olivetti typewriter, his writing hand in bronze and life-sized bronze bust sculpted by Mark Rossi, a photograph of the 1966 Ford Galaxie he called an "extension" of himself, his graduation Bible from his mother, a healing feather and gourd rattle from our Indian friend Joseph Enos. We took this feather and rattle to the hospital with us whenever Frank had pneumonia. Dr. Farr laughed. Now he has sent a jungle of flowers. Someday he'll believe. Flowers in front. Dawavendewa's kachina death painting behind, next to

Marcia Gaiter's renewal snowflake painting. Frank's favorite Indian bowl for his ashes. All of us scatter them.

When Jongewards lived here in the winter, they used this treasure as a salad bowl. They weren't supposed to. The chip they put in it angered Frank. But he seldom rocked the boat by expressing his negative feelings aloud to others. They are shocked about using a salad bowl for his ashes. Some ashes will be buried in a blue tea tin under his monument boulder. Double sacrilege. At least all of his ashes are here. D. H. Lawrence's ashes bounced around the world between France and New Mexico for some time before they finally came to rest in a crypt on Lobo Mountain not far from us. If indeed they are the writer's. Some locals have their doubts.

Blue sky, perfectly blue. Brilliant red Indian blankets. Wind speaking through the trees as it did that day in 1969 when first I stood on the bars of the locked silver gate in front. Frank was attending his sister's funeral in Sedona. Now it is his turn. Full circle.

"Someday this place will be yours to preserve," the wind-tossed trees whispered way back then. "You will be its guardian."

Frank thought I was "fey," or otherworldly. He liked the word "fey," and he liked fey women. He said his sister, Naomi, was fey too: "a fey soul with intuitive promptings." Maria, his enduring protagonist in *People of the Valley*, is fey. Fey people understand what the wind is saying. They pay attention. One day I shall ride away on the wind. Maybe today.

Up again, Old Heart! Courage and courage; we will win in the end. Emerson, maybe. Something like that. He's right. My heart feels old. He means, *Get with it, Barbara.* You read next.

Guillermo Rosete's Aztec conch shell echoes through the mountains. Repeatedly it trumpets, "Behold. He is coming. Make way!"

His Way

His position in death could not have been more fitting. He did it his way. As always. Not Storm's, who wrote *Seven Arrows.* On

Friday, May 12, 1995, Wolf Storm presented Frank with a painting from Storm's recent visit to Hopiland—a kachina stepping through the Doorway of Death. Surprisingly, despite all his reading of Eastern philosophy Frank had grown fearful of death.

Storm said to Frank, "The time is near. Very near. You must prepare. This will help you to prepare."

"Now wait a minute," I interrupted. "This time has to wait until after June 15, when we go to the premiere of the opera made from *The Woman at Otowi Crossing*."

"Yes, we definitely are going to St. Louis for that," Frank insisted. "We already have reservations."

Storm shook his head. "Well, we'll see," he said. He had to smile. We were so confident.

"You must think hard about *where* you want to spend your next lifetime.

"Which country, specifically. And who you want to be. You must decide now. And think of it many, many times," Storm instructed Frank. "Maybe it will be in China."

"No," I said. "Frank thinks he's done China already."

"Yes. I've done China before," Frank said. "I've lived there in a previous lifetime."

In our small Tucson home, the kachina painting looked dark and foreboding.

"If I had to stare at something repeatedly for such a purpose, I'd take Marcia Gaiter's snowflake painting any day over this," I said after Storm left.

"Me too," Frank said. "Storm's is depressing. I don't like it at all. Let's forget about all this business. Stick that thing in a closet somewhere out of sight."

When Frank died on June 3 in the kiva bedroom he had built with the help of Frank Samora, in the Taos house he loved above all others, on a table at his head lay a *Webster's Unabridged Dictionary*, like a headstone. Above it was a shelf full of books he himself had written. Over these on the wall hung a photo of Ramana Maharshi, whose books on Eastern religion he esteemed, and a photo of himself, the Eternal Youth, taken at Lake Chapala when Frank met poet Witter Bynner in 1933.

To Frank's right rose the bed Mabel Dodge Luhan had given him from her Italian villa. To his left stretched his most precious shelves of research books, with which he would never part. Above these his best kachinas circled the upper shelf next to a Hopi gourd rattle. Kachinas danced in a painting on the wall above the cottonwood spirits. Spiritual peyote fans flanked the painting. From the beamed ceiling above Frank's feet hung a Cheyenne war shield, his heritage.

You see, as always Frank slipped through the Doorway in his own unique fashion. Head toward the East. Face down to the Earth, of course.

2
Ocotillo Odyssey

Taos seems the place to stay this first winter after Frank's death, the place where his spirit will remain closest. Yet during a four-week stay in November at our Tucson home, I find it much with me here too.

He loved this house from the start. We bought it the summer of 1977 before he came down from Taos in September.

"It's small," I told him over the phone. "But it's on four acres in the foothills of the Tucson Mountains. It is peaceful, and it has big trees and lots of birds. Besides, it's all we can afford. If we don't buy now, prices will soon be out of our reach."

As with most major decisions, Frank made up his mind at once. He was game if I was. After he had driven haltingly up the driveway a few months later, he exclaimed with beaming face, "It's a real *house*. Made of *brick*. Why, I expected to find a tin-roofed shanty!"

The part of our Tucson home that delighted him most, he was frequently to say, was its *thermostat*. Compared to the fireplaces and butane wall heaters in our Taos house, it seemed almost magical to have a central heating system at his command with the flick of a wrist.

Frank was also partial to his warped writing table built by some of my English students from Canyon del Oro High School in their workshop class. We decided a ley line extended from Wasson Peak, high point of the Tucson Mountains in front of us, straight through his large table in our living room to the Catalina Mountains, behind us and highest of the five ranges surrounding Tucson. This power helped to ignite his book *Mountain Dialogues* in particular, I am convinced.

One late December we were married in the living room before a fireplace banked with brilliant poinsettias we'd bought in south Tucson on 17th Street. Every anniversary Frank remembered buying those poinsettias. I remembered his pleased, tipsy grin in our wedding photo, snapped by Jane Wallgren. It was a surprise party, but she had come prepared.

Frank's mathematician friend Jack Ryan claims that the Garden of Eden lies a few hundred feet directly under our Tucson house. He says the "Big Bump" flipped our planet and moved the Garden opposite from where it grew in biblical times. Frank thought Jack's work on the Mayan Calendar was sound. Who knows about his Eden? It seemed close to us at both homes.

Esther, a devoted part-time caregiver in Tucson, said to Frank at the end of May 1995, "Now, do your exercises so you'll be strong for the trip home. You want to get back to Taos, don't you?"

Frank surprised us by snapping, "No!"

True, he had taken to calling her "the General." It may have had something to do with that. Or it could have been his automatic inclination to say "no" until he'd finally get tired of no-ing and decided to say yes. The differences in altitude and climate were also formidable challenges to one with his lung problems.

Perhaps Frank never wholly left Tucson, for he died the day after we returned to Taos in June. My first days back in November are filled with sounds of the Arizona silence he loved. It seems as if he is emphasizing them to remind me.

At night from two and a half miles away drifts his favorite, the sound of freight-train whistles wailing their harmonica blues. Frank had been born very near the sooty side of the tracks in Colorado Springs; to him this sound was always both lyric and lullaby.

As a young man his lifetime ambition was to become a ticket seller at the local railway station. There he sold newspapers and acquired his "itchy foot" to travel like those cosmopolitan customers with whom he brushed fingertips. He often mentioned the time he had listened to the famous Jack Dempsey–Jess Willard fight over a loudspeaker there in 1919 and the red-letter day he glimpsed the great man himself, the "Manassa Mauler," arriving on a train. This experience may have influenced Frank to take up boxing and to work out on a punching bag in his attic bedroom.

Rain begins tapping lightly on our roof, as if Frank is saying, "A small job well done, Barbara, getting yourself and the three dogs down to Tucson from Taos in ten hours."

"Well, I appreciate the acknowledgment. But I've been doing a lot of *big* jobs too in Taos these past five months."

The rain beats down furiously. It continues all night and the next morning, Tucson's first hard rain in a month. "A big job well done!"

After Frank's speech at Colorado College's Tutt Library in 1985, a torrential rain accompanied us back to the old mansion on Cascade Avenue where we were staying.

"This means a job well done!" Frank said with a pleased smile. "The same thing happened at my sister's funeral. A big rain on an important occasion means a job well done." His belief gave me some small consolation when buckets of rain poured down upon us during our elaborate outdoor party celebrating Frank's ninetieth birthday in 1992.

Another of his favorite sounds, still much with me in Tucson, is the burbling of Gambel's quail as their black plumed topknots quiver in anticipation of our morning and evening feedings of wild-bird seed strewn on two circular platforms and across the ground. A hundred of them flurry amidst doves, finches, and red-eyed cowbirds while cardinals dart from camouflaging creosote bushes to snatch at their own special sunflower seeds; and witch-beaked thrashers sing siren songs to scolding, redheaded Gila woodpeckers. Then the sudden shriek of a Harris' hawk sends all of them

9

scurrying in an uproar while His Majesty sinks to a solitary bath in the coyote pool outside our worn picket fence. Unperturbed, bees cluster in humming holiday wreaths about a nearby birdbath.

In the evening at the coyote pool, Frank's closest friends howl up their laments for him, including their own version of the "Traveling Song" that Tony Reyna sang at Frank's final ceremony. Frank truly was one of them, an honorary member of the Hopi Coyote Clan.

A year ago someone dumped a half-coyote dog near our house. We named her Trickster, and she lives up to her name every day of her life. Parting with her would be like parting with another fragment of Frank.

"Maybe she came to help Frank with his transition," a friend suggests.

"Maybe she came to help *me* with his transition," I think to myself.

Into the darkness of the night a peacock shrieks like a demented woman, "Help me. Help me." Yes, help me! You will, I know. In a different voice. It's the little things one must listen to and watch for, not the old resonant voice, certainly not a channeled voice. One must listen for the voice of the peacock, the eagle, lizard, and rattlesnake. Some say Quetzalcoatl was consumed by a divine fire upon sacred Orizaba Peak, his spirit mounting through the universe as a peacock. The peacock is a symbol of totality, immortality, and the incorruptible soul. The eyes in its feathers symbolize stars, openings in the firmament through which the departed beam through to us.

Six months from now on my second trip to Tucson alone I will find a gorgeous peacock feather at the godforsaken desert rest stop outside Lordsburg where we always stopped. Frank used to say, "I'm proud as a peacock of you!" I hear him. His eye is on this sparrow.

When the chimney sweep arrives shortly before my return to Taos for the winter, he says, "It sure is quiet here. Is it dangerous?"

I smile. He's old enough to know that *living* is dangerous. It can break your heart. If you let it.

Listening to the soft, knowing words of the wind chimes Ann Merrill gave us, I realize that somehow, someday, there will be a Frank Waters Foundation North and South, like Frank Lloyd Wright's Taliesin East and West. Our Tucson home will retain a part of Frank forever, and of me. And in his name, just as they already do on our Taos property, creative persons will share the spirit of this place for short periods of time as they write, paint, or compose.

We must never forget to water the tall ocotillo out in front, though. Frank said when it went, he would go. It is still alive.

3
Cows

Nature has always been my salvation. I am counting on its healing balm again.

Back in Illinois it was really Gerry's Woods and its inhabitants that raised me. The cows in Gerry's Woods were our closest friends, severest critics, and favorite enemies. At age twelve Frances Gerry and I weren't all that discriminating. Because these brown creatures with scratchy ears and satiny noses were our pals, we crowned them with perfumed daisies and waded gingerly through the slimy ooze of their shit as we navigated the oak-shaded stream shared by all us woodland denizens. Bloodsuckers between our toes we did not so casually tolerate, though they were a given too.

Four-leggeds swished their tails and shook their udders in maternal disapproval while we puffed on jaunty cigarettes until we turned green, at which wretched sight our audience mooed with unseemly laughter that stayed with me for life.

Before we presented our oratory at school, these stern, fly-speckled judges graded us on our delivery of Lincoln's "Gettysburg Address" and FDR's famous "We Have Nothing to Fear but FEAR Itself!" Three moos and several nods of approval was the best I ever got. But Frances won five moos, with snorts and vigorous tail swishings, for Hamlet's "To Be or Not to Be." The radical bovines stampeded when we declaimed the Pledge of Allegiance in unison.

Mock bullfighting they repeatedly shrugged off with bored twitchings of their ears instead of courageously fighting us Hemingway heroines *mano a mano*. Willow switches flicked across their plump rumps set their digestive bakeries into high gear, producing batch after batch of pungent cowpies shaded apple green. Still, the placid Buddhas remained generally huggable.

Today the site of Gerry's Woods is occupied by a sterile housing development. Only the ghosts of our beloved behemoths haunt the decimated land. But they, along with Gerry's Woods, remain a crucial part of who I am.

4
Waves

The first Christmas after the death of a loved one is hardly a celebration. On top of that, spending it in southern California is like taking a bath in tepid smog water. It is triply difficult if you're staying with a close relative who fears displays of emotion.

Like a petulant child, my eighty-six-year-old mother tells Eira, her caregiver, "I don't *want* to take Barbara to the ocean with us. She'll start crying."

After Eira and my mother return from Newport Beach, twenty minutes away, my sister Joan and I go there together for a few hours. Later on I visit the ocean either alone or with Trickster. Had Mom shared her unfounded fear with me, I could have reassured her that for me the ocean is not a place for tears. It is a place to regain perspective. To see the bigger picture. To connect with a higher spirit, as well as with those spirits that have gone before.

It is a place to bond with the same spirit energy that can be experienced in contact with most free-flowing water, mountains, trees, the Grand Canyon, clouds, new snow, stars, and the moon. Frank drew his spirit energy from the sun. Facing east each morning in a reciprocal ritual, he greeted the sun with outstretched hands containing his own breath energy. Then slowly he drew sun energy to his chest with hands cupped protectively around his gift, which he brushed at last against his heart and flicked down his body with an outward half turn of the wrists.

In an article about Peruvian mysticism in the Andes, Joan Wilcox and Elizabeth Jenkins note, "The giving of one's breath is a gesture of reciprocity, asking the nature spirits for their help and guidance and offering the energy of our prayers in exchange."

Eira, who has a strong Christian bent, later admits why she and Mom went to the ocean without me. I explain, "The ocean is my salvation, Eira. For me it's the nearest thing to God. It is what you would call God in all His magnificence. It certainly doesn't make me cry."

Maybe I have been drawn to California to go through a Christian stage of grieving too, I think with a start of surprise. We were raised rather socially in a Congregational church. I'd forgotten how deeply immersed my mother, Joan, and Eira have become in religion.

In *Women Who Run with the Wolves*, Clarissa Pinkola Estés has much to say about tears. They "make the icy heart melt." They call "the spirits to one's side." "Tears are part of the mending of rips in the psyche where energy has leaked and leaked away. . . . I am amazed how little women cry nowadays, and then apologetically. . . . Crying is good, it is right . . . it enables the process to continue instead of collapsing. . . . Some women marvel at all the water their bodies can produce when they weep. It will not last forever, only till the soul is done with its wise expression."

In the course of my grieving, I have cried bucketfuls of therapeutic tears. Tears in public embarrass neither myself nor those who understand this crucial aspect of grief. Usually my tears come in private, though, since they help me more than my companions. I cried for three hundred miles while returning to Tucson the first time without Frank, an odyssey with a hundred adventures built in during our eighteen years of driving back and forth together. It didn't seem possible that one human being could hold three hundred miles of tears. Fortunately, the next three hundred miles of unrelieved driving rendered me comatose, or I might have burst like an overfilled water balloon.

All these Damn Firsts make me cry. Except for viewing the ocean and the Grand Canyon. First Christmas. First birthdays. First trip alone. First shaggy eyebrows like Frank's. First snow without him. First picnic. First setting for one at "our table" in our favorite restaurant. First luncheon with Frank's niece, Susie Arnell, in Del Mar during this visit. We stayed with her twice in the '90s. Frank loved it here. The infinite number of Firsts is always surprising, sometimes overwhelming. Seconds are not nearly so wearing. Except for the sound of ambulances.

My mother lives with Joan, who is involved in an intense two-year Bible study at a Reformed church in Orange County. Over the holidays Joan lets me read her ten-page paper, "God's Covenant of Grace with Abraham, the Golden Thread That Runs Through the Old Testament." At the ocean it becomes clear to me that our Covenant of Grace is actually the great partnership that a higher spirit extends to each of us. Somewhat like a good marriage, this partnership makes us spiritually one. An aspect of our oneness is that bond with spirit energy derived from nature, among other places. Frank's sun ritual is a perfect example of both partnership and oneness related to energy.

"When I conducted a devotional service at the Crystal Cathedral last week, it wasn't me at all," Joan says. "It was God coming through me. All creativity is God coming through us."

"It is not just Him coming through you," I reply. "Most often it is His fire igniting in you what you have made ready to be ignited. This includes your willingness to stand on the firing line and *do it*, no matter how badly your knees shake. For us mere mortals, this working together is the great gift of partnership."

Splashing barefoot through the grasping tide, I consider exceptions such as Wolfgang Mozart, a child prodigy who can't really be understood or explained. As Goethe wrote, "A phenomenon like

16

that of Mozart remains an inexplicable thing." Such geniuses are open to this partnership and oneness without much preparation, if any. They are ready sooner than other people, perhaps due to the uninterrupted flow of two consecutive lifetimes at the same level. Generally, we have to work at it longer.

Frank, who too was touched with genius, spent years preparing for his role in this partnership. His was not the way of academe. First, during his growing-up years in Colorado Springs he read every book he could get his hands on, including much of his grand-father's esoteric library, which opened Frank's mind early to a variety of spiritual and metaphysical possibilities. While he was still a little boy, his father—who died when Frank was twelve—inscribed to him a small notebook that I still have. In it Frank listed titles of a hundred or so of the first books he read. Susie has kept a few of his favorites from those early years.

Next, as a young man he quit college to work, travel, and live in Wyoming, California, and Mexico. On these travels he absorbed experiences, observations, and knowledge, and he kept his language free of deadly professor-ese.

His grade school friend Charles Hathaway once asked him, "How do you write a book?"

Frank said, "Charles, first you have to have something to write about."

Frank hadn't made himself fully ready to become a great writer when words began pouring through him. They started while he was living in El Centro, California, in a desert shack with canvas flaps for windows. This first torrent of words was basically one big description of the stunning desert landscapes that had swept the Colorado mountain man off his feet at first sight.

To create a book from these words, he later said, he first had to visit a library and find out what size paragraphs were supposed to be. He never did learn what adjectives and adverbs and all that nonsense were about, he claimed. But somehow he yanked the words around right as his next step in the partnership. Finally, he threw in some human characters and wove them through a slender plot. The result was his first novel, titled *Fever Pitch*, also called *Lizard Woman*, published in 1930 by Horace Liveright.

Frank loved the Pacific Ocean beaches too. It is another way we stay connected. On his days off in the mid-1920s when he was living in southern California, then a pristine land of milk and honey, he would take a Red Car trolley from Los Angeles to one of these same beaches, most often Santa Monica Beach, and sun or wrestle in the sand with friends. When he gave a talk at a Santa Monica bookstore in 1990, he was shocked to learn that Santa Monica Beach has a problem with street people and can be a dangerous place nowadays.

A sun worshiper, Frank was never overly keen about actually being in water itself or on a boat. Surprisingly, he wrote in a *South Dakota Review* article about Los Angeles, "On my first payday I went to Santa Monica and for the first time saw the Pacific Ocean. It looked quite unimpressive as I stood on the beach."

Frank's deep tan from sunning on these beaches helped to make him look handsomer than most movie stars of the day. A few years later Spud Johnson was to call him "the Gary Cooper of Taos." Yet Frank never set much store in his looks or thought of films as his path, with the exception of short script-writing stints for C. V. Whitney Pictures in the '50s. In late life he had some vicious bouts with skin cancer as a result of all those Sundays at the beach. Some gift from the sea.

Anne Morrow Lindbergh's classic *Gift from the Sea* invariably comes to my mind at the ocean, and with each visit a search begins for the special treasure cast up on its silvered beaches just for me. This Christmas I hunt for a finely etched circular sand dollar. The young couple ahead of me is gifted with one. Instead, I receive a perfectly ridged pink seashell, along with the awareness that we do not choose our gift. It chooses us. Shells are related to the moon, fertility, and water. To Andean descendants of the Incas, the half shell is the divine feminine.

Greatest of all gifts from the sea is the ability to see.

Soon after my untimely birth in Oak Park, Illinois, my mother "got sick," she says, and sent me to her wealthy parents' home in nearby LaGrange to stay for a time. Thirteen months later Joan was born. During the height of the Great Depression in the mid-1930s, three brothers and another sister came along. One brother died. The rest were sent to an orphanage after Dad had a nervous breakdown half a dozen years later. My maternal grandmother insisted on raising me, along with Joan, until my marriage. I have always felt a special fondness for this grandmother, who from my birth gave me a mother's uncritical love, appreciation, comfort, understanding, and forgiveness.

California mirrored my grandmother's inner beauty and my grandfather's imperturbable tranquillity when my two boys and I first began traveling out from Illinois in 1960 on Santa Fe's Super Chief to visit them and my parents in Fullerton, California, where they had moved. One train menu I've saved featured on its cover a fascinating print of a peculiar place named Taos Indian Pueblo. It looked so strange and so foreign to a Midwesterner that it might have been from another continent, or another planet. It captured my unconscious immediately and forever. Eight years later, to my amazement, I found myself living five miles from this marvel and teaching English to its young people.

For forty years, oddly enough, a romanticized oil painting of Taos Pueblo had hung unnoticed and unrecognized in my grandparents' living room. It was painted by our friend Otis Bunker, from whom they had bought some Indian rugs, a couple of which I now own. In 1908, the year before Mom was born, my grandmother first rode the Santa Fe herself to visit her father, who lived and worked at the Mt. Wilson Observatory above Pasadena, California. She took my mother for a visit there in 1914 and periodically thereafter. Their train stopped in Albuquerque, New Mexico, where they ate at the famous mission-style Alvarado Hotel, pride of the Fred Harvey chain. Then they visited the Indian museum, workshop, and curio shop made memorable in

1902 by Mary Colter's unusual Indian decor. In addition, Mom remembers Indians selling merchandise beside the railroad tracks.

In *Mary Colter: Builder upon the Red Earth* is a photograph of a slender young woman looking at crafts displayed outdoors at the Albuquerque station. Her hair is done up in a Gibson Girl hairdo, and she wears a long white dress. Gibson Girls have a tendency to look alike in old photos, yet I like to think this is my grandmother. It resembles other photographs of her. Later she also traveled throughout the Southwest with the Bunkers, I learned after her death. It was as if my genes absorbed an affinity for this region.

Of all her children, my mother has bonded closely only with Joan. As a first grader, after a visit to Joan's kindergarten class I would wonder, "Last year why didn't Mom send me to that magic place where my little sister goes?" And much later, "Why does Mom make a handmade quilt for Joan and not for me?"

After obtaining a psychotherapy degree, I understood at last that much of our conflict derived from my mother and me being typical firstborns. Unconsciously, we locked horns over our reflected, innate characteristics: independent, stubborn, critical, perfectionists. Mom bonded more comfortably with my sister's secondborn characteristics: not so perfect, not so rigid, more uncertain, less interested in being best.

Joan and I bonded because she was my baby sister and I her big sister, and perhaps because of a meshing of our characteristics—similar to Joan's with my mother's. We played and suffered together. We remain connected, probably because I consider Joan the closest thing to a saint walking through my life today. My brothers and younger sister agree.

In retrospect, I see my Window-Jumping Incident at age four and a half as one of the early blueprints of the relationship between Joan, my mother, and me for much of our lives. While playing "house," Joan and I had accidentally locked ourselves inside a deserted second-floor apartment next door to ours in LaGrange. After we discovered our predicament, Joan panicked and began crying.

"Don't cry, Dodie," I comforted her, patting her short, silky ringlets and using the nickname I'd given her at birth. "I'll jump out the window and save us. Don't *worry*."

As she sobbed harder, I somehow raised the dining-room window and crawled up on the sill. It was a long, long way down. And a wicked-looking windowbox jutted out from the first-floor apartment.

Altering my plan a bit, I stood up in the window space and began yelling, "Help! Somebody catch me. My sister needs help! Help!"

Neighbors quickly came running, along with our mother.

"Don't you dare jump, Young Lady," she said. "I'll get the janitor's key and let you out. You *wait*."

Joan's lamentations reached a new crescendo. I was sniffling myself by this time.

"I'm jumping. We need help right now."

"You jump and you'll get the spanking of your life with my hairbrush and go to bed without dinner. Do . . . you . . . hear . . . *me*, Young Lady?"

I always hated being called "Young Lady." I jumped, ripping my side on the windowbox.

She caught me. Sure enough, I got the spanking of my life. And crackers for dinner in *Joan's baby bed with side slats*, the supreme punishment for a grown-up heroine. It remained the unkindest cut of all, not my wounded side. After eating a regular dinner, Joan commiserated with me.

Forty years later, I finally cured myself of acrophobia.

My face looks open but without its customary smile in a formal photograph taken of us two sisters about this time. We sit close together on our grandmother's outdoor bench, two curly-haired blondes, shy little Joannie wearing a jumper suit and sandals, myself in overalls and practical oxfords with hair flying and the same bangs as now.

Since then Joan has grown far from "Dodie." We both have grown. Yet I sometimes catch myself about to threaten Crystal, our balky sheltie, "You come in here this instant and get your muddy paws washed. Do . . . you . . . hear . . . *me*, Young Lady?"

Pounding ashore, waves foam between my toes, then vibrate through my soul. The stray thought of Mom's quilt-making transcends to thoughts of the soul quilt each of us on earth is piecing together patch by patch.

My quilt is far different from my mother's. They are not to be compared; each is uniquely perfect.

I am a bit of stitchery here and there in my mother's quilt; Joan is a bright recurring motif. Mom is a thread stitching together many of my patches, sometimes dark, sometimes golden with hope. This is right and good. Her quilt is OK. My quilt is OK. Your quilt is OK. Although we may interweave, what matters most is piecing together the whole of one's own pattern.

If I'd had to raise my two sons during the Depression, how different my patches would be, how different my entire quilt! I feel eternally grateful for the pattern that is mine alone. "It has ramifications and interweavings that reach out through all the persons I meet and all the events that come to me, and the best way to put myself in harmony with the Divine Plan within myself is to accept with radiant acquiescence all the individuals and events that are drawn to me, seeing in them perfect instruments for the perfect unfoldment of my perfect Plan."

It amazed me how people volunteered what I needed when I needed it, particularly as work began on my next challenging quilt patch—without Frank beside me. Like him, I tend to shy away from words as Christianized as "God" and "Divine," favoring more abstract terms with the same essence, such as "Higher Spirit," "Higher Power," or "the Light." Nevertheless, it resonated with my beliefs and needs in this Christian phase of grief recovery when Mary Saler, an Episcopalian and a close friend, sent me a tract titled "The Divine Plan" by Glenn Clark.

Besides the preceding quotation, I was drawn to these four concepts, in which Clark's plan is another metaphor for my "quilt."

1. When we are attuned to ourselves and what is ours within, we're free from greed. When we measure ourselves against each other, or compare, we cut ourselves off from receiving our due.

2. Those we need to complete ourselves have been selected. We find them, or they find us, through "proximity, mutual attraction, or need."

3. Negative happenings are not part of the designated Plan. They are caused by failure to harmonize with the Divine Plan. Inner peace results from harmony with the Plan and leads to creative activities that unfold our individual Plan, or to patience that helps others to begin this unfolding for us.

4. Closed doors point to bigger and better open doors ahead. Blindness or deafness within us causes failure to see ahead and walls us from God. But He uses our failure to help guide and inspire us so that we may overcome defeat and find these larger, planned doors.

Unused to receiving such pamphlets, I was surprised to tune into another helpful tract given me by Joan and written by Rev. Robert Schuller. He refers to getting "through the valley"—a Slough of Despond and loneliness for the departed, in my case. "Through" is the key word here. It implies coming out on the other side rather than sinking into a quagmire of self-pity, blame, bitterness, resentment, or despair.

Schuller warns of desertion by formerly close friends on our difficult trek through the valley. This warning helped when several of our acquaintances defected, persons who had used their friendship with Frank for personal advantage. On a Christmas card to remaining friends, I wrote words of appreciation for their "help through the valley." It concluded, "May your Christmas memories sparkle like Frank's favorite Pleiades, where surely he is now one with the universe." The card was a photograph snapped at his final memorial celebration as Tony Reyna, our Indian friend from Taos Pueblo, sang and drummed Frank's "Traveling Song." Looking bleakly hopeful, poet Keith Wilson and I stood together near Tony under the oak tree where some of Frank's ashes had just been scattered.

At my bedside Joan has placed a book titled *The Joys of Christmas*. In it one writer expresses her wish that readers will find people they love with whom to share the holidays.

A broken wave hisses beneath my feet. "Are people really necessssary?"

"Yessss and no," its successor seems to reply with a spent sigh. "Sssome people help."

As do some books. And oceans. And Light.

In a chapter called "When Christmas Isn't Welcome," another bedside book has counseled, "If you can't say 'Merry Christmas,' maybe you can whisper, 'Welcome, Light of the world, Shine softly in my darkness.'"

At a Garden Grove bookstore I have searched to no avail for *To Heal Again*, recommended in a friend's Christmas letter. What popped into view instead was a book named *Hope Springs from Mended Places*. For several days after seeing this title I wondered vaguely, "Where *are* my mended places?" Nothing felt mended. Hemingway said the world breaks everyone, but "many are made strong at the broken places." It's hard to believe that the death of Frank can ever make me feel stronger anyplace.

Running beside the crashing waves with wary Trickster, I suddenly realize that she is one of my mended places. Appreciation of Trickster and of Morgan and Crystal, our other two dogs, is a mended place. They have gotten me laughing and loving again. My resurrected appreciation of nature and of classical music, literature, and an ever deepening intuition are other crucial mended places. Horseback riding on either of our Missouri Foxtrotters is another mending. Getting dressed in the morning is becoming easier, a nearly mended spot.

Run, run! Run, Barbara, run with the waves! Run as if your life depends upon it. Your life *does* depend upon it. This is joy. Joy is *life*.

If you let it, the ocean may bring back joy. The Pacific, so rightly named, is one of this planet's ultimate mending places.

Were I a psychotherapist in California instead of in Taos and Tucson, I would bring all my clients to the ocean. In the same 1981 issue of *South Dakota Review* as Frank's article about early Los Angeles appears a piece by C. A. Salter on the possibilities of Los Angelenos using their landscape as therapy. Salter writes, "The ceaseless thrusting of ocean waves conjures up a continuity to the forces of nature that enables the seeker to put his or her particular anxiety in a slightly less painful perspective. Things do go on. Nature has seen these plights before. The comparison between human effort and natural power tends to have the seeker reconsider the scale and magnitude of his or her own complications."

Like joy and the ocean, laughter mends. To my delight, I can laugh at the name of the seaside breakfast nook where we pause to eat after Trickster agrees to stop chasing seagulls in exchange for a vigorous patting by three resting surfers. Where else would a restaurant be named the "Stuft Surfer"? Where else would squalling seagulls scarf up my leftover pancakes, as the owners have warned? Maybe they should change the name of this place to "Stuft Seagulls."

Much to her tail-wagging pleasure, one of Trickster's new admirers enthuses, "A coyote dog! Cool."

Surely our coyote dog did come, with her ancient topaz eyes, to help both Frank and me with his transition. Once a coyote, always a coyote. These clans stick together. Perhaps Trickster too is an extension of Frank, like his car. Rollerbladers and bike riders greet her with smiles and pats. Sailboats flash white welcoming wings, beating back the blue. Hope tangs the sea spray salting our lips.

Southern California remains more than simply smog and tepid bathwater, after all. As part of America's last frontier, it too is piecing together its own eccentric pattern. And for me personally it shines softly in the darkness of this First Christmas, alone.

5
In Touch

Free again! Free to be me, independent me again. Untie those apron strings, Mama.

Up through the bumper-to-bumper traffic, filthy smog, and stench of Riverside, where Frank once marveled at walnut orchards, flowering orange groves, and clear air. On to Route 40 at Barstow, where he was deeply affected at the sight of his first palm tree in this "Promised Land." Climbing again, back into God's clear and vibrant country. Seventy-five miles an hour past signs pointing to nearby "Historic 66."

Historic, indeed. Frank wrote in his Los Angeles article about his first trip to California along a New Mexico section of this famous route in the fall of 1924 and about Mr. Garth, whose Star roadster they were riding in with Frank at the wheel: "Highway 66 was an unmarked and unfenced dirt road over which we traveled at some thirty miles an hour. Every evening we turned off to camp in the sage. Mr. Garth, a dead shot with his .22 rifle, was always able to supply a rabbit for the pot. Occasionally, another car would come along, and seeing our campfire its occupants would turn off to join us."

On up to ever green Williams, white-mantled San Francisco Peak reigning in the distance. Then north to the Grand Canyon at sunset, fifty-eight miles to go, blazing red clouds singeing my left shoulder, frosted full moon silvering my right with fairy dust. In 1900 it took all day to get here from nearby Flagstaff in a dusty stagecoach, and it cost $20 besides. Imagine being stuffed into a stagecoach, Trickster. Why, you could *run* faster than that.

Free again! In touch again. Free from California! Howl to your heart's content, Trickster. My heart feels the same. I hear them too, your sisters and brothers welcoming us back, back to kachina country! Pine scents our joy. Musk of the eons penetrates our beings as we approach the edge of creation.

"It is the sum total of all the aspects of nature combined in one integrated whole," Frank wrote about the Grand Canyon at the end of *The Colorado*. "In its heart is the savage uncontrollable fury of all the inanimate universe, and at the same time the immeasurable serenity that succeeds it. It is creation."

If you never read another description, read the last fifteen pages of that peerless book. It is so typically Frank. He begins the chapter, "No writer of worth has ever seriously attempted to describe Grand Cañon. . . . None ever will." Then he does it! I can see his own first sentence getting under his skin, challenging him to do the impossible, hear his hearty caught-in-the-act laugh, ending with that guilty-but-glad-I-did-it boyish grin everyone loved.

Besides describing the Canyon's majesty, *The Colorado* gives readers important clues to Frank's personal life. As Joseph Gordon of Colorado College observed, "In a way it is a record of his own physical and spiritual search for his homeland, and his discovery of the real and imaginative landscapes that informs his life and work."

For many Southwest Indian tribes, the Grand Canyon is the Place of Emergence, the prototypic *sipapu*. Their kivas, or underground ceremonial chambers symbolic of the universe, contain a small hole also called the *sipapu* to represent this Place of Emergence; it leads down into previous worlds from which all have emerged. Caked with pink clay, spirits called Mudhead kachinas *(koyemshi)* are said to have emerged from the Grand Canyon.

Mudheads are clowns and game players, but they also accompany other kachinas. Thoughts of their emergence here at the

Canyon remind me of the Mudhead attending a giant Zuni Shalako kachina pictured in my Christmas present to Frank this year.

For years a frayed, unframed watercolor depicting those two figures has hung over his file cabinet in our bedroom. On its back is printed:

"The Zuni Shalako and the Mud Head"
by Percy Sandy
Taos, New Mexico
Zuni Tribe
Indian Name—*Kei Sa* (Red Moon)

Below this, taped to the file cabinet, is another unframed but more tattered Shalako print, number six of ten done by Miriam Birmingham. In it two Mudheads attend a towering Shalako, watched by Indians on the left. The head of a deer appears in the upper right corner. It symbolizes the death at the end of this dance cycle of the Shalako, which is transformed into a deer.

At dances Shalakos themselves are usually seven or eight feet tall with rayed eagle-feather headdresses, bulging eyes, curved buffalo horns, black clacking beaks, and thick ruffs of raven feathers about their necks. In addition to these standard attributes, our Shalako painted by Red Moon has long, sagging breasts and is robed in a white Hopi mantle trimmed with green-and-black designs and embellished with two feathers. Its moccasined feet dance on ground shadowed the same shade of burnt red as the Supai red sandstone emblazoning the Grand Canyon.

For some reason I took Red Moon's painting with me to Tucson in November and had it matted in this Supai red sandstone color, covered with glass, and framed in dark brown wood matching our bedroom furniture. Thoughts of how happy its refurbished beauty would have made Frank at first filled me with regret. This feeling vanished when a sudden sense of his appreciation for his belated but caring gift flooded my being.

On this trip to the Canyon one or two ravens follow me everywhere, even to the gas station, as if they are protective spirits connected with Frank and keeping watch over me and the three dogs. In part they may represent that Shalako raven ruff, it occurs to me later.

Ten days after returning to Taos from this trip, I am to see Frank's spirit for the first two times since his death in June 1995. These viewings both occur after late-night sessions of writing, when I step outdoors to inhale fresh air and stars. It almost seems as if he has found yet another way to encourage me with "a job well done" in my search for illumination.

The first specter is a twelve-foot-high sheath of white light as tall as our front-yard apricot tree, its backdrop. Curved slightly, like a crescent moon—as are the Shalakos in our paintings—it reminds me of a Shalako without facial features. It has width and depth, weaves slowly toward me, then back.

The second vision appears two nights later at our backyard entrance, where three twelve-foot poles are structured like goal posts. The horizontal pole extends a foot past each vertical pole, seeming to transform them into crosses. This time a wide sheath of curved light resembling the first encompasses the entire twelve-foot height of the lefthand "cross." It too billows slightly forward and backward.

The cross symbolizes far more than Christianity. Symbolically, the left side represents intuition or the unconscious. Closely connected with the vertical, this illumination is also tied to an emphasis on *life*—even in death. As Cirlot observes in *The Dictionary of Symbols*, "The most general significance of the cross is that of the conjunction of opposites: the positive (or the vertical) with the negative (or horizontal), the superior with the inferior, life with death." To the Andeans it represents the divine masculine. The cross in the backyard is also the Tree of Life, as could be the apricot tree in front.

Light is most often equated with spirit. Cirlot writes that its whiteness alludes to "the synthesis of All" and that psychologically "to become illuminated is to become aware of a source of light, and, in consequence, of spiritual strength." The Tree of Life and the Light of Spirit are yet another union of opposites, a blending that is All.

When I look up the Shalako dance in Frank's book *Masked Gods*, everything comes together. In his opinion, the combined Zuni Shalako rituals before the winter solstice are, above all else, a ceremonial for the dead.

Frank's description of the sacrificed Shalako rivets my attention: "The Shalako is then laid down as a ceremonially killed deer, his head to the east and sprinkled with meal. The act is suggestive of sacrificing the Shalako who thus becomes a deer and imparts luck to his 'killer.'"

After his oxygen line broke, Frank died alone on the floor in a space beside our bed with his head primarily pointing east, like the Shalako. His novel *The Man Who Killed the Deer* has connected him symbolically with the deer ever since its publication. When sculptor Ted Egri was searching for a symbol to represent Frank on his three-thousand-pound memorial boulder, I chose one of the ancient Mimbres deer from petroglyphs. Its seven-pronged antlers and head sweep up onto the boulder's upward-slanted face. On the straight lower face below is the deer's body, carved inside with Frank's positive words from *Deer:* "We will meet again. As equal parts of one great life."

In *Masked Gods* Frank does not agree with Elsie Clews Parsons's theory that the main purpose of the Shalako death is to bring "hunting luck." It may be more of a blessing, an affirmation that death is not to be feared. Death is simply one more step in our evolution toward a greater spiritual whole—a greater oneness. And it is a reassurance that no one is ever truly lost to us. "We will meet again. As equal parts of one great life." Our visiting Shalako Light Spirit is a blessing to me. It comforts and reassures.

"This business of spirit is perplexing," Frank wrote in *Mountain Dialogues.* "One can't doubt that an invisible other-world impacted with unimaginable powers lies beyond our world of the senses." He had his own preknowledge of physicist David Bohm's theory that we are all part of one implicate ocean of interpenetrating energy waves organized into our potential as human, rock, or flower—the explicate order—by a superimplicate order.

Regarding a reported ghost seen in our home, a Catholic priest once told me, "I have lived too long in New Mexico to disbelieve anything." Suspending disbelief works best for me, as it did for him.

Pueblo Indians at Acoma bury the dead with the head pointing toward the East to ensure rebirth. Our Aztec friend Guillermo Rosete says the direction of the head at death indicates characteristic attributes to which the spirit will be drawn. Since the East is a place of hope, for example, Frank's spirit will be a positive one with an emphasis on hope that should manifest in his next lifetime.

East is also the home of the old Aztec fire god Huehueteotl, a favorite of Frank's, and "home of the mountain spirit," according to Rosete. Beside our back door, by coincidence, hangs a piece of aspen wood etched with the calligraphy, "Home of the mountain spirit, *Aspen-san.*" Artist Michio Takayama executed this piece years ago. He called my husband *"Aspen-san,"* for he was tall and thin and white with all-seeing eyes, like aspen. Ever since hearing Michio's pronunciation of *"Aspen-san,"* I have thought of Frank as "Aspen Son." He frequently was photographed beside aspens, his favorite trees. His monument and most of his ashes rest in the Sacred Aspen Grove next to our home.

Frank died the day after our return to Taos from Tucson. It seemed imperative that the mountain spirit return to the home of the mountain spirit in the Sangre de Cristo Mountains to the east for eternal union. He also lived with one fire sign and departed with another.

It is fitting that his spirit continues to pursue his interest in the east. If his Shalako spirit is one with the East Warrior, he is called Yamuhakto and twinned with Warrior of the West. Their Indian name means "carrying wood," further denoting "you are a tree and under your body the deer lie down to rest at your feet." Cottonwood sticks adorn their heads, and they carry deer antlers.

Frank's deer association and his love of all trees, especially aspen and our huge cottonwoods, would make this an appropriate connection. He thought our friend Helen Blumenschein, daughter of a famous Taos artist, had gone out of her mind when she said, "All these high old cottonwoods and aspens make this place of yours look like the house of a *sorcerer*. Get rid of them, Frank, like I did. Chop 'em all down!"

Similarly, our Jungian friend Jane Wallgren said of a tree in Tucson, "You'll have to cut down that olive tree outside your bedroom window, Barbara, so Frank can face east every morning and greet the sun."

I thought, "Well, he usually performs that morning ritual outdoors. But she met him before I did, and she's a Jungian. Maybe she knows best."

I told Robert Dolan, the tree man next door, to cut it down. At the time he barely knew his new neighbors. Nevertheless, he snapped, "Are you *crazy?* That's a valuable Russian olive tree! You don't see many that shapely and tall, and it's taken years for it to get this way. No way am I cutting down that tree. You can't pay me enough money to cut down your tree."

A tree lover myself, I could tell we would become good friends. Right away Frank took to Robert too, and agreed with him that *both* Jane and I must have been crazy. Frank had his own ways of reaching the East without our help. Always the East drew him. He liked the idea of Navajo hogans opening to the east. He liked the East known as the Orient. He studied Eastern religion extensively on his own. In his fine book of essays *Mountain Dialogues*, one of the most interesting chapters—"The East Is Red"—is about his trip to China in 1976. And his longest essay there contrasts the analytical Western psychology of Jung with the Eastern spirituality of Ramana Maharshi, representative of the "East's mystical belief in one universal reality."

Frank's granite monument chair was carved in China; his monument boulder came from Colorado. This joining of East and

West is symbolic of the "one great life" he envisioned, or "one universal reality."

In a masterpiece of writing and original thought for which he has never fully received deserved credit, Frank parallels in *Masked Gods* the forty-nine-day Zuni Shalako death ceremony and the forty-nine-day transition period after death called the Bardo of Becoming plane, described in that bible of Eastern religion *The Tibetan Book of the Dead*. The Shalako process ultimately illustrates that "life may be renewed with freshness, increased vigor and a deep sense of its continuous flow," Frank writes. It fills the gap between one type of lifetime and another, one season and another, just as bardos do for those of another belief.

In a new interpretation titled *The Tibetan Book of Living and Dying*, Sogyal Rimpoche defines the Tibetan word "bardo" as "a 'transition' or a gap between the completion of one situation and the onset of another." There are four: the natural bardo of a current lifetime; the painful bardo of dying; a luminous bardo of afterdeath; and a forty-nine-day Bardo of Becoming that lasts until a new life is taken on.

One "expert" claimed that after forty-nine days Frank would make his choice between being reborn or becoming pure spirit for eternity. If released energy transforms itself into permanent Universal Spirit only when sufficient growth has been experienced through enough lifetimes, then Frank may experience further lifetimes chosen for growth—in the specific area of relationships, for one. I was his fourth and most enduring wife, but marriage was still a challenge for him—more so than for the typical man or woman. He usually was not there for his relatives either, and sometimes not for his friends.

He once told his school chum's bride, who later earned her doctorate and had an illustrious career in education, "What do you want a college education for? You will always be a scrubwoman."

He told a large group in Colorado Springs that before his fourth wife came along he "thought all women were good for was the bedroom and the kitchen." Not necessarily in that order. The I-ness of Frank's Leo and Aries natures was a deterrent to effective relationships. He once admitted with a sheepish grin, "When I finally looked up from my typewriter, all my wives were gone." True, good intentions count; and he had plenty of those, generally.

It is said that survivors can most effectively help departed ones during the first twenty-one days of the forty-nine. The deceased is holding on to life impressions then. What worries me is that some can "get stuck" in this fourth bardo plane, as Rimpoche warns, and become spirits or ghosts remaining overly long with someone or something that has attracted them. This delay blocks the flow of spiritual evolution. I hope this did not happen to Frank. One year and twenty-five days after his death I will have a vivid dream about the birth of a vibrant baby, a boy it seems, that gives me the strong feeling Frank is reincarnating.

Helpful meditations and loving thoughts of the dead will help them through "stuck" spots, according to Rimpoche. We must not selfishly hold our loved ones back, he writes. It is all right to utilize Frank's energy in the universal pool of energy, for instance, but not his evolving spirit energy. Frank believed that his energy would continue to be used. One way to experience it still is through his books. He felt that a crucial goal is proper exchange of energies between individual or group and the universe, resulting in oneness.

It is particularly important to transform the suffering of one who has experienced a traumatic death, as Frank did. For spirit release and progression Sogyal Rimpoche recommends a four-part meditation. First, through visualization, invoke a favorite spiritual guide or Higher Power brimming with compassion and light. Second, pour out your troubles and pain to this power; release them. Third, fill your heart with the Higher Being's bliss—its love, peace, compassion, wisdom, and power. Visualize these attributes as light. Finally, beam this light of healing compassion out to the loved one who has died. Surround yourselves with enlightened love, forgiveness, and optimism desired for the loved one's future lives, and your own. Then relax. Open your heart. Be patient. Persist.

Spectral Shalakos soothe my soul as I stare ever deeper into Canyon shadows, for kachinas return annually after their Going Home dance in late July to the place of emergence here or beyond San Francisco Peak, antenna for human prayers and messages. Unlike Poe's ominous raven spirit, these compassionate spirits leave behind promise of surcease from sorrow, ever more.

6
Sipapu

The Grand Canyon is the greatest meditation temple in the world. To get the most out of contact with it, one needs to be alone at some point in order to sense and absorb what it has to offer. It takes time to appreciate. If one hikes across it with another person, as I did twenty years ago, the memory remains always a magic carpet to hop aboard and fly back upon—alone. As J. B. Priestly wrote, "Even to remember that the Grand Canyon is still there lifts up the heart."

Here as elsewhere, participation with one's senses, imagination, and empathy sets up the partnership that leads to understanding and oneness. Frank mentions in *The Colorado* possible pitfalls of coming here with another and advises temporarily severing the connection with other humans if they intrude upon one's introspection: "Simply take your look, turn on your heel and leave. The cañon will be there if you ever return. And if you are drawn back, you will know then that it is a great experience not to be taken lightly, and not before you are ready for it."

The Canyon did not come into my life until I was forty. I did not expect it to live up to its outsized reputation. It did, like Machu Picchu, which I visited some years later. It is, after all, North America's Machu Picchu—right here in our own backyard. No need to traipse off to South America. I first visited the Grand Canyon alone, and never with Frank; nevertheless, we had a shared affinity for it. I was ready.

Spirits from the entire universe have gathered at Mather Point to greet Trickster and me this morning. She sits quietly, appreciatively, head held high with big ears perked, eyes sparkling in anticipation. Unchained, she wears a wide red collar, Frank's favorite color, to keep from being shot as a coyote. She knows this place is special. Perhaps she senses the presence of Frank's energy, always strong in the locale of one of his book settings. At nine o'clock we watch the great spirits marching past below, footed in the Canyon floor, shadowed on its turreted sides: giant Shalakos, Osiris and Isis, two-legged Egyptian jackals striding erect, Quetzalcoatl, Zoroaster, Thor and Freya, Merlin, Spider Woman, and the War Twins—first to emerge here eons ago.

Trickster seems to watch the jackals most intently. She is fantasizing about the lifetime when she too will walk erect on two legs with a crown upon her head. I can tell from her secret jackal smile. It's a crown or nothing for Trickster. None of these asps coiling up from headdresses shadowed on the walls. Ever since a rattlesnake bit her on the lip last year, she has hated snakes almost as much as cats.

I snap a photo of this unearthly Spirit March back to the Place of Emergence. It is the last of my film, reminding me that I should not have taken it. Like those snapshots of an Indian dance in our home, it is not likely to turn out. Against my wishes, a visitor took photographs of two women friends, myself, and Isabel Concha, dancing in our living room after dinner one evening as Frank watched. We were dancing to the singing and drumming of Isabel's husband, Pete, a Pueblo religious leader.

At the airport two days later the would-be photographer wailed to our guest Ann Merrill, "None of my pictures turned out!"

Ann replied, "That will teach you some things are sacred."

Nearly thirty-five years ago Colin Fletcher walked the width of the Grand Canyon from Havasu Canyon on the west to the Little

Colorado on the east, swam the Colorado, and exited at the head of the Nankoweap Trail on the northeast. In *The Man Who Walked Through Time* he described freeing himself from the tyrannies of haste, clothing, and finally photography, after his camera broke. "Photography is not compatible with contemplation," he wrote. "Its details are too insistent. They are always buzzing around your mind and clouding the fine focus of appreciation. . . . Now, when I came to something interesting, I no longer stopped, briefly, to photograph and forget; I stood and stared, fixing truer images on the emulsion of memory."

One of the last things Fletcher did before leaving the Grand Canyon was to visit the Place of Emergence, or at least one of them, in a side canyon of the Little Colorado four and one-half miles from its confluence with the Colorado River. He found rising from translucent aquamarine water a smooth travertine mound approximately forty feet across, thirty feet high, and two hundred feet in circumference. On top a round yellow spring bubbled out of its center, the heart of the *sipapu*. Fletcher calculated that the brown mound was probably only fifty thousand years old, a mere youngster on the Canyon scale of time.

Since Indians are not inclined to reveal their most sacred places, this may have been a red herring to mislead the curious. Yet Fletcher tried to feel some of the awe that the first Hopi must have felt at discovering this astonishing spot, whether *sipapu* or not. He failed. He blamed this failure on a friend's jarring four-day visit, which threw off Fletcher's fine attunement to his surroundings and the things of nature. Too, he had other agendas on his mind, like writing a commercial book about his feat.

All the rainbowed colors of the world mass before us during our morning meditation here at Mather Point. Some boldly glaring, others faceted with light, the most vivid hiding themselves until sunset. Joaquin Miller wrote of this vast rainbow, "Color is king." In *The Colorado* Frank views the Grand Canyon as a "celestial symphony of color" and as characters in a drama. One can't help but mix metaphors on this magnificent stage, and superlatives are the rule. Frank describes its dramatic hues as "royal purples, angry reds, mellow russets and monkish browns, soothing blues, shrieking yellows, tragic blacks and mystic whites, cool greens, pale lavenders and anemic grays." He has fun with his description. Like the ocean, the Grand Canyon is not a place for weeping.

As the "madding crowd" begins to close in around us, Trickster and I turn on our heels and move on to Yavapai Point, leaving Mather Point to others, to those greater spirits we had watched march off in the bright sunlight, and to the spirit of Stephen Mather, who gave more than his name to a piece of this Canyon. The first director of the National Park Service, Mather gave much of his borax fortune and his life to the cause of conservation. His memorial here acknowledges: "He laid the foundation of the National Park Service, defining and establishing the policies under which its areas shall be developed and conserved unimpaired for future generations. There will never come an end to the good that he has done."

Another crowd soon closes in around us at Yavapai Point although the park is officially closed until a government squabble is settled. We move on to the South Rim's Hopi House, El Tovar, and Bright Angel Lodge. After this we'll stop at the more private East Rim, more private in winter at least, to finish our meditations. Chained to a thick pine, Trickster lies down and yawns, "Back to the old chain gang. How boring. No cool spirits either."

On the contrary, Hopi House is full of spirits, sad spirits not ancient at all. Indian spirits of those who lived and worked here at the turn of the century. And that of Mary Jane Colter, who must be saddest of all. In fact, she must be spinning like a top in her grave, not just turning over. Hopi House, her indestructible stone building, has become a hodgepodge of cheap crass commercialism as well as expensive crass commercialism. In her time this business was termed a "partnership between commercialism and romanticism," but that commercialism was tasteful and museum quality.

Colter's massive version of stone houses at Old Oraibi in Hopiland is terraced upward with tall wooden ladders integrating

39

its three levels. The porch of each level is the rooftop of the level below. It was built of local stone by Hopis, and Hopis originally lived on the upper floor. In the attractive workroom here they made fine rugs, jewelry, and pottery, all for sale to visitors. Valuable old Indian items were displayed in another room. Colorful Navajo rugs, pots, and baskets served as decoration throughout the building, along with Hispanic relics and other Southwestern antiques. Rare replicas of two Hopi ceremonial altars and an authentic Navajo sandpainting were highlights of Colter's ingenious interior.

Today the T-shirt mecca of giftshops is located in Bright Angel Lodge, originally another monument to Mary Jane Colter's vision. No longer is the focus on her striking "geological" fireplace that began at its base with water-worn sandstone from the Colorado River and proceeded upward, including every rock layer of the Canyon, topped by gray-white Kaibab limestone. Gone are the pioneer furniture and warm Indian decor. Now the focus in the garish largest room is on T-shirts, sweatshirts, sunglasses, commercial pottery, and postcards, to mention a few of the more unsightly items swirling before one's eyes. In January, the rest of the lodge resembles a cold, deserted barn. All in all, it's a place where one wants to whirl on one's heel and walk away fast.

Moviemakers contacted us in 1995 about a documentary production featuring Mary Jane Colter's life. A letter in her biography by Virginia L. Grattan mentions Frank. They wanted to interview him; his second wife, Janey, had gone to work for Colter in 1947. They waited too long. All that lingered was a scrap of memory about Colter ordering steak while Janey was expected to order cheaper cuts of meat. They ate out together when necessary, but Janey remained the underling, Colter the boss. Possessively, she called her help "my boys" and "my Jane." Colter was not an easy woman for whom to work, her employees unanimously agreed, yet they all admired her grit and talent. Frank liked her.

Frank and Janey were married in 1947, and in April Colter wrote Mesa Verde naturalist Don Watson, "What did you think of my Jane? Well—she got a fine man in Frank Waters! I really believe his 'Man Who Killed the Deer' comes closer to hitting the Bull's Eye than any other book on an Indian subject I have read."

Frank used to tell people that it was "love at first sight" when he met me. This is partly because both Janey and I were projections of his first love, a blue-eyed blonde named Leslie Davis whom he loved and lost in grade school. Janey was more high-strung, extroverted, and voluptuous than I, and not so tall; local Hispanics thought she must be a movie star.

John and Evelyn Sinclair, a writer and an artist, respectively, were astonished at how much Janey and I looked alike. In 1973 at the Santa Ana Corn Dance, Frank and I stood with the Sinclairs on a rooftop. I wore a blue-flowered squaw dress, as we called such full-skirted two-piece outfits back then. When the wind blew, I tied a blue chiffon scarf loosely about my blonde hair. John and Evelyn stared at me. Frank stared.

Finally I asked Evelyn privately, "Is something the matter? Am I doing anything that's taboo?"

Evelyn, who had only one arm, hugged me and whispered, "You can't imagine how much you look like Janey. You look exactly like her! John and I can't get over it!" Apparently Frank didn't either.

I've never seen that much resemblance myself, except perhaps in my portrait painted in August 1970 by Dirk Van Driest. I was to spend the night with Frank after Van Driest had finished painting my mouth; it has a Mona Lisa twist of a smile. Later, of course, the whole thing changed after Mr. Van Driest ironed the painting when its frame warped. Today, though still lovely in its own strangely wrinkled way, my portrait resembles the "Picture of Dorian Gray" after one of his bad nights. Maybe Janey had a Mona Lisa smile too.

She met Frank when they backed their vehicles into each other at a party given by Mabel Dodge Luhan, a wealthy Taos patroness of the arts. It must have been another "love at first sight." They soon married, then honeymooned on Lobo Mountain in a cabin called "The Tower Beyond Tragedy" after a poem by Robinson Jeffers. The title was a hint of what was to come for Janey. Frank began writing *Masked Gods* there. In it he called her "Queen of the Bandits" because she later hung around with a local gambler collecting money from slot machines while Frank submerged himself in writing.

Thirty years after their honeymoon I found an injured butterfly up on Lobo Mountain that seemed to me imbued with Janey's spirit. I brought it home with us, fed it, and nursed it back to health in our guest room, where Janey had lived during the late '40s. Frank marveled that I was able to catch and to heal a butterfly. Eventually it practiced flying outdoors for two days, spiraled higher each time, and flew away for good. It may have been duplicating Janey's own spiritual evolution. In meditations meant to fill her spirit with light, I asked for her blessing. She seems at peace now. Someday I shall add Butterfly Maiden to our collection of kachina etchings, to keep some of Janey's bright energy with us always.

Frank and Janey moved from "The Tower Beyond Tragedy" into an apartment above Harwood Library in the heart of Taos, and he began remodeling this Arroyo Seco house, purchased in 1947. As Frank carried in Janey's clothing, artist Lesley Brown craned her neck out the window of a nearby apartment to get a good view. Noticing her, Frank shouted with a happy laugh, "Don't worry, Lesley. It's legal. We're married!" This was, after all, back in the good old days. And above a library.

Janey was an artist, came from a wealthy family, had traveled and lived in Europe, spoke French and Italian, owned two chow dogs, and was exotic enough to suit Frank. Isabelle Larrinaga, from whom Frank and I rented a house in Alamos, Mexico, over the Christmas holiday of 1976, once told me, "Everyone loves Frank. But his wives have all been so . . . so *flamboyant*."

The marriage lasted only a couple of years. Then a psychoanalyst treating Janey told Frank he was stifling her creativity and they needed to separate for a time. Janey soon divorced him, married again, had a fight with her unfaithful husband, and was found bruised and drowned in their pool in 1960. The only time Frank lied to me was when he said they never had divorced. I don't think he ever got over that heartache. Until his death he carried in his wallet a glamorous photo of Janey looking like a blonde goddess couched on her throne beside one of her chows. Having always felt that her energy was with us in a positive sense, I didn't mind. Being me, however, I added to his wallet a photo of our sheltie and me sitting at Frank's feet, which appealed to him.

Coincidentally, Frank and Janey had spent time together in Tucson, where her mother lived in a luxurious home. This Tucson residency was to be another duplication of roles between Janey and me. One of the many times Frank "went broke," as he called it, Janey and he picked apples in Washington state, where she showed him the impressive estate owned by her father prior to his death. I always felt grateful that Frank went through his apple-picking stage with a previous wife. This role Janey could keep for herself!

A friend who worked for Frank's third flamboyant wife in her art gallery told me that Frank had begged Rose not to divorce him. Ten years later when I asked him why he had done this, knowing they were ill suited for one another, he replied, "Well, you put so much energy into a relationship like that. It seemed a shame to waste everything we had put into the marriage." This appears to have been the case with Janey and him as well. Her letters indicate that in her own way she felt as much regret as he over their parting.

After Frank's death, Larry Torres recalled in the *Taos News* that local people thought their famous neighbor had been married to a movie star in the '40s.

"How did a story like that get started?" I asked.

Larry shrugged. "Frank Waters was the first stranger to move into our closed little community of Arroyo Seco, you know. He was so different. A writer! In our minds, writers and movie stars went together. It seemed natural."

Today, this little community eight miles northeast of Taos has so many rich Anglos living in it that it's called "the Beverly Hills of Taos." But Frank retains the distinction of being the First Stranger here, the first esteemed stranger. Janey was a fleeting butterfly who earned respect here by swearing in Italian at Mrs. Quintana, a village matriarch, for letting her loose pig dig up Frank's stone walk. After that the two women became fast friends. What counted most in Arroyo Seco then was respect, not money.

I sometimes wondered if Frank's "love at first sight" concerning us wasn't really sex at first sight; it took him seven years to get over his marriage snakebite and ease into his fourth, with me. "One of these days you'll wake up," I would tell him with my Mona Lisa smile. "Number four is the Indian number of completion. Pythagoras called it the number of totality. Four is going to be your new lucky number!"

He informed me, "Right now five women are in love with me at the same time. They are all beautiful and all have very successful careers."

Was I one of his lucky, lucky harem, I wondered? I didn't give him the satisfaction of asking. Besides, it sounded like hyperbole to me.

Instead of sitting around twiddling my thumbs until Frank came to his senses, I went hiking all over Arizona and parts of Utah with Pete Cowgill, then outdoor editor of the Arizona Daily Star. He was a very physical man. Hiking across the Grand Canyon with Pete was far different from floating above it on words with Frank. There is something to be said for both. Frank never did hike across the Canyon. He tended to fall silent at any mention of my achievement. And achievement it was beside Pete. Pete liked to do things the hard way, or not at all.

When we climbed Rainbow Bridge, for example, we had to use tiny finger- and-toeholds used for centuries by the Indians. Most people don't know this route exists. Indians have alarmingly small fingers and toes, I learned from experience. The best things about it were touching terra firma again and finding Zane Grey's autograph scratched on a stone hidden off to the left side of the bridge under a rock.

Pete's seventeen-year-old son was with us at that time. He was shaking so hard he couldn't begin to climb. "I'm not *that* scared," I

44

decided. I could trust Pete. He always knew what he was doing when we were out in nature. He had talked me across more than one sheer face of a cliff. I had finally gotten over my fear of heights in order to climb with him. Again I followed his instructions.

The kid must have decided, "If that old lady can do it, damn it, I can too." And he did.

Solidly built like a Rock of Gibraltar, Pete was muscular but spare of excess flesh. About five foot ten, he shaved his head bald and wore glasses but had soft brown eyes and a wide, sensuous mouth deeply grooved at the corners from smiling. He had his dour moments back in civilization but seldom out in nature. He often spoke in a misleading growling tone, as good humor sparked from his eyes. He wrote the same way and had a big following.

Pete and his friends always crossed the Grand Canyon at least one way in a day. They strained to see how often they could cross it both ways in one day, or how long it took for four consecutive crossings. They were fanatics. Pete knew I wouldn't put up with that nonsense, nor could I measure up. The plan, therefore, this third week in May was to park our vehicle at the South Rim, sleep in it, hitch a ride at dawn 215 miles to the North Rim, hike down, and sleep outdoors at Phantom Ranch next night in our sleeping bags. Beds were not in Pete's vocabulary. Next morning we would climb up to the South Rim on the more challenging Kaibab Trail. The easier Bright Angel Trail was a "goddamned highway" upon which Pete would not set foot.

Now, you may be one who thinks this journey sounds like a breeze. Believe me and Canyon employees *and* signs, it is not. The Canyon's 1996 winter newspaper, called *The Guide*, carries the notation, "July, 1990: 26-year-old fatality near South Kaibab Trail—Hiker ran out of water." Other remarks warn, "In a recent three-year period, 750 hikers in the Bright Angel and Kaibab Trails were able to return to the rim only after seeking assistance from park rangers. . . . The Grand Canyon is so demanding that even people in excellent condition often emerge sore and fatigued. . . . The overnight backpacker must be equally prepared for the lack of water, extreme heat and cold, and isolation characteristics of the Grand Canyon. . . . Two quarts of water per hiker is the minimum; one gallon is recommended in summer."

The south Kaibab Trail is steeper than Bright Angel and has no shade and no water. Before the upward climb, numerous signs warn of danger ahead and of the need for specific, increased amounts of water. Yet two young German men almost died after overhearing our hiking plans while seated nearby at one of Phantom Ranch's long dinner tables. With *one cup* of water between them in broiling late May and without our knowledge, they attempted to follow us up next morning at a distance. They collapsed a thousand feet below the rim. They might have died there if a couple of Sunday morning breakfast hikers hadn't found them and revived them with water and oranges.

The Germans staggered past us at the rim as we sat waiting for our ride back to Grand Canyon Village; with Pete's customary zeal we were two hours ahead of schedule. Later they returned with a case of soft drinks and sat in their car near Yaki Point "waiting to help anyone else who makes the same mistake we did," they told us.

The Canyon is roughly ten air miles across and a mile deep. We began at an altitude of 8,240 feet and ended at 7,260 feet, a big contrast to the 2,000-foot elevation we'd just left in Tucson. Our total vertical descent from the North Rim was 5,760 feet, our ascent to the South Rim a mere 4,780 feet. "Thank God for small favors," I learned to pray around Pete. On paper, our shorter ascent figure looked better than our longer descent. But that rugged ascent caused me ever after to hate switchbacks. Not counting side explorations, our hike covered twenty and one-half miles starting early one morning at 35 degrees above zero in snow and finishing next day in puddles of sweat at 75 degrees after climbing in 100-degree heat. Overall, we traveled from the climate of southern Canada to that of northern Mexico. Surrounded at first with tall spruce, fir, and aspen, then ponderosa, we ended at the South Rim in an environment studded with low piñon and juniper.

In between, at the bottom we encountered a desert scrub community interspersed with a habitat of seeps, springs, and streams. Overlapping these lay a river and riverbank environment. Water, water everywhere below! Water brought the greatest, unexpected joy. From above the Canyon floor had looked dry and arid. In reality it was paradise. Winter snow on the North Rim highlighted summer below.

Down Roaring Springs Canyon we quickly descended five miles to Bright Angel Creek, named by Powell's party in contrast to the Dirty Devil, which was even worse than the Colorado River, at that time "too thin to plow, too thick to drink." The name Bright Angel comes from John Milton's *Paradise Lost*, but it was Paradise Found by the time we reached Cottonwood Campground two miles from the rushing conjunction of Roaring Springs and Bright Angel.

Most exquisite of all were the deep pink blooms of redbud trees, incongruously reminding one of cherry-blossom time in Washington, D.C. Besides shady cottonwoods, at this oasis we found willows, box elders, and cattails. One and a half miles ahead we came to heaven on earth, Ribbon Falls, the best of three waterfalls we visited. Pete later ran a large photo in the *Arizona Daily Star* of the Falls with me on top, wearing my bikini, most practical uniform of the trip after our descent. Fortunately, I was a mere speck on top of the tumbling cascade curtained with travertine. Fifty feet below, a limestone stalagmite slowly built itself upward, cutting in half falls once one hundred feet high.

Spray flung silvered crystals thirty feet into the air, creating a green fairy dell filled with Venus maidenhair ferns, watercress, scarlet monkey flowers and seep-spring yellow monkey flowers, golden columbine, mariposa lilies, and purple filaree. I wanted to stay here a week, if not forever. Splashing, bathing, laughing, perfuming each other with flowers, we had found Eden. Like the photograph of me, it put into perspective how insignificant we are. What specks of sand we appeared at the foot of those looming mesas and buttes!

Pete's schedule and our empty stomachs dragged us away at last so that we arrived at Phantom Ranch's main house and clustered cabins before dark. We were ready for this cheerful place after emerging from the gloom of the Box, where one thousand feet of black Precambrian schist towered above us in vertical sheets of brooding stone. We'd had an unforgettable day of fairly easy hiking along crystal-clear Bright Angel Creek, its banks scarlet with monkey flowers and cardinal flowers. Just as fascinating had been the juxtaposed desert foliage: prickly pear cactus, agave, yucca, burrobrush, and Mormon tea, or *Ephedra*, with some blue grama grass and Apache plume. Canyon wrens, desert sparrows, and a mockingbird had serenaded us. Blue-winged piñon jays scolded. Finally, the spicy fragrance of barbecued chicken firmed my faltering steps.

After dinner the roar of the Colorado River clashing with Bright Angel stimulated me with renewed energy and excitement that kept us talking and laughing in our sleeping bags much too late into the night. I identified with Joseph Krutch's story about the lady who had just been helped out of her saddle here at Phantom Ranch. "That wasn't too much," she said. Then, as her knees buckled, she added, "But it was plenty."

At first the ghost of John Wesley Powell prowled my dreams, sparked by words from his diary quoted on signs along the trail. Powell, who pioneered conservation here, charted this vast domain, named and measured its every byway, survived its rapids, triumphed over fear of the unknown. Powell, a man to match the Grand Canyon's domed splendor. A one-armed man to study and to emulate when the going gets tough. After a time the sound of roiling water flooded my soul with a Beethoven symphony, and I grew ready in dreamless sleep for our emergent climb next day.

Up through brown Tapeats sandstone to gray-green and purple Bright Angel shale, more slowly onward to gray Muav limestone stained red, then step by dragging step past gray-blue Redwall limestone with scarlet streaks.

Supai red next, red as my face and body. Up through the hell of steep, long, red switchbacks, down for a few blessed strides, back up

48

ever more steeply. Nearly naked, dripping wet, face contorted with effort, caked with pink earth like a panting, emerging Mudhead kachina. Pink as the tiny rattlesnakes here, symbols of the underworld, the emerging unconscious.

Red is hardest. Only from afar is it most beautiful. Red symbolizing the flesh. Life. Life versus spirit. To be or not to be. To be is hardest. To be left behind. While the other goes on.

Pat D'Andrea said the only way she made it up the Kaibab was by mantra-ing herself into a soaring raven that watched the toiling human speck below. Nevermore, Barbara! You are stuck with doing this yourself.

One must not fall back alone into the abyss, into the colossal *sipapu*. Coming up this trail, even mules stop every three or four minutes to catch their breaths. Not with Pete, they wouldn't.

He'd growl, "This ain't a tea party."

Right. Like grieving. Grieving is no tea party either. Right foot. Left foot.

It is a time of birthing. Agony. Rebirthing. Blooming. All so painful! Yanking one's being from the chasm of the unconscious. Coming out is much harder than going back down in, returning to the *sipapu*. Do not go gently into that good night. Rage. Rage! Against the dying of the light. A rage to live! Frank raged so admirably against the dying of that bright light. Like Powell, he was a man to match our mountains. Frank is on his own rebirthing journey now. Light. He needs light. Remember to send light. Release him into light. *Light.*

Water. Water everywhere, shimmering pink water, a shimmering, wavering lake of water. And not a single drop to drink. This isn't a tea party, you know. Drink. Drink from your canteen. Pete does believe in drinking water, thank god. *Drink.*

Energy is the first to go while grieving, last to return. Energy and laughter. That is the challenge: climbing in the dark out of a Grand Canyon without energy. Without purpose.

Pale brown sandstone next. So near and yet so far from the rim, from emergence. A man's reach should exceed his grasp. Or what's

49

a heaven for? Something like that. Browning? And what are stars for? Your spirit to shine through. Upward to the Pleiades. Onward. *Adelante y arriba*. Hayfoot. Strawfoot. *Reach*.

It is said the Pleiades will signal the return of celestial order. Descendants of the Incas believe nature and the cosmic energy of the Pleiades will banish chaos and establish order here on earth by 2012. Our individual energy will help. Energy? Frank said 2011 is the time for the coming sixth world of higher consciousness. He is one with the Pleiades, his special constellation. He is order. We are all one. One. One with the Pleiades. Reach. Like the seven aspen in our backyard. Toward the Pleiades. *Reach*.

Gray-white Kaibab limestone. The final test. Grief is no tea party, indeed, at the bottom of the Canyon, the bottom of the personality looking up. The true measure of success is how you overcome the obstacles. You may come out on top if you climb steadily—or unsteadily—past these obstacled black schists, Tapeats sandstone, Bright Angel shale. Past Muav limestone, Redwall limestone, and Supai red to pale brown sandstone surmounted by Kaibab limestone.

Gray-white Kaibab limestone above, like the top of Mary Jane Colter's geological fireplace. Gray limestone shaded with juniper. Out of the canyonic depths. Out of the fissured unconscious into integrated consciousness. On top at last!

Emergence. Emergence is the eternal goal.

7
Place of Spirits

Creative vibrations are much higher in Taos than in Tucson. Perhaps the thinner air with less oxygen at eight thousand feet thins the curtain between human and other than human. Ions carom about from water to earth to trees to mountains to sky and light to animals and humans in a cauldron of intermixed energies that make up the heightened vibrations here. An important ingredient in this cauldron is spirit energy. Like the Grand Canyon, Arroyo Seco is a place of spirits. It feels comfortable, therefore, to live in a house of spirits. Certain houses, as well as locales, may make the implicate order easier to access.

One category of spirits is the witch, the female *bruja* or male *brujo*. In northern New Mexico, three types of witches have made their presence felt: the bad witch; the good healing witch, or *curandera*; and the witch who can both cast spells and take them off, the *arboleria*, connected with the Tree of Life, or the Tree of Good and Evil. Other spirit categories are spirits of the departed and ghosts. The latter have to do more with entertainment. Before the tube was invented, they were the old-time equivalent of today's television stars. Many persons here still tell a good ghost story.

In casual conversation, these terms are used interchangeably. For instance, I told a local art gallery director about the latest "ghost" seen in our house; more accurately, it was the unhappy spirit of a deceased person who had once lived here. After overhearing my story, the new owner of artist Andrew Dasburg's old adobe home said, "We've turned Andrew's place into a bed-and-breakfast. Now we'll have to dream up a respectable ghost like yours to entertain our customers." And they did.

In creaky old houses around Taos, ghosts aren't too hard to come by; most houses with any character have them, almost as a prerequisite to authenticity. But they don't come guaranteed "respectable." In the little adobe that became Brett House Restaurant, for instance, the ghost of its former owner Dorothy Brett was said by John Manchester to smell of urine.

Born of minor English aristocracy, as a young woman Brett first traveled to America with D. H. Lawrence, whom she idolized, and his wife, Frieda. After his death both Frieda and Brett settled in the Taos area. In later years Brett, an artist, called Manchester the "Lawrence of my old age."

I disliked Manchester, a dilettante and homosexual who was once a close friend of Frank's; John preyed upon local boys and Brett in her old age. As her self-appointed "caretaker," he treated Brett shabbily until a month before her death in 1977, when he left town, taking with him most of her valuable paintings and her few personal possessions of slight value. The feeling of dislike was mutual between John and myself. He said bitterly, "If it weren't for *you*, Frank Waters would be living with me for the rest of his life." This was news to Frank, and amused him. John was the one person I've had to associate with whose negative spirit prompted me to keep a protective shield of light around myself at all times in his presence. And it felt as though in death his spirit remained just as malevolent.

Frank and I spent the night in Manchester's house after his funeral in 1987. Frank went to bed early; I stayed up, finding it difficult to sleep in John's bed. Suddenly water began gushing through the kitchen. It splashed and bubbled and gurgled merrily in an ever widening stream. Armed with thick bath towels and mops, I spent the night holding it at bay, trying to keep the adjacent carpet dry.

John was an Aquarian who considered water his element, and he collected frog artifacts.

Above his fireplace hung the most stunning early R. C. Gorman painting I have seen, a portrait of white-haired Brett done mostly in white on white with a single scarlet flounce slashing down the front of her white blouse. As I collapsed on a couch opposite it, I seemed to hear Brett say in her clipped British accent, "Now, John, *do* be a good boy. You are simply too, too Aquarian. Stop this nasty flood at once and get on about your new concerns. Naugh-ty man!"

The morning after John's deluge, workers whom I'd tried unsuccessfully to raise during the long nighttime siege found that the main water pipe beneath his house had burst. As with most emergencies, Frank slept through the entire proceedings.

The absence of a urine odor during Brett's ghostly monologue refueled my dislike of Manchester; he had even maligned Brett's ghost! Moreover, none of us ever detected such an odor when we ate at Brett House Restaurant near the blinking light five miles west of Arroyo Seco. True, restaurants have failed three times since 1977 in that house. And John's old house next door was just as jinxed, passing from one owner to another, bouncing to and from his heir; it is now involved in major litigation connected with title companies and Indian land claims. Owners of a children's school currently rent the building. As a student project, perhaps they should consider building an ark. Or they might try reinstalling Brett's coat of arms on the north wall of her place close by; removing it was a big mistake. Perfumed sachet bags to ward off the devil's burning smell of sulphur might be another handy project at Manchester's former home, I muse wickedly.

As far away as Columbus, Ohio, people know of Arroyo Seco's reputation as a town of witches and spirits. My neighbor Linda Ann read in a book on Southwestern witchcraft while attending college in Columbus that Arroyo Seco, New Mexico, was one place *brujas* could be found with certainty. Other books pinpoint Llano Quemado at the south end of Taos as the most famous haven of witches. In both places they are said to turn themselves into balls of fire, fly out of their conventional homes, and dance madly about the hills. It takes a good man with the first name of Juan to get rid of a fireball dancing with the devil. He must draw a circle around it with a long stick and wither it with a special incantation that boils down to, "I'm a better spirit than you are. I am the spirit of John the Baptist. My name is John too. In the name of God, I call thee witch! Now get lost."

Witches northeast of Taos traditionally are the most bizarre, although on Friday I would never say that, even if it is my lucky day. On this day, traditionally, people dare not speak against them. On Fridays witches hear whatever is said about them. Then watch out! At El Salto waterfall, about a mile east of us on the west flank of the Sangre de Cristo Mountains, *brujas* are said to turn themselves into jackrabbits, tumbleweeds, and wild animals, as well as fireballs. Frank thought the mountain had a negative feeling about it. It could be an accumulation of legendary negative feelings and events connected with this area that he was picking up on.

Taos Indians steer clear of El Salto waterfall. They are said to believe that at least one person died in a leap or fall from atop its cascade and that sacrificial deaths occurred there in the distant past. D. H. Lawrence used this belief in his novella *The Woman Who Rode Away*, based on El Salto waterfall and its recessed cave but transposed to a fictional setting in old Mexico. Frank was amazed to learn that I'd thought he and his friends—especially his Indian friend Tony Lujan—had picnicked there in the early days.

"Tony wouldn't go near that waterfall," he said. "He thought it was jinxed. All the Indians did. We would never *think* of picnicking there."

Illustrating the thinness of the veil in this region were the death cries Frank and his sister heard at the base of the mountains on Taos Indian Reservation across from us. As they hiked toward Lucero Canyon, they suddenly heard a frantic cry for help. Frank shouted back. Then came "one last despairing, agonizing death cry," both earthly and unearthly. It seemed to them to have been uttered by someone "who had been pushed or jumped to his death from the cliffs," Frank wrote. During this time brother and sister felt themselves held immovable in some sort of force field. When they could move again, they hurried to the Pueblo, where Frank told his friend Albert about the suspected accident. The Indian said he would look into the matter and advised him to come back the next day.

Upon Frank's return, Albert said briefly, "Long time ago that happen. You just hear it now." Naomi and Frank for a time had gone behind, or gone beyond, our explicate order.

Ann Merrill's daughter Blandy experienced much the same phenomenon in Pilar, twenty minutes south of Taos, where the Rio Grande thrashes down the canyon, sometimes almost level with the road, often separated from it by cliffs. Blandy was helping friends mend their roof not too far from the site of an accident in which a woman had died the year before. Trapped in her car after it had crashed into the river and landed on a submerged boulder, she drowned as her vehicle slid slowly underwater before help could reach her.

Distinctly Blandy and her coworkers heard a woman's voice call over and over again from this same deserted spot, "Help me. Someone help meeee! Help!" It was not the first time, neighbors said, that she had been heard.

In her book *No Lloro Pero Me Acuerdo*, Josephine Cordova records another incident in which a restless spirit made itself heard and read. A local World War I veteran whom she knew well had returned home safely from battle but died of an illness before fulfilling his wartime promise to give thanks at the Sanctuario in Chimayo near Santa Fe for his safe return. Soon his spirit began walking the floor of his former home, knocking on his wife's door, wailing and sobbing all night.

A group of *espiritistas* who talked to departed souls agreed to help the widow. In a dark room they gathered one night around a table upon which they had placed paper and pencil. They then asked the man's soul to write down what his problem was. Soon they heard someone writing. After relighting the lamp, they found in the veteran's handwriting his explanation that his soul could not rest in peace because of his broken promise. His friends visited the Chimayo Sanctuario for him and prayed to the Holy Child there, as he had promised to do, thus freeing his soul.

In her book Josephine also tells the tale of a man on horseback who one day followed a strange-looking coyote near Arroyo Seco. "Before the coyote could escape, the strange animal changed himself into a man and warned the man who was after him not to disclose his identity." Such shape-shifters were not uncommon.

Josephine claims that towering La Larga "dressed in black and carrying a wand or a walking stick horrified everyone who saw her." She was another spirit not to be taken lightly. "At midnight this horrible creature would come out of nowhere weeping and wailing for all she was worth."

La Larga seems to have been a sister in suffering to internationally feared La Llorona, "who came out at night wailing and scaring people off the roads." La Llorona is thought by some to stem from Aztec mythology. She is frequently connected with the spirit of Malinche, Cortez's Indian mistress and interpreter. After a time he deserted her for a Spanish love, took their two sons away from Malinche, and may have had them killed. In some versions of this story, she herself drowned them. As perpetually weeping La Llorona, she wanders the world searching for them. In Tucson she is seen and heard wailing beside a wall on Main Street near the old barrio section. Her children are thought to be walled up here. Other times she sobs her heart out along the Santa Cruz River. Two of her favorite hangouts are Old Mexico and New Mexico, where again she usually appears near water.

Another legendary local witch had the habit of taking out her eyeballs at night and laying them in a dish as if they were false teeth. There was hell to pay when her black cat licked the dish clean one night as the *bruja* slept after an exhausting evening of jetting about on her broomstick. In a fury, next morning she snatched out the eyeballs of her dog and plunked them into her own sunken sockets, for she needed eyes of the animal kingdom to see in the dark in order to perform her evil deeds.

Indian and Hispanic beliefs often parallel one another to a surprising degree. In *Mountain Dialogues* Frank writes that the Hopi name for "witch" or "sorcerer" means eye, walking, doing "because he uses the eye of the animal kingdom for evil purposes— destroying crops of his neighbors, bringing winds, driving away snow and rain, shooting ants, insects and glass into his victims, and causing the deaths of even his own relatives in order to prolong his own life."

During his extensive research for *The Book of the Hopi* at Hopiland, Frank was exposed to the Indians' strong belief in witchcraft. It didn't touch him because he didn't believe in it. "I don't believe in witchcraft and I told them so," he said in 1978 at the University of Arizona in a discussion group that included Leslie Silko, the well-known writer from Laguna Pueblo.

She agreed. "The first step for someone to get to you is for you to be able to be gotten. So it sounds as if that's what you've done. You've done the very best thing that you can do. That's a very good protection. So maybe you do believe."

Frank also told about two ghosts who came to him in Hopiland while he "was pretty much awake." He thought they were "two traveling salesmen . . . a pair of bums."

They assured him, "Oh, we're ghosts. But ghosts are just like people, you know."

Frank explained further during this taped session written up in *Frank Waters: Man and Mystic:*

They just gave me a little lecture. One of them wore a brown suit, and one of them wore a kind of blue suit. And they said, "Well, we're just ghosts and we're just here. We just dropped by to tell you to stay on the line." Now, one of them was stationed at the North Pole and one of them was stationed at the South Pole. So every so often, at periodic intervals, they had to travel up and down on their routes. And they would send out warnings and messages. And apparently, New Oraibi, my house, myself, at that time was on their route, on their line. So they said, "Now,"—and each of them said it very vociferously, emphatically—"now you stay on the line!" So I took that to heart. If I wanted to get this book done, and get anything I had better stay on the line. . . . I took it to heart I better behave myself. Stick to business and stay on the line.

Although Frank ended this remark with a laugh, another participant said, "Yeah, it wouldn't relate just to his book, but to his whole life."

Leslie Silko added, "I've always had a difficult time understanding people's terror of dying, because at Laguna it never seemed like anyone was gone, really died, that they were still about in some sense."

In a serious vein, Frank said of his stay at Hopiland, "There was one friend of mine; he was scared to death of a woman there. He thought she was *powaka* (a witch). Scared to death of her. And I pooh-poohed the idea. He said, 'That's my woman. She's going to either take seven years of my life or destroy me.' I said, 'No, I'll tell you what you do. You get us together and you just tell her to exercise her witchcraft on me, and she won't be able to do a thing because I've got power that'll throw this off.' . . . I just don't accept this negative power idea."

Frank believed in positive power. This conviction helped to bring him a long life. He elaborated at this meeting on his belief that some illnesses, accidents, and even broken bones can occur from one's being out of harmony with "all the forces" around one. "Maybe what's wrong with us when we get ill is that we're just not in tune. We get out of tune," he concluded.

I spent a lot of time reminding him of this belief during his final years. To a degree, it helped.

Frank told Dennis Hopper that the incense smell of burning copal, used in Guatemala's sacred places, would drive away unwanted spirits present in Mabel Luhan's house after the actor purchased it. If ever anyone was out of harmony with "all the forces" around him, it was Hopper at this generally negative time in his life. He was soon to become a very sick man. Mabel had said that after her death she would punish "whatever uncouth or vulgar people" mistakenly tried to invade her house. Hopper's original intent had been a creative one, but the situation deteriorated in the late '70s until the place became almost a commune for freeloaders, some of whom didn't recognize their generous host.

Positive spirits are welcomed at our place. Frank bought our Arroyo Seco house from Josephine Cordova in 1947 for the going price of "$100 per acre, $100 per room," although he rashly paid for more acreage than he wound up with. Josephine had inherited the place from her mother, an enduring matriarch named Maria de las Nieves—Maria of the Snows. Upon marrying a man from the nearby village of El Prado, Josephine abandoned her Arroyo Seco property. At this time it did look like the house of a sorcerer, a tumbledown three-room adobe with roof caving in, thicketed trees, pastures, and streams stretching back to mysterious depths on fourteen and one-half long, narrow acres. Josephine left behind more than her stories.

After his purchase, Frank told his friend Ralph Meyers about it with some pride. Ralph was the trader fictionalized as Byers in *The Man Who Killed the Deer*, and a friend to the Indians. To Frank's dismay, Ralph told him he wouldn't last a month in Arroyo Seco. "The damned location is no good," he said. He thought it was too close to El Salto waterfall, which had an "Indian jinx on it" and was "full of Spanish brujas." What the house needed to take away the jinx and propitiate any wayward evil spirits, Ralph decided, was "a piss and a prayer."

In *Mountain Dialogues* Frank described the ritual: "A copious urination was followed by the sprinkling of sacred cornmeal from a small buckskin sack hung around his neck. Apparently that did it. I have never been troubled by evil spirits."

Like Brett's ghost, by the way, Ralph didn't seem to think much of having restaurants in his former home, adjacent today to El Rincon on Kit Carson Road. At least two restaurants have gone broke there since his death, and every so often his son hears old Ralph clumping around inside. Ralph may not be too happy with his ex-wife, present owner of El Rincon. After Mabel Luhan died without buying a plot in crowded Kit Carson Cemetery, Ralph's ex said, "That's all right. I know Ralph would be glad to move over a bit to make room for her." And this is where Mabel is buried, squeezed between Ralph and the cemetery boundary fence.

Mabel was a busybody in real life. And she hasn't stopped meddling. I've felt her friendly energy myself, vibrating off the valuable Spanish Colonial furniture she gave Frank long ago. We also had an old couch with coil springs that used to talk and sometimes radiate music. Either it picked up radio waves or it tuned in on Mabel's bygone harangues, it seemed. Finally, to get rid of its clatter, I gave the couch to old Mrs. Quintana. I never wanted to frighten her by asking if its built-in entertainment had moved in down the street with her.

David, Carolyn, and Crystal Jongeward lived in our home seven winters from 1977 to 1984. In his book *Weaver of Worlds*, David confirms, "The House of Waters is a house that talks." After discussing a few of its utterances, which often frightened little Crystal, David adds, "During the first winter I distinctly heard gentle crying sounds in the corridor outside Crystal's bedroom. Thinking it must be wind in the trees, or some animal, I'd check outside, only to find another mountain of silence, canopied by more stars in the Milky Way than I have ever seen."

Energies from the other world never bothered Frank in our house or in his childhood home. He grew up with two ghosts that became part of the family in his grandparents' three-storied home in Colorado Springs. The house had been built against his grandmother's wishes at the wrong end of town on land where two old trappers camped when they came to town to sell hides and wild animal carcasses from door to door. A father and son, the Kadles were "smelly old men" dressed in tattered clothes. In *Pike's Peak* the woman who was really Frank's maternal grandmother prophesied indignantly, "We'll be carrying the Kadles' name with us to the grave.

60

Why, the ghosts of those two old men with their bloody clothes and tobacco juice runnin' down their white beards will be stompin' through the house in their smelly boots as long as it stands."

Sure enough, the Kadles spent their ghostly afteryears tramping up and down the third-floor stairs and checking out the house. When rebuilding the stairs didn't help, the occupants learned to live with their extended family. Years later when Frank's mother, called Ona in this book, became frightened by a recurring other-worldly light on the third-floor landing, she wanted to scream out to the Kadles for help, "trusting to those two old faithful family ghosts to make their nocturnal rounds and set the seal of their benediction upon the house. . . . She only knew that this gaunt old house on Shook's Run was haunted by specters of the unforgettable past and the dreaded future, by the ghostly flow of time; haunted by worries and doubts and futile hopes; haunted, oh haunted, even by the aimless ancient winds forever prowling about the creaking timbers which stood where once tall slim lodge poles raised firm and straight."

Like the Jongewards, other winter renters learned to go with the flow of spirits here at our Taos home—as Frank and his relatives had done in Colorado Springs. Most visitors and renters agree with Carlos Vasquez, who said, while he was director of oral history at the University of New Mexico, "I don't know whether this house has affected Frank's writing or his writing has affected it. But it has a wonderful feeling about it."

Nevertheless, one renter did have a problem. A likable fellow named Jim from the Chicago area, he was gay at a time when people were running especially scared of AIDS after Rock Hudson's death. We have a large gay population for a small town, but Jim just didn't make friends easily. When he grew unbearably lonely, he would call us at our Tucson home. "Your old friend Nan McCarthy at the hardware store is the only friendly person in this whole town," he reported at Christmastime. "I bought $200 worth of moccasins from her at El Mercado because she's the only one here who will give me the time of day."

Jim was approaching forty. Nan was pushing eighty-five and about to be spirited away by her family to a Santa Fe retirement home. Jim and Nan needed each other. But Jim decided he needed something more.

"This house is jinxing me," he complained in January. "Maybe it has put a hex on me. I talked to an old Indian in the plaza about this, and he agrees. He said hang an eagle feather above the entrance door in back. Is that okay with you?"

"Of course it's all right with us. That whole house is already full of eagle feathers, though: surrounding the Cheyenne warshield over our bed, on the *pahos* hanging in the living room, dangling from the antique light fixtures in both main rooms, to say nothing of all the eagle feathers in our peyote fans."

"Oh. Those are eagle feathers?"

"Of course."

"Well, they look pretty beat up and dusty to me. Some are moth-eaten. Can I hang up a clean one?"

"Every little bit helps."

"Yeah, I guess I'd better buy two, for extra good luck."

As it was by then against the law to sell eagle feathers, we figured Jim would have a hard time ridding himself of his hex. Yet he hung on in Taos through February and March. The two feathers he had hung in the shape of a cross over the back door appeared to sustain him. Then in April he called to say he was moving to La Jolla, California, where he could grow red bougainvillea and hot-pink hibiscus on the terrace of an apartment overlooking the sea.

When we returned to Taos, we could see why Jim's hex had never lifted. His two "eagle" feathers had come from a large white hen, about the size of one of Mrs. Quintana's chickens! For quite a few years we kept that feathered cross hanging above the back door. It added laughter to the other positive vibrations of our home, to glad ghosts like Janey, Brett, Nicolai Fechin, Strawberry Jim Suazo, and writer Victor White. Helping to keep their energy alive here are paintings, photographs, and books by or about them. In a sense Chief Seattle, foremost speaker and diplomat of the Duwamish tribe, could have been speaking of our place, which the Indians used to call "*La Isla*," when he said, "At night when the streets of your cities and villages are silent, and you think them deserted, they will throng with the returning hosts that once filled and still love this beautiful land."

8
Maria of the Snows

"Spirits used to be a common thing around here, you know," Josephine Cordova assures us, her dark, hooded eyes flashing above a cup of tea. "My uncle's spirit rattled and turned the doorknob of my bedroom door the night he died. And two of our relatives to this very day are *brujas*. Yes. witches. Oh, I could tell you stories. . . ."

Petite, brown, and wrinkled as an apple doll, with wispy tufts of hair, Josephine is beginning to fail mentally and physically. One kidney is already gone, and she has other ailments that she doesn't dwell upon. Born the same decade as Frank, she is much loved and honored by Taoseños who remember her as a dedicated teacher for twenty-six years, principal for thirteen. Now she repeats herself, talks to herself, and remembers most clearly her early years at this house, when she hid in the apple tree beside the front stream to read voraciously and to get out of helping her mother in the house. Josephine's apple tree today is fighting the losing battle of old age as valiantly as she.

Murmuring *"Que bonita"* as she strokes the top of our beautiful coffee table inlaid by Frank and his sister with Indian potsherds, she slips into thinking this house still is hers. In her day it was simply two stark rooms separated by a small kitchen, which is now a bathroom. The west room is a guest room, the east a large kitchen. The deep-silled window between them was once a door.

Josephine is visiting us this August day in 1991 with her daughter-in-law Kathy Cordova to discuss in more detail an apparition seen standing in this long window by Frank's niece, Susie (known to outsiders as Arleene). A successful middle-aged businesswoman with a logical mind, Susie has done well in real estate investments and as an administrator with the Los Angeles park system. In her spare time she is a wood carver, violinist, stamp collector, golfer, and swimmer. Ordinarily she is not one to hobnob with ghosts or spirits. Yet she has written us of a vision etched in her mind on the last morning of her most recent annual visit with us.

"I woke suddenly, feeling as if someone were staring at me," I read aloud from her letter to Josephine and Kathy.

I sat up and looked toward the guest-room door, which I'd left open. I thought, "How nice; Barbara came to wake me early because the shuttle leaves at 7:00 A.M."

I saw, thought, and felt this all at once. I saw a tall figure of a woman dressed in an old-fashioned long full skirt and a shawl that covered her head, shoulders, and arms. Her clothes were shades of black and gray. The figure filled the deep window in the hallway. Her feet brushed the low blue window sill. She was facing in, but looking toward the kitchen to her right. I knew now that it was not Barbara, nor was it anyone I knew. It all felt so natural and calm. During all this time I felt no fear, just a mild curiosity as to what she wanted and how I could help her.

As I mulled these thoughts over in my mind, the figure made a slight turn toward me. She had a straight back and moved in a graceful manner. Now she extended toward me her left arm and hand, waist high and palm upward, as gracefully as if performing a dance movement. Right after this, she rotated in a three-fourths turn toward the front yard. Then she extended her right arm in a gesture suggesting that I follow her.

As I watched, the figure seemed to drift away and vanish into the wall.

I went back to sleep and woke refreshed at 5:30 A.M. with no memory of this appearance. I recalled it while riding the shuttle bus down to Albuquerque. I don't know what to think. I only know I saw the figure and how it moved. My friend Lauri says it may have been death. The feeling I had was of calmness and quiet. What do you think?

The note of alarm at the end of this letter had led me to call Susie soon after receiving it. "I'm pretty sure it wasn't a death figure you saw," I'd said to reassure her. "Around here, death is personified as a grinning skeleton with stringy hair and a shriveled, bony chest. She's named Doña Sebastiana after St. Sebastian, who was martyred by arrows, and she rides around in a rickety wooden death cart with an arrow strung in the bow she clutches in her bony fists. It's this aimed arrow we have to worry about. It warns us to live right. Any moment it might strike us dead! You'd recognize her a mile away. No, your figure must have something to do with a person who once lived here. Maybe it's connected with that ghost child your mother saw years ago in a cradle suspended from our guest-room ceiling beams. I'll go over and see what old Mrs. Quintana has to say. Josephine's mother was her aunt."

Laying down Susie's letter after reading it aloud, I turn now to Josephine and pat her wizened hand to get her attention. "I went down the street to see if Alicia Quintana or her daughter Amada had any idea about who this figure was. Isn't Alicia your mother's niece?"

"Yes, my mother, Nieves, was her aunt. Alicia's mother and my mother were sisters. Nieves's mother was Josefa Martinez, wife of Juan Julian Martinez. They were my grandparents. In her old age I took care of my little mother right here in this house. Nieves, people usually called her. Her name was Maria de las Nieves."

"I know. Maria of the Snows is one of the most beautiful names I've heard. I wish it were mine."

"Oh, you wouldn't take my little mother's name away from her, would you?" Josephine draws back in alarm.

"Of course I wouldn't. Still, it is *muy bonita*. Anyway, down at Quintanas' I told Susie's story to Amada so she could retell it to her mother in Spanish. I didn't expect Amada to say anything. You know how she is. Most often all she says around her mother is, 'Myyyy. Imagine *that!*'

"To my amazement, I had no sooner closed my mouth than Amada exclaimed, 'Of course, that has to be Nieves, Josephine Cordova's mother! Maria de las Nieves Martinez was her real name, but everyone called her Nieves. She lived to be ninety-two. She was widowed young, left with five children to raise. After her husband died she always dressed in black or dark gray, just as Susie says, with long skirts and a shawl. Most women wore mourning clothes for only a year or so after their husbands died, but Nieves dressed like that the rest of her life. She had a long, hard life, but she always stood very straight like that.

"'Nieves and my mother's mother were sisters. My mother's brother Onésimo Torres felt sorry for Nieves. He told her to go over to Tres Piedras for five years and homestead some land there. Then he would trade properties with her. After five years, he took her land there and gave her this land in Arroyo Seco where you and Mr. Waters live. She and her children moved here. Two of her little ones died when they were about two years old. Mr. Waters's sister must have seen one of their spirits in that hanging cradle.'

"'What was Nieves doing with her hand held out to Susie?' I asked Amada.

"Again without a moment's hesitation, Amada replied, 'She wants Susie to pay for some masses to get Nieves out of Purgatory. She probably is still down there and needs a contribution. We believe dead people go to Purgatory before they get to Heaven. Masses help get them out. From another story I heard, I guess it takes about seventy-three masses to get out of there.'

"'According to what Susie says, though, Nieves seemed too calm and peaceful to be in Purgatory,' I interrupted.

"With one of her rare laughs, Amada said, 'Yes, she must be just about out!'"

My Cheshire-cat satisfaction with these remarkable sleuthing results is short-lived. Like most Taoseños, the Cordovas like a good ghost story—the more complicated the better. As Josephine daintily sips her tea from a pink-flowered cup, Kathy puts her cup firmly down on the coffee table. She is going to nominate a new candidate for our Ghost of the Year. As she draws a deep breath, we can tell it will be a long nomination. "Perhaps as Amada says, the ghost was that of Maria de las Nieves Martinez," she begins.

"Nieves was my little old mother," Josephine interrupts, slowly nodding her head up and down as if grieving. "She lived to be ninety-two, and I took good care of her in her old age. I loved her very much."

Patting Josephine into silence, Kathy continues, "Josephine's son Arsenio, my husband, has a different idea. He thinks this spirit could be that of Josephine's grandmother, Josefa Garcia Martinez. She owned land here, and it is possible she roams the El Salto area in search of a lost item."

"Life was very hard for my mother, who died at ninety-two," Josephine says. "When we homesteaded at Tres Piedras for five years, she baked cookies, and I sold them at the train station. Such a little girl—to be selling cookies! Passengers on the Chile Line bought them and stuffed money into my pockets. I was so proud to go home with my pockets full of money!"

"According to family oral history," Kathy resumes, "over a century ago Apaches or Comanches kidnapped eight-year-old Manuel de Atocha from his yard in nearby Mora while he played with a friend. He was Nieves's brother. Josefa Martinez, their mother and Josephine's grandmother, mourned the loss heavily. When her husband, Juan Julian, finally accepted the fact that Manuel would never return, he moved his family back here to Arroyo Seco in an effort to ease his wife's depression. Josefa, in turn, became easy prey for traveling gypsies and con men who swore they could help her find her lost son—for a fee, of course. Some say she went mad for a time. She and Juan spent their last years living in houses separate from each other."

"*Su casa es muy bonita*. Your place is very beautiful. *Su casa es mi casa*," says Josephine, her eyes sparkling like hummingbirds as she takes in the rare paintings, pottery, Spanish Colonial chests, and Indian rugs. "You take good care of Mr. Waters, as I did my little old mother."

"*Gracias*."

"Out of desperation, the grieving mother waged a vendetta against the Blessed Mother," Kathy finishes after a flurry of pats for Josephine. "'As long as my son is captive, so shall yours be,' Josefa said. Then she removed a sacred statue of the Christ Child from Holy Trinity Church and buried it near El Salto waterfall, never revealing the exact site. Josefa died, leaving the Christ Child captive. Perhaps she suffers still from a guilty conscience and wants Susie and you to dig up the Christ Child and return it to Holy Trinity. This would explain her signaling with her right hand to come outdoors.

"That's what Arsenio and I think this is all about. We think Susie saw Josefa, not Nieves. Of course, Nieves's spirit could be worried too; this all has to do with her lost brother. But we just have a feeling it was *Josefa* standing in your window.

"By the way, the kidnapped boy was never found, but Arsenio thinks he has located Manuel's grandson in Oklahoma. He thinks the Indians dragged the child clear over there. Maybe this belated family contact will help to quiet Josefa's troubled spirit."

After the Cordovas leave, I again call Frank's niece in California. "You'd better play it safe and cover all the bases, Susie, since you're the one who saw her. Why don't I go over to the church for you and buy two Sunday masses to be said for Josephine's mother, Maria de las Nieves Martinez, and two for her grandmother Josefa Garcia Martinez? I feel as if our ghost really is Nieves, but just in case it was Josefa signaling you to come outside and dig up her captive statue, we'd better help *her* out of Purgatory too. She may be stuck there a lot longer than Nieves! It will cost only $20 for all four masses. And next summer during your visit we'll scout around the waterfall to see if we can find any remains of the missing Christ Child."

We did just that. Combing the waterfall area, we peered into crevices, crawled under rocky overhangs, dug into cool, sandy hollows. Not too surprisingly, we found no trace of the purloined *santo*. But it was moving to hear the names of these two women from so long ago uttered aloud again before the Holy Trinity congregation. It seemed a touch of immortality.

Josephine said later, "It made me cry when Susie and you bought all those masses for my mother and grandmother. I hope Mr. Waters won't mind, but I am going to buy some masses for him so he'll get well. Do you think he will mind? He is such a fine, sweet man. And as I tell you every visit, he is so luck-ky to have you; you take such good *care* of him—like I did my little mother."

Five years later I feel Nieves's energy with me more than ever. It is a sustaining, comforting energy, not a troubled one. The spirit of Maria of the Snows has gone on. She has left me, however, that part of her energy that can be helpful. Part of it has to do with appreciating the sheer joy of winter, her time of year. She too read the ancient calligraphy of shadows cast upon new-fallen snow by moonlit cottonwoods. Nieves too delighted in royal-blue Steller's jays, black-and-white magpies with blue-sheened tails, sparrows chirping their hearts out. Smiled at the sight of crystal icicles gingerbreading our house. Inhaled the pungent perfume of piñon fires at dawn and dusk. Reveled in glistening moonscapes when mountains turn to giant white Shalakos dancing above the Ancient Ones, the sage and piñons mantled in snow. Oddly enough, both Frank and Nieves died at age ninety-two. Perhaps she was forewarning us.

What joy it must have given her to be named after this winter wonderland, this *nieves*. Her name surely must have lifted the heart of Maria of the Snows from the drudgery of her daily existence, from the grief of losing her husband in 1914. Josephine reminds us that for her family the widow constantly provided "health, happiness, and success without having to depend on anyone for support."

Josephine's book contains moving vignettes of Nieves's family carrying bouquets of summer flowers to blessed Mother Mary, of Nieves and her little brood kneeling every night before their *santos* to say the rosary. "We were all very willing to kneel down to pray," Josephine recalls, "because after the rosary was recited, we had something very good to eat: piñon nuts, candy, cookies, or pies."

I call myself "Queen of Kindling" now that I have mastered simply the art of chopping kindling wood and hauling it in a wheelbarrow to the house, along with loads of logs chopped by someone else. Maria of the Snows gathered all her own wood in the summer and chopped every bit of it herself. Like me, she fed the animals daily, but hers were not pleasure animals. She fed her cows so her children would have milk, butter, and cheese. She fed sheep for clothing and pigs for food. She sold eggs laid by her chickens, and she butchered her own cows when the time came, along with her sheep, pigs, and chickens.

Nieves made all her children's clothing, crocheted rugs from sheep wool, embroidered, and quilted. She grew a large garden; canned; and made jams, jellies, and chokecherry wine. These things Maria of the Snows did routinely. Other, seasonal tasks included making brooms from tall field grasses that she and her children scythed at harvest time. Josephine writes, "She was a very religious but proud woman and she sincerely believed that everyone should work for a living." Nieves was never a welfare recipient. It is hard to think of her ever as "little." Reading about a typical day in the life of Nieves shakes me out of bed and the doldrums, through what is a snap of a day by comparison.

When Francisco Martinez, a widower, sent his formal letter requesting the consent of Juan Julian and Josefa Martinez to marry their daughter Maria de las Nieves, he described her as "good, moral, and beautiful." In a photograph taken just after her marriage Nieves's thick hair, drawn up in a knot at the back of her head, falls in a loose puff about her face. Large, soft eyes beneath straight eyebrows beacon out above a dainty but firm nose shadowed on the right by an emphatic line. She has full, heart-shaped lips, with a dimpled cleft between her mouth and chin. Her earrings are thin gold circles; a starburst is pinned to the top of her yoked blouse. About to smile, she looks like a gentle woman.

Indeed, Maria of the Snows in her youth is a vision of loveliness. Today I feel like honoring her with a monument, her kind of monument: a snow lady. Frank was amused and pleased one rare winter in Tucson when it snowed enough for me to make a midget snowperson stacked only waist high. My little carrot-nosed alien lived in our carport to protect it as long as possible. Unlike Frank, it was not a sun worshiper.

Not too far from Frank's ashes in our Sacred Aspen Grove, I build my monument to Nieves and to all the wonderful matriarchs of Arroyo Seco and Taos. She stands beside our first small house for writers and artists. One can tell she wants to be part of the Frank Waters Foundation. And of course she always will be.

My Nieves is fashioned of snow crystals glistening brilliant as diamonds in the cold, bright sunlight. Pleased at being a diamond snow lady, she is about to smile. Her stomach is firm and round, her bosom fashionably buxom, her head life-sized with large sparkling rhinestone buttons for eyes, two smaller rhinestone buttons for nostrils, and red lips the same heart shape as those of the real Nieves. They are cut from a red plastic bag and dimpled at the corners. Over her head, Nieves wears a black lace mantilla, like the one old Mrs. Quintana always wore to Holy Trinity Church. It is pinned with a starburst. In Nieves's pierced earlobes are thin, wired circles covered with gold paper. *Que bonita*, Maria of the Snows. You are indeed a beautiful woman!

As for me, I am sweating and worn out. Whew! Making a snow lady at eight thousand feet is not child's play. More accurately, it is child's play, and I am no longer a child. But play is good for us at any age. Maria of the Snows deserved some play. She worked entirely too hard. Staying beautiful in itself was a major chore. Nieves made her own makeup. She ground burnt deer antlers into powder, then compressed it by hand into "little loaves." Rouge for cheeks and lips came from *maravilla* weed. Her face cream was a mixture of mutton fat and piñon pitch, her hair shampoo amole root.

You are captivating, Maria of the Snows. To me the word "widow" formerly had a frightening, lonely sound. As a model widow, you give me courage to go on. Alone. In a sense. Although I don't have your beautiful name, I have the inspiration of sharing this house and land with the remaining, positive energy of Maria of the Snows.

I cry. For all of you are gone, and by the wind grieved. Gone! Both you and Frank gone at age ninety-two. Old Mrs. Quintana gone at age one hundred. Josephine in a Colorado nursing home, her mind all gone. *Yo lloro y me acuerdo.* I cry and I remember. And through these memories, your enduring energy sustains.

9
Queen of Kindling

Actually, compared to those of an average suburbanite, my days in Arroyo Seco are no "snap," especially for an elderly wench. Mornings start off with a bang. The two shelties and Trickster leap against the side of my high bed, shaking it until I roll out and fix their breakfasts of dried dog-food pellets and low-fat cottage cheese. Meanwhile, Ginger and Golden Girl wait impatiently at the corral gate for their hay. Their breaths billow white in the frosty air. They make a wonderfully comforting sound down deep in their throats, a repeated "whuuuuuh-whuuuuuh" with a vibrato to it. It is lower-pitched than a whinny, and more affectionate.

Ginger is a greedy pig. She grabs her thick flake of hay as I lift it over the fence, starts pulling and gobbling while it's still aloft. When she is fully engrossed, it's time to throw Golden Girl's hay flake over the gate fifty yards away. Golden Girl is a lady, standing patiently by until it is her turn, even allowing Ginger to run over and grab some of this second breakfast if she feels like it.

Incredibly, Golden Girl has four-inch-long icicles hanging from the sides of her brown winter coat. Two icicles longer than the rest dangle from her jaw. They hurt her when pulled off whole; I break all of them into smaller and smaller glittering beads. The last beads touching her body she won't let me remove. She too wants to be a sparkling diamond lady, like my Nieves snow lady.

Moonset turns the horizon to Neapolitan ice cream, layered blue beneath rose beneath a white-gold full moon. Piñon smoke incenses the crystal air. And teasing magpies raucously dive-bomb Trickster until I feed them their suet. Trickster has dragged a piece of sheepskin matted with dirt into the yard. As I lift it up to put it into a garbage bag, a black tail soft as silk caresses my hand. I would like to hang it Davey Crockett fashion from the back of my black hat trimmed in fur. But it makes me feel too sad to do that. The sound of sheep bells next door reminds me that this silken tail may have belonged to one of Salomé's Black Faces, as I call them, and just weeks ago twitched gaily up and down the long pasture adjacent to ours. His sheep have black faces, black legs, and black tails. Black spruces up the ordinary off-white wool covering their bodies.

Luis Torres butchered a week ago. Now our yard looks like a meat-packing plant each morning before I dispose of the latest treasure Trickster has carted home: one morning a jaw with thick yellow teeth, another day a skull, the next a long, bumpy spine, then several times calf legs thick with stiff black hair. Hooves are another delicacy. It is gross.

Luis is Nieves's great-nephew. He is short but wears a dashing cowboy hat with its brim curled just so and expensive cowboy boots made of finest leather. As I wheel into the house my first eighty pounds of gnarled piñon logs for the day, an amazing synchronicity dawns upon me. This is probably the very wood that Maria of the Snows homesteaded in Tres Piedras when Josephine was a child. Luis had sold me wood before, so this year I had him deliver and stack two cords of fine piñon. He told me it came from their Tres Piedras land, twenty miles from here. The connection did not sink in until now. How fitting! Astonishing, these wheels within wheels, turning, ever turning.

Luis and his wife, Bernice, a former bank executive, were extremely caring at Frank's final celebration. Luis is Onésimo's son.

Onésimo too thought a great deal of Frank. Once he asked Frank to buy his big place down the road for a song. But Frank didn't have enough money at the time for even a "song," and he did not want the added responsibility. Nevertheless, he always felt extremely honored by this offer, as he told Onésimo and others. A major character in Frank's *People of the Valley* is called Onésimo, a name that sings with the music of northern New Mexico. Luis and Bernice have turned the old house and grounds into a showplace. They raise Charolais bulls and have a dozen buffalo and a couple of llamas and a gazebo and some fake white swans floating on a tiny lake. Now they call their place "Hacienda de Los Torres."

Tell me, Maria of the Snows, was your wood system as complicated as mine? Someone said I'm like my car, an Acura, with front-wheel drive instead of rear. On the snowy path between the barn and house I don't have the strength to push a wheelbarrow loaded full with logs, but I can *pull* it walking backward. Planting one's feet firmly for each backward step is the most crucial element of reverse pulling on ice or snow. The idea is to trundle the wheelbarrow up to the back door, somehow, then carry twenty-five-pound loads in a log carrier to each woodstove.

The secret for top-notch fires is to have three different sizes of wood. Basic are logs fourteen to sixteen inches long and cut into at least fourths in diameter. Aspen is no good; it burns too fast. Most people here use pine nowadays; on the average it costs $120 for a cord four by four by eight feet, delivered but unstacked. Rare oak and cedar cost too much in this part of the country, or they would be best. Piñon is best here, but most expensive of our three main types. It burns slowly and exudes the fragrance of wood sprites. Another help in starting and nurturing a new fire are lumber-yard reject lengths of pine approximately sixteen inches long, three inches wide, and one inch thick. A third type of wood needed is kindling about the size of fat spaghetti. It is the key to easy fire starting. Some of my own kindling is chopped so fine I can set a match to it and start a new fire.

Generally, it's best to avoid such hubris and tent six pieces of kindling over one crumpled sheet of newspaper, with three or four lumber reject lengths tented above that and a small log held in readiness for rip-roaring flames. A beginning fire must be properly shaped in some such fashion.

My first chopping efforts looked more like French fries than kindling. Luckily our plumber, Gilbert Tafoya, was working here that day. I had seen a man casually shaving lumber rejects with a large ax to make his kindling, but Frank's ax was too heavy and un-wieldy for me. Then I found his precious tomahawk abandoned in the beat-up cardboard box that serves as our toolbox. This little hatchet reminded me so much of Frank's wood-cutting days, and those of Nieves, that I used it in Boulder, Colorado, as a show-and-tell item for a speech in February 1996 about tapping into Frank's energy.

Although I tried to hide my shaved French-fry efforts from Gilbert, during his trips back and forth between house and truck he saw what was going on and came over to the barn. An open shed-like structure built of wood, it is wide enough to shelter two cars, three cords of wood, and a hundred bales of hay.

"See, this is what you want to do," he said kindly. "In the first place, you don't want to swing down on the wood. You might chop yourself in half that way! You want to balance on one end, against a solid surface, a piece of pine without bark or knots on top. Now you lift up your *log*, see, not just the hatchet. Then pound the log down, up and down, over and over again until your hatchet works itself all the way through. Okay?"

Well, okay. It works! What you are doing is *hammering* wood against a solid surface, not chopping it. Your hatchet is embedded in the wood you're banging against a surface. If the hatchet isn't embedded, Gilbert's system doesn't work. No one ever told me before about *hammering* wood.

Things were looking up the next time Gilbert passed by. "It might make it a little easier for you," he said with careful diplomacy, "if you used an old stump as your base instead of this metal wheelbarrow." He circled his arms around the heavy tree stump we use as a mounting block for riding and carried it inside the barn for me. What a difference! The sound factor alone made this change worthwhile. When it came to chopping wood, this plumber knew what he was doing.

As I crashed the hatchet handle down against my thumb, a little later he cautioned, "Always keep your work gloves on when you're doing this. It may save you a finger or two."

Confidentially, I would recommend knee pads too, but I didn't want Gilbert to know that my log frequently jumped away from me and whammed me in the knees, for most of one's hammering occurs at knee level. I couldn't see Maria of the Snows wearing knee pads, though. In fact, I've never seen any wood choppers using knee pads. It doesn't appear to be the "in" thing. One learns to tough it out. And logs begin to behave more properly after a few days, or weeks.

The final step is to hammer any kindling pieces as thick as one's thumb to the desired fat spaghetti size, still using Gilbert's embedded-hatchet technique. If the piece is pointed, forget it; there is no space for embedding, and everything goes flying or smashing about.

The first day one small log will work up a horrendous sweat on a novice at an altitude of eight thousand feet. And you will feel like saving this first kindling for some worthy museum. After that, it's often fun to wrap a dozen pieces of vintage kindling loosely in a piece of bright giftwrap and give it away as a very special present. A few of my more amazing pieces I've given individually to friends as bookmarks. People are dismayed.

With woodstoves goes the added chore of emptying ashes. Our catalytic Avalon in the kitchen is a gem. It is easy to start, simple to keep going, and snugly heats up half the house without any pampering. It has no ash pan, though. Emptying the ash bed can be a pain. A fine curtain of white ash quickly veils all the furniture in our combined kitchen–dining room. Learning to live with this ash curtain is better than becoming a full-time drudge.

The Dutch West catalytic convection stove in our master bedroom also is easy to start, but it takes constant pampering to produce and sustain the desired temperatures. Its saving grace is a pan underneath that simplifies ash removal every few days.

The corner living room fireplace is another ash headache. All these ashes must be transferred to metal buckets. They in turn are lugged outdoors through muck or deep snow to a dumping spot near the stable. Despite the labor involved, mankind's primal fascination with fire remains. One dreams before its tapestried mythology. Without a good-sized stack of wood to nurture one's imagination, however, reality sets in quickly.

During ash removal, while fortified in my waterproof Sorel mudboots, it makes sense to cope with garbage and the horses' second daily feeding. Garbage disposal complicates my days almost as much as heating. Its five basic steps consist of burning papers in an aluminum garbage can with holes out near the stable, throwing leftover food over the fence there to Celestino Quintana's animals, taking recyclables to the recycling center, if it's open, carrying the remainder of our garbage to large cans in our car-hay barn, then hauling them when full to the county landfill.

Appreciate your garbage service.

Somehow, garbage disposal lacks the creative zing of wood chopping, and it shocks one too quickly into left-brain activity from the right-brain work of writing. Hammering fine kindling and chopping wood ease the mind from right-brain creativity through a new type of creativity into left-brain activity and physicality. Frank did his writing in the morning. As a younger man, in the afternoon he chopped wood and involved himself in similar projects, such as gathering rocks from a riverbed to make a striking walk that extends almost the length of our house in front. After thirty years of neglect, that walk had silted over, by the way. I discovered it while attempting to plant petunias there. It was almost as exciting as excavating Pompeii to uncover Frank's stone walk one summer. It seemed that the rocks began to speak when liberated. And they continue to do so. They speak of a man and his pride in doing a job well, of his creativity, and of his love for beautiful Janey, who inspired him to build this stone monument.

Frank believed a writer should never speak in public of creative work in progress for fear the energy will be "all talked out" of it, and it will never see the light of day in print. Isabelle Larrinaga told me of an amusing incident that occurred over cocktails during an art show opening. Someone asked Frank, "How is your work going these days?"

"Oh, fine!" he replied. "We dug thirty post holes yesterday and got the new fence halfway up this morning."

To ease out of the right brain after writing, in later years when he was physically worn down, Frank drank more than he had during his wood-chopping days. Perhaps writers like James Joyce and Ernest Hemingway would have had less of a problem with alcohol and depression if in midlife they had taken up wood chopping, or kindling hammering at least. Kindling hammering would have been perfect for Joyce, who shunned the physical. He would needle a person in Hemingway's presence, then duck behind his friend and cry, "Deal with him, Hemingway. Deal with him!" Joyce could have dealt with chopping kindling and felt good about this achievement.

To really enjoy it, one should come to wood chopping in midlife or later. It's like living in an adobe house. It can get old. For two summers in the early '70s after school was out I rented a house on a hill two or three miles west of Frank's house. It had been renovated by Judy and Mike Wallner. One day a man stopped by with his family and asked if they could see the inside. His ancestors had owned this house for generations before Wallners bought it.

"How could you sell a house this beautiful?" I asked.

"If you had been born and raised in an old adobe, you would get sick of it too and want to live in a clean, modern mobile home," he said. "In an old adobe, dirt is always falling in on your head and getting into your food and everything else. An adobe never stops falling apart and needing fixing somewhere."

At first I called Wallners' place "the House of Rainbows." Almost every afternoon I saw out its east windows a rainbow arching from Frank's house to the Indian reservation. *Our* house really is the House of Rainbows, therefore. The end of the rainbow lies here.

Wallners' adobe had a brass bed that Frank and I both appreciated. I wrote a forgettable poem about making golden love there in a golden bed with golden sheets, and eating golden popsicles afterward. The bed had belonged to my visitor's great-grandparent. He showed me how to unscrew the top of one bedpost and peer down into a secret hiding place for valuables, of which none remained, not a single Spanish doubloon.

Over Guatemalan coffee at Casa Fresen one morning this winter, my young friend Valerie confides, "For five years I lived in Woodstock in a house heated only by a woodstove. I've had it up to here with chopping wood. Today my first priority is a thermostat!" Frank would have empathized with her.

Chopping wood from childhood on, for a lifetime, must be like having adobe dirt ceaselessly falling on one's head. I admire those human goddesses who did it, like Maria of the Snows, old Mrs. Quintana, and Elizida Duran next door. Elizida could hold her own with any man chopping wood, though she was a slender woman only five foot three, no Brünhilde. We're talking chopping when it comes to Elizida, not hammering. She had a swing like Joe DiMaggio and was twice as accurate. She didn't like people to see her chopping wood, which is regarded as a none-too-genteel pursuit in some circles. Yet hers was an art that should have been preserved on film. She died of cancer several years ago. Since then Salomé only halfheartedly keeps his hand in at the woodpile. I miss seeing them out there side by side, taking turns at reducing a mountain of chaos to an ordered woodpile, or Elizida chopping while Salomé made kindling.

Mrs. Quintana was built much the same as Elizida, only shorter. She and her husband had both been teachers. They retired after inheriting a flock of sheep from her parents. During the summer Mr. Quintana herded their flock from Arroyo Seco through the mountains to a valley near Red River, about forty miles away.

Little Mrs. Quintana would ride over on horseback with supplies and cook for a day or two. Back at home she did everything, or ordered about whichever of her sons was available.

She chopped many a cord of wood in her day. And she had the lifetime muscles to prove it. When she was ninety-five and angry at her nephew Luis for making her grandson move her fence two feet back from the Luis O. Torres Road, I watched her lift Luis's impossibly heavy post-hole digger. She raised it over her head and threw it over the fence toward Luis's house next door with a disdainful "Paaagh!" At ninety-seven, she was still planting and tending a garden despite dizzy spells connected with her diabetes that caused her repeatedly to fall flat on her face. At one hundred she flew to California to attend a wedding.

Once when she was middle aged, during the absence of her husband Mrs. Quintana dragged an entire deer carcass out to the back of her acreage and burned it. She had stopped by our house and found a note on our back door. It read, "We've come looking for the Man Who Killed the Deer." This was a joint reference to Frank and his book. Alicia Quintana mistook it as a note from the law, which she presumed must be looking for her husband and his illegally killed deer.

The wood-chopping tradition goes on, with its fans and its detractors. During a hippie stage, my younger son and his friends traveled to the high, isolated mountain town of Truchas, where they had heard pot was easy to come by. Single young women there greeted them with open arms. And axes. "We got so sick of chopping wood for those damn women that *nothing* made it worthwhile to stay long," Bill said. "We never wanted to see northern New Mexico again after we took off from there." And he didn't, until Frank's death.

Reverence for wood chopping has been built into our community. The patron saint of Taos Indian Pueblo is Saint Jerome, or San Geronimo in Spanish, protector of the wilderness and wood choppers. A fifth-century doctor of the church, Jerome (Hieronymus) is credited with translating most of the Vulgate version of the Bible.

82

As a noted biblical scholar, essentially he had nothing to do with wood choppers. For four years between 374 and 378 he did retreat to the wilderness desert of Syria, with only scorpions and wild animals for companions. In later life he and some followers exiled themselves to Bethlehem, where Jerome lived part of the time in a rock-hewn cave while helping to establish a school and a hospice. A cultured man with a caustic wit, he remained an outcast from Roman society by choice.

Nevertheless, our artist friend Marcia Gaiter painted him as a barefoot, disheveled hermit wearing a rough red mantle. In the *santo* she did for us, St. Jerome looks as if he is yodeling to himself or God as he ventures a two-step. I nicknamed him "the Tipsy Saint," much to Marcia's disapproval. We did not know until her death that she was Catholic. Our San Geronimo ("g" is pronounced as "h") holds a crude cross in his left hand; a thin halo circles his head. His face is turned toward a trumpet extending on his right from an upper corner of her painting. This trumpet is said to represent his communion with God. They may be talking, therefore, not yodeling. Near his left foot is a blond-headed raven. In some versions Marcia painted a scorpion near this bird. San Geronimo is sometimes depicted with a lion from whose paw, one legend says, he has removed a thorn. Had I known such liberties were taken with the saint protecting my wood chopping, for our *santo* I would have had Marcia sling an ax over his shoulder instead of a cross.

Sixteenth-century Spanish priests appear to have grafted Jerome's saint's day of September 30 onto a traditional Indian harvest celebration at the Pueblo as the most convenient way to get Christianity's foot on the ladder of the kiva. Although Jerome the intellectual might have shuddered at the thought of wood chopping, his Indian worshipers could identify with his supposed love of it—and them. I can too, with a willing suspension of disbelief.

On San Geronimo Day his statue is attired in a fine yellow dress and carried reverently to a high golden aspen bower at the beginning of the racetrack on the northeast side of the Pueblo plaza, where he bestows blessings upon footraces being run to honor the sun. Frank writes superbly of this important feast day in chapter ten of *The Man Who Killed the Deer.* He views as the heart of this celebration a tall pine holding aloft food and a sacrificial deer or sheep. At the climax of the feast day, strong men attempt to climb the slick pole and bring down this food. It is considered a bad omen when no one succeeds or major setbacks occur. After describing the respect and wonder of the woodsmen about to chop down this great ceremonial tree in the forest, Frank gives their intuited prayer and its purpose:

> *We know your life is as precious as ours. We know that we all are children of the same Mother Earth, of Our Father Sun. But we know that one life must sometimes give way to another, so that the one great life of all may continue unbroken. So we ask permission, we obtain your consent to this killing.*
>
> So they cut him down, he in their midst who had stood here tall and sound and proud before they were yet grown. And it was well with them and with him who had spiritually assented to their ritualistic request for his sacrifice.

In our lives we would do well to pay such homage to wood, honoring it rather than taking it for granted. Throughout most of human history, wood has been highly respected or worshiped for its life-giving aspects: fuel, shelter, furniture, walking supports, protection, medicine. Symbolically, wood stands for the mother, or female, and is associated with fertilization and rebirth. Burnt wood also is identified with wisdom and death. In sacrificial fires, the remaining ashes and charcoal themselves are imbued with these magical, fertilizing, and rebirthing connotations. To help with renewal and growth of trees, early ceremonial rituals included the pruning of saplings with ritual axes.

Our hatchet, made by Estwing, is thirteen inches long. Its handle curves in a slight "S" shape with four inches of unadorned steel above almost seven inches of leather wrapped tightly in thin hori-

zontal strips that once were varnished. At the top and bottom of the
leather section, two thin bands of white surround a black strip. Its
head is silver, five inches across, three and a half inches at the highest part, two inches at the narrowest.

In the oldest religions, ritual axes like ours belonged to goddesses. Minoan goddesses used them to mark holy places and the
initiate's path. Croatian sacred women used them to free newborn
children from the underworld by severing their umbilical cords.
The double-headed ax is associated with the labyrinth and thus
one's pilgrimage in search of the center, as is the single-headed ax in
my case. Used as a hammer, like mine, such an ax would be "en-
dowed with the mystic power of creation," writes J. E. Cirlot.
Regarded as a celestial ax in Asia, the ritual ax was used symbolically
to cut away the unillumined self. Cirlot states that it is a symbol of
celestial illumination and a symbol of the power of light.

The hard work of chopping, or hammering, wood can
be equated with developing one's inner resources. Estés states,
". . . chopping of wood symbolizes vast psychic resources, the ability to provide energy for one's tasks, to develop one's ideas, to bring
the dream, whatever it be, within reach."

From Swiss peasants C. G. Jung learned to respect the innate
renewing power of wood cutting and stone carving. Into his old age
he cut all his own firewood at his private retreat, Bollingen. Wood
cutting relaxed him, made him happy, and constellated his creative
Personality No. 2 "that lives in the centuries."

Who would suspect that the backyard woodpile is such a power
spot? People don't have to trek to far-off Tibet or Machu Picchu
for enlightenment; I have long been advising them that they can
find it in their own backyards. But to me it had previously seemed
that this state would be attained through contemplation of beauty
rather than panting, inhaling great gulps of air, sweating, and
smashing wood. Live and learn.

This brings to mind a favorite cartoon featuring two good old
boys rocking on a porch. One is saying, "I searched the whole
world over before finding happiness right here in my own back-

yard." He smiles complacently at the oil derricks honeycombing his property.

My tomahawk and my wood are my oil derricks. They open me to further interaction with the energies of bygone wood choppers and to increased creativity, cornerstone of our Foundation. They help to provide centering, illumination, and sustaining light for Frank's continued journey and my own. The art of wood chopping is a great humbler at the same time it makes one greater than one.

As the New Testament promises, "Cleave the wood and I am there."

10
Roses Are Blue

I weep for Adonais—he is dead!
　　—Percy Bysshe Shelley

The blueness of another Damn First crept upon me last night. Today the blue-black of our first Valentine's Day apart has struck with full vengeance. It will take some doing to get through this day, including Shelley, Donne, Shakespeare, and whoever else flickers through my troubled mind. All the world's poets and all the king's men cannot piece my heart together again. Believing Christmas is the only stumbling block for lone survivors, others seldom stop to think that Valentine's Day can be a very blue one. Most send Christmas cards to the grieving, not valentines.

My sister Joan does send an old-fashioned valentine picturing two young girls who look much as we once did, except that they are from the Victorian age. Back in 1970 another man named Frank told me I was a "throwback to the Victorian age." At the time it seemed a compliment. It sounded as if he were comparing me to my beloved grandmother. Now that I feel as old as Queen Victoria in her dotage, and nearly as dumpy, this valentine is not so comforting.

An ex-admirer who dislikes the West sends my second valentine, titled "Summer Lawn." It looks like Martha's Vineyard, with sailboats in the distance, an American flag flying from a white porch, and a pink-flowered picket fence stockading a lush green yard. His card has a lot of blue in it, like me, only light blue. Light blue water, lighter blue sky, light blue shadowed porch. Inside, he has drawn the black outline of a heart pierced with a black arrow. No wonder he is an *ex!* Talk about blue. I threw it in the garbage last night. Then retrieved it this morning. To make myself feel sadder, I suppose. We torture ourselves this way.

> Roses are blue
> Violets are blue
> Shadows are blue
> Water is blue
> Waters is black and blue
> With blueness.

I didn't win today's poetry contest on radio station K-TAO, but then I didn't submit my poem. All entries had to begin with "Roses are red." I could have done a lot better with "Amaryllises are red." My amaryllis is brilliant valentine red today. Irene Davies sent the knobby brown bulb last Christmas. Its third trumpet blossom opened this morning, just in time for this blue-black Valentine's Day. Now Irene too is dead. Suddenly. Unexpectedly.

Why do we celebrate death this day? Saint Valentine is thought to have been a Roman priest beheaded in 270 A.D. as a Christian. If instead our honored saint was Saint Valentine the bishop, he also was martyred around the same time. For our gift one year, Marcia Gaiter painted a striking *santo* of Saint Valentine the Bishop robed in holy pink. Now she too is dead, martyred by poverty and living exclusively in the right brain.

Today—this most unlikely day—death closes in like a shroud of ash veiling my soul, stifling my being, shutting out the light.

Death, be not proud. . . .
One short sleep past, we wake eternally,
And death shall be no more: death, thou shalt die.

Yes, die! Turn instead to light and life: snapping fire in the kitchen woodstove; plucky red poinsettia left over from Christmas; Frank's green shamrock plants with delicate white flowers; my scarlet amaryllis—a Georgia O'Keeffe valentine in itself; lunch with Ann Merrill at Lambert's; poetry of the greats.

Love alters not with his brief hours and weeks . . .

Charles Adams once referred to the "peculiar but deep attraction" Frank and I had for one another. Ours was a "marriage of true minds" for eternity. A woman who sees through time glimpsed Frank and me as two male merchants crossing and recrossing a desert with our pack train. Perhaps this explains his fascination with the desert and mine with burros; the protagonist of my children's manuscript is named Don Burro. In the guise of merchants, this seer said, before Christ was born Frank and I were secretly spreading the Essene faith—an interest of ours in this latest lifetime.

People were always claiming chunks of Frank; there wasn't enough of him to go around in one lifetime. In our desert scenario Ann Merrill played no role. Nevertheless, she claims to have been Frank's first wife in another lifetime, probably in China. She has grown into a solid earth-mother type, the Crone with a thousand lifetimes carved into her face. She looks Indian now, her long hair drawn straight back in a bun. Frank had four planets and I my moon in Ann's sun sign, Cancer. We are simpatico, following "knowledge like a sinking star, beyond the utmost bound of human thought." In the '60s when she arrived in Taos, Ann's goals were more socially superficial, and she had personal problems. Frank served as a surrogate father to her vivacious young daughters, Lolly and Blandy. I later suggested that he dedicate *Flight from Fiesta* to them, which he did.

Ann was more important in my life than I at first realized. In March 1969, six months after coming to Taos, I had a psychic experience connected with my son's wounding in Vietnam and Frank's book *Masked Gods*. The first semester of 1970 I began teaching in Tucson but spending my summers in Taos. Needing money that summer, I went to work selling paintings for Western artist Kelly Pruitt at his Spanish Steps Gallery on the plaza where the Garden Restaurant is now. Working with me was a salesman named Pat, friend of bookseller Anne Nagle from Albuquerque.

Like many women, Anne was extremely fond of Frank. Another Cancer, she called herself his "Girl Friday" and tried to promote his work by selling his signed books out of her home. On July 21, four days before Frank's sixty-eighth birthday, she came up to Taos to have lunch with Pat and to have Frank sign books filling a couple of boxes.

"Frank Waters!" I exclaimed after meeting her. "You're going to see Frank Waters? Oh, I've been wanting so much to meet him. I feel that he inadvertently helped to save my oldest son's life in Vietnam."

"Well, why don't *you* take the books up there to his house?" Anne said with her quirky little-girl smile. "It's about time Frank made some new friends. The woman he's going with is not at all right for him. Besides, he's depressed about getting false teeth. And his sister died less than a year ago. They were close. You go perk him up!"

For several years afterward, I had no idea Ann Merrill existed or that Anne Nagle had wanted to make sure that Frank did not get serious with anyone, especially Merrill. Nagle's plan boomeranged in a big way. Frank did indeed perk up. We were both smitten, but I was astonished when he kissed me good-bye. Anne had given me the impression that he was a reticent person.

From the start I never thought of Frank as a famous author, only as a *man*. We knew we'd been together many lifetimes; the twenty-seven-year difference in our ages was nothing. I feel eternally grateful that we did touch lives this time, however late. We came so very close to missing each other.

How strange it is this difficult Valentine's Day that Ann Merrill and I have spontaneously decided to share lunch. Mashed potatoes and down-to-earth meat loaf with a Southwestern bite for me, a chicken sandwich for her. She shows me how to squeeze the scratchy dried garlic clove so that moist points of garlic pop out to enliven our homemade French bread. At home I've been existing mostly on frozen dinners. For the first time in thirty-eight years of being a part-time housewife for two different husbands, I do not have to cook! Moreover, grief deadens the appetite. I do miss the Mrs. See's chocolates we used to gorge upon this day and Mary Ann Torrence's fudge from Texas. Later I buy a candy bar, for old time's sake.

Our grief we set aside. Ann has pictures from her meditation stay in Hawaii. She talks with animation about her acting lessons, dream group, and movement therapy. Tonight she will join a drumming group.

I tell her about my Boulder visit and speech and about my unhappy friend there who said, "You know, Barbara, I have recently come to realize that I've never in my life had a *passion* for anything. I have missed the *passion*. Now it is too late."

"Can you imagine anyone saying it is too late?" I say to Ann. "And never having a passion! Remember when I accidentally said Peter Wood is building a front 'church' on our writer's studio, instead of a front 'porch'? A Freudian slip, you said then. In Boulder I suddenly realized that the Foundation is a *passion*."

Yes, Ann Merrill and I remain simpatico. We have *passions*, and we have a shared passion. As Frank did, she helps me to see more clearly on this darkling plain. She personifies my favorite philosophy from Tennyson's "Ulysses":

> How dull it is to pause, to make an end,
> To rust unburnish'd, not to shine in use! . . .

Old age hath yet his honor and his toil. . . .
Though much is taken, much abides; and though
We are not now that strength which in old days
Moved earth and heaven, that which we are, we are—
One equal temper of heroic hearts,
Made weak by time and fate, but strong in will
To strive, to seek, to find, and not to yield.

Imogene and Nate Bolls send a valentine one day late that cheers me after being locked out of the house until 11:00 P.M. and having to go to the bathroom in the snow. I could write a bumper sticker: "Frozen Shit Happens."

The front of their valentine has a hole with a heart in it and the words "Guess what kind of card this is?" Inside, the heart turns out to be part of the three of hearts from a card deck. "No!" it scolds. "You'll never get the hang of this psychic business unless you concentrate!"

The laugh is welcome, as is the synchronicity that I am writing about a psychic experience involving my oldest son, Terry. The biggest gift that goes with age is a marked increase in intuition. It's here to be tapped if only we will trust and use it, and recognize it.

One of the most memorable intuitive experiences I've had is the only time a voice clearly instructed me. In Tucson one morning I woke to a woman's voice saying, "Today we have to do something about Frank's papers."

Within days his collection of letters and writings was to be sold by John Gilchriese to the University of Oklahoma for less than it was worth. John was supposedly an expert in such matters. Frank and I were not yet married, just living together. It seemed presumptuous that early in our relationship to think I could find a more appropriate place that would pay more money. Yet I heeded this voice and utilized its energy.

My call to the University of New Mexico library put me in touch with a top administrator named Paul Vassallo. He was a feeling person, and his voice grew as choked as mine over the mistake about to happen. As a result of this one phone call, Frank's papers are now where they belong. With some further pressing, the Frank Waters Room is also a reality now at the University of New Mexico. Frank had said, "Oh no. They will never agree to a Frank Waters Room. You have to be rich like Clinton Anderson to have a room named after you."

Sometimes I called him "Dr. No." It was his favorite word. Once Ann Merrill asked, "How do you get Frank to go to Mexico and Guatemala and Peru and all those interesting places? Every time I asked him to go anywhere he'd say, 'No.'"

"I just let him say 'no' until he's blue in the face from no-ing," I replied. "Then, sweet as pie, he suddenly says, 'Yes!'"

My sons do not send valentines or call this year. The instinctive bond is always there, though, between mother and son. Never was it stronger than on March 26, 1969, while I was driving back to Taos after taking a friend to the Albuquerque airport. As I approached Santa Fe at sunset, it hit me that Terry was in deep trouble in Vietnam. I must send him energy at once, pray for him in this city of the Holy Faith at a noted power spot, such as Saint Francis Cathedral. Immortalized in Willa Cather's *Death Comes to the Archbishop*, the cathedral has stood on this site for nearly two centuries. Native shrines existed here before that.

I had joined the Catholic church in 1964 to please my former husband. Its rituals did not speak to me, but the power of group meditation in Catholic churches did. When I arrived this crucial day, the cathedral's hand-hewn blocks of stone had turned tawny with sunset fire. Saint Francis seemed more closely connected with nature than usual, a cosmic cathedral. To my disappointment, its massive front doors were locked. A notice indicated that evening mass would begin an hour after my arrival. Turning toward the life-sized bronze of Archbishop Lamy in front, I remembered that Cather had come to consider him "a sort of invisible friend." This was the right spot, whether an elaborate church in more recent times, a rustic adobe earlier, or a primitive Indian shrine in the beginning.

To divert my anxiety about Terry, I crossed to the magazine and book shop in Santa Fe's La Fonda Hotel. Here, for some reason, a thick book titled *Masked Gods* drew my attention. I didn't know its author from Adam, but his words soothed and strengthened me. They were a prayer in themselves, kindling an energy that took me out of my puny self and united me with one great Energy. Today that dated and signed book is kept in a special place. It never loses its magic.

For an hour in La Fonda's dining room, I submerged myself in this book of wisdom. Then I returned to the cathedral. First with others, then alone, I related to the mystery of the vast silence. Mounting the great pillars topped with green stone leaves of life, hope, and rebirth, my higher self spiraled through arches, fortressed walls, and stained-glass windows shafted with twilight dusk until it soared out the white vault crossed above with bands of green and gold.

The helicopters came then, at dawn, to rescue my son. Most of his friends lay dead around him. He said later, "There came a moment when I decided I *will not* die here."

The sound of a hovering helicopter still makes me cry, that life-giving sound of blades chopping the air close above. Enfolded in a universal wave beyond time and space, Terry was not alone that day.

After all these years, mortar-shell fragments pop out of his wounds every so often; his stomach remains stapled inside. His chin is furrowed from the bullet that plowed through from a distant corner of the long trench, his hand a little stiffened. Scars slanting down his body as if blasted from a shotgun are fading. The first time we went waterskiing after his return, I asked why he was waiting so long to take his turn. He said, "It's the unveiling I hate."

Masked gods will have their way. I am unceasingly grateful that his life mission this time around was judged incomplete. Our tuning in to the energy of the implicate order undoubtedly helped to sway the verdict.

Like her great-grandmother in the '20s and her grandmother in the '60s, Terry's twelve-year-old daughter came to New Mexico in 1988. "The first place we have to visit on our way home," I said to her at the airport, "is Terry's Cathedral."

To get a reading on what psychics were doing, some time ago I went to one Akashic Record reader, the one who told me about spreading the Essene faith; one channeler; and one psychic of a type termed "fortune-teller" in Frank's day. My skepticism was somewhat of a handicap.

The channeler went hiking with Shirley Young and me three years ago in an abandoned lepidolite mine about twenty-five miles south of here in the little winery village of Dixon. Tucked into a shadowy pink and lavender grotto that we had climbed into, the woman channeled someone named Michael. He advised me to "hang in there through thick and thin." Whoever he was, Michael obviously knew that being married to a successful man is not all it is cracked up to be. He proved to be more astute than his channeler, however trite his advice.

As we munched our sandwiches in another part of the pink cave, the channeler gushed, "It must be absolutely *marvelous* to be married to a famous man like Frank Waters!"

"No. It is not *marvelous*," I replied.

"Why isn't it marvelous?" she persisted.

Shirley said, her laughter echoing through our pale pink chamber, "Because he is *human*."

It's good to have these profound words recorded in my journal. Often during our grief process we romanticize and forget the down side. Lisa from The Crazy Old Lady shop, *La Vieja Loca*, reminded me of this the other day when she said, "I was just telling someone you're a *pistol!*"

"Me?" I asked. "My mother always said I was the quiet one, like my father."

"Well, you lived with Frank Waters all those years, didn't you?" Lisa replied with her wide signature grin.

Like her assumed Spanish name and her personality, Lisa's shop is fascinating. She is teaching movie star Julia Roberts to sew her own clothes and grown men to knit. At an opening there Irene

Falk, who crochets kinky caps in shades of blues, violets, greens or yellows, oranges, and reds, says of her own grief after her husband died, "I tried this and this and this. Maybe these strategies will work for others; maybe not. There are no guarantees and no formula. You'll be coming along just fine, you think, when suddenly this *thing* shows up." Irene gestures and looks down beside her as if a loathsome stray dog has put in an unexpected appearance.

"This *thing* pops out of nowhere. Why, where did *you* come from? It took me six years before this *thing* stopped springing up in my life when least expected, or welcome."

I recognize this grievesome *thing*. It has slunk in as my valentine this year.

Tyger! Tyger! burning bright . . .

My one visit to a psychic occurred in 1990. I'm glad it was then. It seems best now not to seek miracles or the impossible. If I can feel and use some of my loved one's energy, I can make do without his image, voice, or important messages from the other side. Save your money; cultivate your own sensitivities. Essentially, the psychic's pitch will be the same as Michael's: "Hang in there through thick and thin."

Not long ago, after I'd given a lecture in Santa Fe, a woman approached the lectern. Putting her arms around me, she whispered in my ear, "I just heard from Frank. He said, 'Tell Barbara I love her and not to be sad.'"

If Frank had anything to tell me, he wouldn't need an intermediary. It seemed a cruel hoax, however well intentioned, and made me feel very low.

On the other hand, if I had given more credence to the words of my one psychic adviser, I would have guarded Frank so fiercely in 1995 that he might still be alive. At first glance, neither this French psychic nor her cavelike house were impressive. She seated me beside a candle flickering on a rickety table. Closing her hooded eyes, she surprised me by beginning, "You have two sons close in age. And you have been married twice." She filled in with other accurate details, then added, "Your second husband was a writer."

"My second husband is alive. And he still *is* a writer."

Startled, she flashed open her eyes, then closed them. "Ah, I see. You are standing in front of your second husband. And he is living off your energy. Do you know that he is very ill?"

Of course I knew. That morning I had picked up his first portable oxygen tanks for our trip to Taos. They were hidden under a quilt in my locked car. Unfamiliar with oxygen at that time, I feared the morning sun might explode them.

Her eyes flew open. "He is *very* sick; do you realize this? It is in his chest. Something is very wrong with his chest. Recently he has had some severe illness, perhaps pneumonia. It is more than that."

I nodded briefly, saying nothing. He'd had his first bout with pneumonia. He needed the oxygen for his emphysema.

She drew the strange second hoods of flesh back down over her eyelids. "He will recover from this illness. Five years from now he will not be here.

"As for you, I see another man whom you will later meet, in connection with your spiritual work. I . . . I . . . I just don't know. You could marry him. But I don't see the actual marriage. It's . . . it's up to you."

Her words to this point impressed me. Unfortunately, she went on to diagnose some physical ailments in my back and legs, which supposedly were out of alignment. She recommended a certain chiropractor at an exact address. When I compared notes with three friends who had visited her, we found we'd all been given the same physical feedback. At the time she seemed to me 20 percent bogus. What stayed in my mind over the years was the bogus part, to my regret.

Long ago Frank went to a Taos fortune-teller named Terecita Ferguson. She had a shaky past, but in his book *To Possess the Land* he describes her as having a "curious fey streak which enabled her to read cards or palms." The word "fey" clues readers into the awareness that Frank liked her.

Terecita told him, "You don't need your fortune told."

> It rains in my heart
> as it rains on the town.

On this Valentine's Day I come to the conclusion that we must need Self-Pity Days. All day I have indulged myself. No wood chopping, nothing constructive or deliberately positive except lunch with Ann, and a breakfast roll and Guatemalan coffee before that at Casa Fresen with Linda Ann. Strangely enough, my English literature text from 1961 has helped me most. At 1215 pages *The Literature of England* is a great book with which to be castaway on a desert island. It entranced me when I majored in English literature a few years after my sons were born. Later I turned to teaching Southwestern literature, including Frank's books, an entrancing field as well. Yet the power and majesty of English literature sweep me off my feet again this night, pull me up by the bootstraps out of self-pity into the mainstream of eternity. Strange medicine, but consistently powerful.

> Though lovers be lost love shall not;
> And death shall have no dominion.

Browsing through this weighty tome all evening while listening to Nana Mouskouri's "Falling in Love Again" brings me back to sanity and rainbows and on to appreciation of Linda Ann and her new poem, my best valentine of all. A newcomer to Arroyo Seco, Linda Ann had wanted to attend our July writers' workshop. It was canceled. Instead she and I met at Casa Fresen, then walked out to Frank's new cross beneath the oak tree. In our lower pasture on the way back, she bent to pick up a blue-gray plastic star three inches across. Strange synchronicities happen around Linda Ann. She sees as many rainbows as I. Her plastic star I've tucked next to this fragment of an Eskimo legend that I had read at Frank's funeral ceremony a month earlier:

Perhaps
they are not
the stars,
but rather openings
in Heaven
where the love
of our lost ones
pours through
and shines down
upon us
to let us know
they are
happy.

Like many newcomers trying to make it in Taos on next to nothing, Linda Ann could not send valentine cards this year. Instead she sent this poem composed after our most recent snowfall. Had Frank known her, he would have awarded both Linda Ann Heinke and her valentine poem his gold star of approval: the accolade of being "fey." It lights up my day at last.

Second Snowfall

Walking past Pueblo land at dawn
snow gods rose to greet me
thanking me
for honoring their show

Sagebrush, covered white
appeared to bow
for I was the first to walk
in the new fallen snow

Humbled, I paused to thank
and it was then, with my heart I saw

one thousand ancestors, dancing on the snow
rejoicing, grateful

For with their keen vision they could see
    corn stalks swaying in the summer breeze
    a double rainbow
    grandchildren playing
    near
    clear waters flowing
    from their Sacred Blue Lake
    recycling this bountiful snow

In reverence, I turned away
flute music still playing in my soul
spirit lightened, heart aglow
I walked on, in the morn, of the new fallen snow.

11
The Troops

Frank was a terrible driver. He could have survived only in the Tank. His driving reduced one grown man to tears and threats of leaping from our moving car. Ann Merrill's daughters prayed to those above, "We need you, Troops. We need every bit of help you can muster. Frank Waters is behind the wheel again!"

From these girls I got the idea of calling helpful spirits "the Troops." Summoned during each of Frank's many illnesses in his late years, they never failed to come through. They became very much my own by marriage, and they have been my own special support too, in times of need.

The forces of nature made up one platoon. Another consisted of healers like Merlin, Black Elk, Fools Crow, Father Kneipp, Jung, and Gurdjieff. Spirits of Frank's departed friends made up an important platoon, friends like Mabel and Tony Lujan, Nicolai Fechin, Victor White, Marcia Gaiter, and Janey. The most elite platoon of all the Troops contained Frank's departed relatives, especially his sister, Naomi, and her husband, Carl; his mother, May Ione; his father, Frank Jonathon; his grandparents, Joseph and Martha Dozier; and all their offspring. Readers come to know this group well in Frank's thinly disguised autobiography, *Pike's Peak*.

Photographer Judith Bronner, who is a librarian as well, and I
spent some time in Colorado Springs in February 1996 on our way
to Boulder, Colorado, where we participated in the public library's
second annual "Book Discussion Day." It focused on *The Man Who
Killed the Deer* and Frank.

The Troops were much with us in Frank's old hometown. In
Colorado Springs we visited his former home, Frank Waters Park,
and Evergreen Cemetery. This pilgrimage was as healing for me as
my trip to the Grand Canyon. It renewed my sense of continuity,
besides putting me closely in touch again with another heartland
where Frank's voice can still be heard. It vibrates strongly in the
following excerpts from two of his unpublished letters, written to
his friend Charles Hathaway in 1925 and 1928 and presented to me
by Charles on this trip.

> There's no place I know of, Chuck, where you can find a place
> like C.S. Most beautiful streets, and scenery, and natural advan-
> tages of any place in the world. . . . I'd give my shirt to drop back
> 5 years and go out on our wheels to the Bluffs or tramp out with
> Budd and Joe and you. . . .
>
> I certainly do enjoy letters more than anything. Contact and
> keeping in touch with people means so much more than working
> with an inanimate thing, that I'm just beginning to value the few
> close friends I have. . . . You and I are, and were as boys, too prone
> to live too close to ourselves. I'm beginning to see that that's my
> trouble. You're going to make a good man old top, a damn good
> man, if you'll let them find it out. . . . Thanks for (reading) that
> fool story. I'm going to start sending some around when I get a
> little leisure. What do you think about my nature as to writing,
> or wanting to do it all the time. Mistake, eh? . . .
>
> I'm awfully glad you're continuing studying and going on with
> your invention, and haven't the slightest doubt that you'll come
> through in the end. It's the man who has the drive within there's
> no holding back; and when I think of the two of us from Columbia
> on up, I believe that, for me, success means nothing more than a

justification of those things we felt as boys to be worthwhile. And I'm sure they'll never change. It's not the North End bunch throughout the world that come through. They're no more than snow and hot air. I'll take a back-alley bunch every time.

As Frank himself did, each year his birthplace has grown more lean and gaunt. This trip the house was painted a mustard yellow with earth-red trim. During a previous visit the place next door had been the same color and bore the sign "House of Metaphysics." It seemed as if the energy of his grandfather and his metaphysical library, so crucial to Frank's development, hovered closely about. Now these two and five other houses in a row are owned by Bijou Street Rentals and rented out as separate rooms or apartments.

Although Judith lamented that this historic spot was now a "boarding house for transients," I didn't feel too badly. After all, it was pretty much the same during Frank's youth. Whichever relatives were down on their luck moved in temporarily or permanently with Frank's grandparents at 435 E. Bijou Street. This made life difficult, especially at the end. Many days, bread and white gravy were all they had to eat. For the rest of his life Frank could scarcely stand the sight of white gravy, let alone eat it. Los Angeles was more of the same. He made do with two doughnuts and a cup of coffee for ten cents until dinner, which consisted of "the cheapest bowl of chop suey" in Chinatown.

In his 1972 introduction to a reprint of *Midas of the Rockies*, Marshall Sprague refers to Frank living in a shack near the Springs and starving his way through the writing of this book. His publisher, Covici-Friede, did give his agent a $150 advance. After the agent absconded with it, Frank "had to starve for eight months more in his shack until he finished the manuscript." Some time before this, "he had starved his way through the writing of *The Wild Earth's Nobility*," for which he received a "minuscule" advance. "When the famished Waters finished the book," Sprague states, "he needed money for food right away." He never got over being hungry.

People speak or write of Frank as having lived in a "more innocent" time. They don't realize that he almost starved to death, did not have proper clothing, and lost his father to pneumonia in 1914 when the man had to work in a freezing mine at high altitude and had no proper treatment; all this on top of the mental anguish of being looked down upon by those from the "right" side of the tracks. Frank thought Charles Hathaway was poorer than he. Charles thought Frank was the poorest. They made a good pair and needed each other.

And they both went a long way, Charles as head of school finance for the state of Colorado. During our trip he took Judith and me to brunch at Denver's fancy Wellshire Inn, formerly a country club. With his keen memory, Charles has been able to write eighty-eight pages of reminiscences about Frank. "I wanted to be with him some more," Charles said movingly. "And this was the only way I could do it.

"Writing is *murder*. I don't know how Frank ever stuck to it day in and day out, his whole life long. Who would want to?"

Until his father died, Frank and his sister lived with their parents at 229 E. El Paso Street right beside the railroad tracks and a half block off Bijou Street. Mother and children then tried living for a few months in the farming community of Garden Grove, Iowa, with Waters relatives. When that didn't work, they moved back into the Bijou Street house for good. Frank's mother had lived there as an adult before her marriage. Frank and Naomi had been born in their grandparents' front bedroom on the second floor, a family tradition. Now they occupied the third floor with their mother.

Judith and I learned that today these top two rooms are rented out separately. The other two floors each have three renters with a shared kitchen. The man living in the front Birth Bedroom with its little balcony is a groundskeeper for Bijou Street Rentals. He has cleaned up the Dozier backyard and tends a minuscule triangular flower garden in front. He has two small American flags pasted on his bedroom window. He found them in the street after a Fourth of

104

July celebration. It seemed a fitting synchronicity that the Confederate flag once flew from the balcony a few feet away during Fourth of July celebrations. A brass plaque identifying the house as Frank's birthplace was still nailed to the front door, so the caretaker knew about him, but not about the Kadle ghosts. The news did not sit well with him when I asked if he had heard them creaking about.

"I never hear nothin'. 'Cept real live folks when they go up them stairs and come back down," he said with dour finality. "I don't believe in ghosts neither. Never have."

After he had left, a young man came out on the porch for a smoke. "What are you doing here?" he asked nervously, as if we were pot-smelling canines.

"My husband used to live here. That's he mentioned on the sign," I explained, nodding toward the plaque. "He and his family always heard these two ghostly trappers squeaking up and down the stairs, especially around the third floor. Have you ever heard them?"

"For god's sake don't say anything like that in front of my brother!" he exclaimed, stubbing out his cigarette without smoking it. "He just moved in here two days ago. He'd freak out totally and move right back out! I don't live here. So long. I have to see how he's doing with his shower."

We felt sadder about the Kadles getting the cold shoulder than ourselves. I tried to polish the little rectangular plaque with a Kleenex. Frank was so proud, so happy, the sunny day a group of local historians installed it.

Frank Waters Park across the street was clean and tidy. Brown and icy then, in summer it would be a long sward of emerald grass beside the rocky brook. A gang had defiled the three Mountain Red granite boulders with Frank's quotations and biography etched into them, but they were fairly clean again. This kind of gang work was an endeavor that not-so-innocent Frank and Charles might have relished in their heyday, given the opportunity. Two other couples ate their lunches nearby at the same time we did. It was a peaceful place, both inside linear time and outside.

Originally called Shook's Run, the stream ran north and south the length of Colorado Springs. To Charles and Frank it was the equivalent of Huck Finn's Mississippi River. Near Charles's old home, still standing at 507 E. High Street off Corona, is another grassy picnic area called Shook's Run Park. Surely Frank and the Kadles were holed up in one park or the other, cooking up the book about them that Frank didn't get around to writing in this lifetime. His fascination with these ghosts remained throughout his life. In 1985 when we stayed on Cascade Avenue in the old Bemis mansion, now a bed-and-breakfast, a creaking overhead reminded me of Frank's Kadles stories. After I mentioned this, he included them in his big speech at Tutt Library the next day, as if the Kadles truly had been with us again. Who knows? Maybe they too had begun hobnobbing with the wealthy "North End bunch."

Many of the elite Troops rest at Evergreen Cemetery, where Judith and I headed next. Three years earlier I'd had installed on the family plot two red granite headstones honoring three key relatives in Frank's life. For his father, a modest upright stone gives his name and dates of December 31, 1862, to December 20, 1914, surrounding an antlered deer's head. Underneath are the words "Source and Inspiration." Frank's grandparents share a matching reddish stone headed "Dozier." On the left is Martha, March 3, 1850–July 13, 1927; on the right Joseph, April 18, 1842–May 11, 1925. Below, referring to his grandfather, whom Frank highly esteemed, are the words "Shepherd of the Flock." Until these new stones were purchased, the lone headstone in this family plot was a small one marking the grave of Frank's young first cousin Arleene Ascough, who had died at age twenty-three in 1927 while Frank was living in Los Angeles. His only niece was named after her.

It is a fascinating triangular plot. In the oldest section of the cemetery, one great evergreen stands alone facing down into a wild, wooded arroyo. The wind soughs through gnarled branches, whispering words from Coleridge's "Kubla Khan" as though they were written to honor the Dozier occupants of Plot 38:

Where blossomed many an incense-bearing tree;
And here were forests ancient as the hills,
Enfolding sunny spots of greenery.

But oh! that deep romantic chasm which slanted
Down the green hill athwart a cedarn cover!
A savage place! as holy and enchanted
As e'er beneath a waning moon was haunted
By woman wailing for her demon lover!

Charles first found the plot for me in 1992 after Frank and he had reminisced for the Fall Heritage Series of the Colorado Pioneers Museum. Charles thought it was a shabby-looking place, vastly inferior to the sterile, newer section where lies his family plot. Despite his sensitivity to art and music, sometimes I think Charles stayed too long in the world of finance. This tendency elicited Frank's impatience. During Judith's and my visit to Evergreen, the "savage place" drew me to it after only a minimum of stumbling around, for I identified with that imaginary "woman wailing for her demon lover," so similar to myself, and to La Llorona wailing for her lost ones.

When the two new family stones were purchased in 1993, a search of cemetery and city clerk's records unearthed the amazing news that the remains of twelve persons reside in enchanted Plot 38 at Evergreen! Now, there's a family that sticks together.

Frank's great-grandfather Daniel Lee Dozier is buried there, along with Daniel's daughter, Mary, and his son, Joseph; his daughter-in-law, Martha; her sister, Molly; their mother, Martha; Arleene; and Frank's father. A relative or close friend named Marion "Onie" Smith joined the others. A baby is with them, and two children named Albert and Mamie Dozier, who died in 1880 of diphtheria and tuberculosis.

As mentioned, Frank's father died in 1914 of pneumonia, and, like many, his great-grandmother died of "chronic pneumonia," which was to plague Frank's final years. We feared it. After one of Frank's hospital bouts with pneumonia in Tucson, a big horned owl came to brood in our palo verde tree shading the back porch. Frank believed, "When the owl cries, the Indian dies."

Quite candidly I told this old owl, "Look, I've got enough on my hands right now without worrying about whether you are good luck or bad luck. I've read legends that say one or the other. But we can't take a chance just now. So get lost!"

It did.

I laughed when Frank, with great love in his voice, once called his relatives a "superstitious, ignorant clan." He had more superstitions than a cat has lives: he would die, supposedly, if this apple tree or that ocotillo died, or an owl cried, or his 1956 Olivetti typewriter or his 1966 Ford Galaxie went on the blink for good. Whenever we left on trips, our house that originally had been blessed with "a piss and a prayer" had to be reblessed with a circle drawn around it in the air and dotted in its center with pointed forefinger.

In 1941 Frank's mother died of heart trouble in Los Angeles and was buried there in Roosevelt Cemetery with her sisters, Mattie and Dixie, and their husbands, Doc and Al. Frank too had some problems with his heart. He'd always had an irregular heartbeat, and in 1994 his heart had to be shocked back into proper rhythm before we could return to Taos. The doctors then discovered he had been born with an undetected hole in his heart that prevented proper blood circulation. But they decided, "If he's lived ninety years with it this way, we're not about to start tinkering with it."

Doctors liked Frank. He bore his ills with grace. His favorite physician, Bill Farr, substantiated this, as well as both the psychic's and the astrologer's interpretations of my role, when he wrote after Frank's death,

> I shall always remember, "How are you Frank?" being answered, "Fine!" Even when he wasn't he had such a wonderful attitude, pleasing personality and positive outlook. A gentleness, kindness and humility embraced his personality. I am confident he agonized

over his unwellness these past years. But in true form, Frank Waters carried on no matter how difficult it was for him. . . .

Barbara, you were decisive and responsible for Frank being with us as long as he was. Without you, I am convinced that Frank would have gone long ago. Your attention, persistent caring, and loving added immensely to his well-being. For all of this we are eternally grateful and respectful—it was no small feat! Your energy, in the absence of his, was crucial for his survival. You comforted and prodded him when it was obvious that difficult times were ahead. He appreciated that very much and didn't want to burden you, he told me privately.

I see Frank in his great-grandfather, my favorite of the clan. There exist a daguerrotype of Daniel Lee Dozier as a youthful plantation owner and a patriarchal photograph of him taken at the beginning of this century. In the first he is an eager young fop wearing a wide cravat, starched white shirt front, and jacket. In the second a full white beard and white hair frame saddened eagle eyes sunk deep beneath thick, jagged brows just like Frank's. Rod Goebel said while painting Frank's portrait, now in the Frank Waters Room at the University of New Mexico, "I could paint Frank's *eyebrows* alone and people would recognize him."

Daniel Lee saw too much in his eighty-eight years. Born in North Carolina in 1816, he gambled away the family plantation by the mid–nineteenth century. In *Pike's Peak* Frank has him die almost fifty years ahead of time, perhaps as punishment for losing the farm. Daniel's father was Joab Dozier of North Carolina, his mother Mary Lee of Virginia. Her sister supposedly married Robert E. Lee, who would therefore be Daniel Lee's uncle. It seems doubtful that Lee married a Lee, but it makes a good story and has not yet been researched. Frank's southern grandmother and great-grandmother were the ones who insisted upon flying the Confederate battle flag every Fourth of July from their front balcony. This custom kept young Frank busy with his fists and could be one reason he took up boxing lessons and worked out with a punching bag in his third-floor rear bedroom.

Daniel had two sons, Romulus and Joseph. Daniel moved to Colorado Springs with Joseph in 1873 and lived to see his son a success as a contractor and builder of local churches and schools, including Cutler Hall, the first building on the Colorado College campus. Frank attended this college for three years. He majored in engineering but resented having no English or writing classes and dropped out to work in the oilfields of Salt Creek, Wyoming.

In his novel *Pike's Peak*, and in the trilogy from which it is condensed, all these characters live on, made wonderfully immortal by Frank's poignant words. Fictionalized as March Cable, Frank heads at the end of *Pike's Peak* toward Evergreen Cemetery with an armful of prairie wildflowers: "white wild onions, bluebells, scarlet Indian paintbrushes, sand daisies, columbines and lupines."

"But when he reached the cemetery he had some difficulty finding the family lot. It was unmarked, sunken grave [his father's] and fresh one [his grandfather's] devoid of headboards pending the erection of small stone markers which March had ordered. He flashed a look down the gulch. It was filled with tin cans. The pines soughed faintly, a magpie screamed. He knelt and self-consciously but carefully spread the crimson flowers over [their] graves, side by side."

To think it took sixty-eight years for those markers to be placed at last! In 1993 I had not realized that my idea to erect them may have originated in Frank's books, where they were only an unfulfilled dream. Frank had remained unusually noncommittal and had not encouraged their purchase.

Three years later my heart leaped up as a joyous flock of black-and-white magpies, Frank's favorite bird, circled and recircled above Judith and me, crying out approval of the headstones and shared love of this magical spot. Judith kept a feather as a souvenir. After cleaning the stones of magpie offerings, I broke a dead antlered branch from the sentinel pine. Some spring I too shall return with bluebells, columbines, and crimson wildflowers.

12
Purring in the Sun

Like Frank, I am basically a tranquil person. Even in paradise, however, tranquillity is not a given. Each day it must be fought for anew. Both woodstove fires are out. The house is freezing. Trickster battles Crystal for something's leg. Two and a half newborn lambs are lying dead in the Sacred Aspen Grove. Three gorgeous peacocks must be rescued from canine jaws of death. Peacocks? Only a romantic would bring *peacocks* to Arroyo Seco. This is the original Town Too Tough to Die. It is predominantly a place of dead lambs, hungry coyotes and mountain lions, fatal car accidents, failing businesses, BB-shot windows, and keeping our home fires burning.

It is a relief to learn that these lambs were born prematurely, that Trickster had nothing to do with their deaths. Their presence in the Sacred Grove is another matter. Feeling much like old Mrs. Quintana with her illegal deer, I hustle the two and a half bodies off to the dump before matters grow complicated. If anyone goes through my garbage, I shall be pilloried as a witch, wearing a scarlet letter "T" for Trickster. The third leg belonged to a lamb, but the fourth that shows up looks a little large for a lamb's leg. If a fifth appears, it may mean hanging or burning at the stake instead of simply the stocks. Innumerable witches were hung at certain New Mexico pueblos well into this century.

Salomé eases my mind a bit by explaining that three of his lambs lived, three died at birth. Each of the dead had been a twin. It is early for them. They stand only a slim chance of surviving the rigors of Arroyo Seco so soon, even if winter has been spring-like so far. Everyone is worried already about a lack of water next summer without enough snowmelt. The horses and Trickster are shedding their coats in mangy clumps. Plump buds festoon plum, apricot, and cherry trees. Tufts of green grass spring up, along with bunches of red willows in front of the new studio.

Sparse snow separates into crystal marbles instead of bonding. A foolhardy skier has been killed in an avalanche outside official ski valley limits. He skied alone in the wrong place at the wrong time. He broke all the rules, but he owned two popular businesses. He was popular. Four hundred persons attend his memorial service at Taos Ski Valley. The difference between skiers and writers gives one pause for thought. Why do four times as many persons attend a skier's service as that of a writer who has influenced the lives of thousands and will continue to do so? I watch countless men hug each other and shed a tear for the skier. Hardly anyone hugged for Frank. Perhaps for writers the tears and the hugs and back-pounding are meant to come out as shining words. "The medium is the massage," said McLuhan.

Poet Imogene Bolls wept in this fashion:

The Walk to the Upper Pasture
For Barbara
In Memory of Frank

Our shoulders soaked in sunshine,
our feet in the cold, water-swollen grass,
we pick our way slowly
across to the higher tufts
then back to the path, sinking
anyway, and not caring.

All around us the trees are talking,
you had said, listening
to the cottonwoods,
the grove of sacred aspen.

Especially the old oak—our goal
in the upper pasture where
the ashes, two weeks without rain,
encircle the trunk in a formal act
of completion—is eloquent.

It says: Listen. I am here
I am rooted. I will last for as long
as you will need me.

It says: Listen to me. Give up
your pain to the wind.
What is past is here,
but the future is the wind
that sings in me and everywhere.

Even you will sing again.

And John Rainer, an elder from Taos Indian Pueblo, shed these
words:

With You Forever

The historical hurt of the past is still in our hearts. Frank, we
come to you today because you have tried so hard to explain our
culture through your research. You have made an effort for the
Americans to appreciate us, and we are here to thank you. The
Taos Pueblo members are deeply grateful for all the effort you
have made to have the Americans understand us. We are thankful for your pen and the books you have written on the Indians in

hopes there will be an understanding, not only of Pueblo Indians, but of the Indians of America and humanity. You are here, Frank, and we are deeply thankful. You will be with us always, always. We love you, and we will be with you forever.

White tears of snow drift down for both men, for diminished mankind, as three black lambs hippety-hop for joy between snow-flakes: the yin and the yang. A flock of gray-headed juncos chirp their own particular joy over finally being remembered at breakfast. They are actually slate-blue with rust-colored wings. They must be a cheering section sent specially to Arroyo Seco, for they are bluer than most gray-headed juncos but have rufus wings, which slate-blue juncos do not, according to Peterson's *A Field Guide to Western Birds.*

Bluebirds of happiness are a paradoxical gift this winter. Steller's jays with their royal-blue crowns, stubby-tailed piñon jays, necklaced scrub jays, the rusty-chested western bluebird, these special slate-blue-and-rust juncos, and the beauty queens of the lot, mountain bluebirds with turquoise breasts. Judith claims to have eastern bluebirds visiting her home. The difference between eastern and western bluebirds is hard for some birdwatchers to distinguish; her visitors are probably westerners. If they are indeed transients escaping a bad eastern winter, they must be the happiest bluebirds of all.

Our birds are content with ordinary wild bird seed from Wal-Mart. Our shelties are the same way. Stuff them full of Wal-Mart's bite-sized Ol' Roy and they never leave home. This is not a gourmet establishment. Our horses are ecstatic over their three-year-old hay. Only Trickster leans toward French cuisine. She is a weird chapter in herself, thanks mostly to Casa Fresen. Casa Fresen is her kitchen and her office. Like Trickster, the rest of us True Believers can barely get through a day without a meditative fix from this funky little deli-bakery in downtown Arroyo Seco. One must visualize its surroundings in order to understand why this deli stands out prominently.

Beverly Hills our village is not; it is infinitely better than any-thing California has to offer, its defenders will assure you. Unless they are of the growing number who do not wish you to know Arroyo Seco exists. They will say it is a figment of your imagina-tion, this truncated town in the middle of nowhere. It might well be named Rinconada, the corner of nowhere, except that another corner of nowhere not too far away is named that. Zip right on through. Neither place can be for real. Yet I have lived in both and loved them. Both Arroyo Seco and Rinconada were "honeymoon" spots for Frank and me before our marriage.

In her 1935 book *Winter in Taos*, Mabel Luhan wrote of the "hamlet" called Arroyo Seco, "It really breathed of coziness and contentment, like a cat purring in the sun." Wildcat is more like it. Mabel doesn't appear to have realized just how lively block-long Arroyo Seco has been over the years. Once it had a pool hall and an American Legion Hall, schools and a butcher shop. It has had sev-eral dance halls, even a nightclub. With the help of his parents, local historian Larry Torres has brought back the energy of bygone people and days by composing a map of some fifty buildings that have surrounded the two plazas of old *La Iglesia de La Santísima Trinidad* this century. Most were private residences, their various owners all known and named. Torres's map is titled "The Plaza of Arroyo Seco as It Was Before the Growth of Modern Times." The growth of modern times here is about as easy to detect as the daily increase of a cottonwood tree.

The most important directional building in our hamlet is the post office at the east end of the block. "Turn sharp left behind the post office if you're going on up to Taos Ski Valley," we say. Or, "Go straight ahead beside the post office if you're driving up El Salto Road, the road without a name sign." The populace may go berserk a few months from now when the post office is moved two blocks from its longtime landmark location in "downtown" Arroyo Seco.

East of the post office and across the road is the school; south is a deserted sunken adobe that seems weighted down with sorrow since its owner, mother of Abe, the former postmaster, died some dozen years ago, taking all her cheerful petunias with her. Abe's adobe comes next, continuing west, and then Abe's Bar & Grill, where one can get green chile burritos for breakfast, and green chile fries with cheese. It has a cheery green chile sign hanging in front that helps to make up for the departed petunias. An abandoned Quonset hut snuggles between Abe's and *La Vieja Loca*, which will move into the old post office building this summer. Once a dance hall and post office occupied this Quonset hut spot. Across a vacant lot beside *La Vieja Loca* is an outsider's vacation dollhouse, a little A-frame trimmed in blue and decorated with a tile of Our Lady of Guadalupe inset for good luck and protection from vandals.

At the west end of the block, facing the post office, is a hostel named the ABOMINABLE SNOWMANsion. On the north side of the street loom two tall adobes with second floors. The first was originally the home of Andres and Margarita Martinez, who rented out the back rooms. The second belonged to the Trujillo family, then to two Martinez sisters before becoming the Gay Nineties nightclub owned by Gil and Helen Corbeille some twenty-five years ago. In 1995 it was the Bistro restaurant. Now empty, it is slowly being converted upstairs into apartments, for change happens as slowly as possible in Arroyo Seco. Then comes Casa Fresen deli and the Art Lab, a hole-in-the-wall gallery with heart that displays local artwork. Next door the old Song of the Wind Gallery, across the street from *La Vieja Loca*, is currently an antique shop named Annabel's. Finally, in what was once mesmerizing Twining Weavers, some Texans have established a fading barbecue restaurant west of the post office.

Behind the restaurant and Annabel's looms ghostly old *La Santísima Trinidad* Church with a crooked wooden cross that teeters upon a crooked wooden steeple rising above obdurate adobe walls. Everyone says "something should be done" with the beautiful old building. Recently some restoration has slowly begun, while artists continue to immortalize its tumbledown beauty and Christianity carries on in a newer Holy Trinity Church, which no artist has cared to paint. In bygone days an adobe fortress wall interspersed with houses circled the old church and its plaza as protection against marauding Indians. Two protected paths provided access to the stream behind Abe's.

In back of Casa Fresen is the Taos Cow Ice Cream parlor. It was once a general store belonging to Ramoncito Fernandez and before that, beginning in 1903, served as a hall for meetings and wedding dances. This is the sum total of "downtown" Arroyo Seco, including all the "growth of modern times."

The former Song of the Wind, long ago a butcher shop, still sings to me of Helen Aufderheide's energy. A spiritually oriented artist, she lived here in the early '80s with her teenaged daughter, Aukie, while building "My Center" in the woods up the road from us. Helen designed and built her center in the shape of an Egyptian cross, or ankh, as a spiritual retreat for everyone to share. She claimed that her vision saw her through construction of this retreat, then deserted her before her dream was fulfilled. She anticipated that someone else with another vision would get it functioning purposefully. Helen returned for a time to her home in Connecticut, where she died of Lyme disease acquired from ticks in the woods there. Aukie committed suicide. Ever since, the orphaned "My Center" has floundered. Sadness flutters like a doomed moth about it and the Song of the Wind building.

In negative-positive fashion Helen serves as an example to me of how one must persistently pursue one's impossible dream, based on vision, past impossibility and possibility, to sound functional reality. Our Foundation goals will be achieved in this fashion. As well as completion *and* publication of this book.

Debra Cole has succeeded this way with Casa Fresen, the best little bake house in the West. After the skiers leave for the slopes each morning, Casa Fresen is the in place for out people. The out people are my salvation when grief threatens to take me too deeply into the unconscious and abandon me there. The out people appreciate this unique oasis and what Debbie is accomplishing in the midst of competition, financial problems, personal loss, and unique recipe challenges at seven thousand feet.

"The cool people," artist Paul Pascarella calls these employed and unemployed workers who are trying to hold on to a dream that is Taos and Arroyo Seco. Paul resents the presence in our valley of a person such as actress Julia Roberts. "She buys up all these houses around here as investments and forces the cool people, the workers who have been renting them, to move out so her people can move in, her 'help,' she says. One of my friends is moving today because of her."

We are seated outdoors in front under the budding apricot tree at a round green metal table with slatted green chairs. Most of us are drinking organic Guatemalan coffee. Linda Ann is eating a long garlic breadstick, "the best buy for a dollar." I am attacking my usual pecan roll with unladylike gusto. For the ladylike, croissants are more the ticket. Julia Wrapp is here from Boulder with Marga from Switzerland. Barbara drifts by with her brother, Pat. He is wearing a gorgeous cap of many colors made of sarongs from Thailand. He has been there recently; his sister has been living in Ireland for four years. A woman from Adams State College in Alamosa, Colorado, recognizes me and comes over. She remembers the next-to-the-last public appearance Frank made. He was supposed to read there from *Mountain Dialogues*. We needed the $1,000 they were paying. When Frank ran out of breath almost at once, I wound up doing most of the reading. That was a worrisome trip, but we got to stay one last time at Crestone, a power spot that long was one of our favorite places.

In the gravel around us sparrows pick at our leavings. Trickster and her boyfriend Seco roughhouse and box, standing on their hind feet facing each other. Though both are "fixed," they are in love. Seco, a small young stray, used to be called Petrie. Now that Heidi has adopted him, he has a new name. The black-and-white part of him is Australian shepherd, the rest Arroyo Seco, especially his spooky white eyes. Even the pupils are white and glittery. One wonders if they were acquired after a witch stole his original eyes.

We do not realize that he is soon to lose his present right eye to infection.

When I tune in again, Paul is saying to Julia, "Eating places in Taos all serve mediocre food and charge ungodly prices. Now, this place, this place is good. It's good happening."

I think of Michael Uptmor, who lived in our house five winters and calls Casa Fresen "the hoppenin' place" or "CostsaFortune." He doesn't know that to make ends meet Debbie or one of her employees must drive down to Santa Fe and Albuquerque four times a week to wholesale breads and bakery goods.

Marga laments, "Food isn't the only expensive thing in this part of the country. My friend Jenna says land has shot up to $70,000 an acre along El Salto Road near her house. I've seen it happen before. Arroyo Seco will be ruined if you let all these wealthy part-time people come in. Santa Fe has gone down the tubes the same way. You have to get together as a community, set up strict regulations, shut out these rich ones, keep big airplanes and jets away, and *stay small.*"

"It's not that simple," I explain. "Some time ago when we tried to get zoning here to keep out condominiums, Luis Torres swung the major faction to his side after he said, 'My sons aren't interested in ranching. If they want to build a Holiday Inn on our Arroyo Seco property, I'm going to see to it they can.'" And last week's paper tells about Taos landowners who defend the right to have billboards on their property because rent received from billboards pays their taxes so they can keep their land. Everywhere you turn, people are trying to destroy this place in one friendly way or another.

Fifteen years ago our Santa Fe lawyer wouldn't let me set up a Frank Waters Foundation. He said, "Some day there will be condominiums to the left of you running the length of that property. There will be condominiums running the length of the property to the right of you. And you will want condominiums running the length of your *own* property to ensure a comfortable old age for yourself." I got a different lawyer, needless to say, and tied up over half of our land with the Taos Land Trust as watchdog so that it can never be changed or developed. At least Arroyo Seco residents are now working on a "vision statement" that may ease us into some zoning protection against uncontrolled growth. But I'm not counting on it.

Dione stops by to share with us the woes of restoring an old adobe, as if we weren't already familiar with them. Whether you're restoring, building a little studio like ours for creative persons, or building a big house, Casa Fresen is the perfect place to eavesdrop or to make construction contacts. Experts on straw-bale building hang out here, as well as builders of "earthship" houses with tire walls, and every other type of builder you may want to talk to, with the exception generally of adobe builders. The best commercial adobe builders in Arroyo Seco are Hispanic. They most often go to Abe's Bar & Grill instead of Casa Fresen.

Dione lives in the house formerly owned by Claire Morrill, who bought Taos Book Store in the '40s with Genevieve Janssen and wrote *Taos Mosaic* in 1973. Dione doesn't realize that the spirit of Claire speaks straight through her from chapter four of that book. It's hard to believe she hasn't read the book yet. In it is my favorite Laura Gilpin photograph of Frank, taken about the time I met him. It looks exactly like the man with whom I fell in love and affects me the same way all over again every time I see it.

Of restoring that same house back in the late '40s Claire writes, "Restoring an old Taos adobe house is a lifetime affair."

Dione says, "At this point my project is thoroughly discouraging. I think it's going to take a lifetime. And it looks like it's going to get worse before it gets better."

Claire writes, "At this point in such a restoration project, an adobe house is a thoroughly discouraging mess. . . . It all got a great deal worse before it got even a little bit better."

Dione says, "The floors are giving me fits. They are adobe, you see. They're the biggest job yet."

Claire writes, "But the greatest task still lay before us—two new adobe floors." She describes the process as beginning with Indians tamping the ground with a cottonwood cross-section to which handles were attached. From time to time they sprinkled the earth with water and tamped some more until it was firm and level. Then a woman on her knees kneaded a mixture of adobe mud and straw for the next layer. After it had dried, cracks were repaired until the surface was perfectly smooth and ready to be painted with red-brown earth pigment from a nearby cave. Finally it was stabilized with linseed oil and kerosene until it resembled dark marble.

Our guest room still has a similar type of floor. Some people used linseed oil and kerosene to harden their floors to marble-like consistency. Frank and Janey did it the oldest way. Charles Hathaway recalls: "Frank then took us to a room in which we were to sleep. The floor was the color of deep red mahogany with a high polish. Frank explained this shining maroon-colored floor of hand-polished adobe. Janey and he had obtained buckets of ox blood at the slaughter house in Taos, hauled it home, mixed it with adobe, carefully applied it to the floor, smoothed it level and, as it hardened, they on their hands and knees polished it with sheepskin for hours."

In her book Claire writes of Frank that he sees the "exchange of energies between the individual and the universe as the secret core of all Pueblo and Navajo ceremonialism."

As I sink into one of the meditative musings characteristic of Casa Fresen, where snow-peaked mountains stretch the gaze, I realize my whole book is a ceremony celebrating my exchange of energies with the universe. Perhaps it will point the way for others to do the same. It should be encouraging, at least, to know that this exchange is possible without any formal ritual or the intercession of some modern high priestess or priest. By simply remaining open, and by opening the unconscious, powerful synchronicities occur.

Dione stops by Casa Fresen this morning and sounds like Claire Morrill, now dead. I open Claire's book again and out jump those few words about Frank—for Claire wrote very little about him—that reaffirm my path and reassure me. And I get the bonus of touching his energy again through the vivid Gilpin photo there.

By definition, synchronicity is a "meaningful coincidence" that connects an outer incident with some inner or greater development. It cuts through time and space. This definition could well be expanded to include, "It is an exchange of energies between the individual and the universe." Like finding that plastic star near Frank's cross with Linda Ann.

This morning I have brought with me a grooming comb and a bird book to identify two rust-black-and-white evening grosbeaks I hadn't recognized at first sight. While combing Trickster, I comment to Linda Ann, "I brought this comb and book along to keep from feeling guilty about wasting time here at Casa. Away from my writing project."

Later she calls to report that she has been listening to Thomas Moore on the radio. "Moore says 'project' is a bad word. He says to forget about projects. Erase the word from your vocabulary. Instead, he recommends nurturing your soul. And one of the best ways to do this, he says, is through the *fine art of conversation*. Barb, Casa Fresen is just what the doctor ordered for you. *Without* Trickster's comb."

13
The Coyote and the Croissants

She came to help
her master
Kukutema
of the Coyote Clan,
He Who Saw Afar,
when he made his transition
to another realm.
And she helped her mistress
view this parting
in perspective.
For Trickster's
gleaming topaz eyes
gaze far into the future,
and beyond.
"Always Looking Forward,"
instinctively
she too is
Kukutema
of the Coyote Clan.

Trickster nudges me hard with her wet black nose until she knocks my right hand off the typewriter.

Stifling my laughter, I order, "Go away, Trickster!"

This encourages her to knock my hand off the keys several more times.

"Oh, you're just like Frank!" I tell her, with the big hug she's expecting. "He never gave me a moment's peace when I was trying to write. I know you're inside this dog, Frank Waters! You can't fool me." Realizing she wants to type her own life story, a story of bad karma and good croissants, I give her a kiss. I can sense her words through her topaz eyes.

The main part of her story right now has to do with Casa Fresen. Trickster is the mascot of Casa Fresen. Each morning she checks out its tantalizing smells and tastes. She is not a Pecan Roll Fanatic like me. Trickster is a Croissant Freak. She prefers to sink her fangs into flaky croissants with the crisp consistency of two-day-old snow, another favorite. Cream-cheese-and-fruit-filled croissants stick to her sharp teeth. As Frank did, therefore, she prefers plain croissants.

He used to tell her, "When it comes to croissants, *we* are purists."

Trickster's passion for croissants sometimes causes her problems. Lisa, who owns *La Vieja Loca* down the street from the bakery, has disliked the coyote dog ever since a blond kitten that resembled a croissant showed up at her store. Trickster was as surprised as Lisa was mad when it didn't taste one bit like a croissant. If she'd gotten a chance really to dig in, it might have tasted much like a jam-filled croissant. But Lisa put a stop to that meal fast.

Her kitten later was hit by a passing car, a more fatal encounter than being mistaken for a croissant.

Three kids broke Lisa's front window; another shot out her porch light with a BB gun. "Both times I called the cops *and* their parents," she told me. "They're doomed!"

Trickster shuddered all over as Lisa looked at her speculatively, and a shiver ran down my own spine. We could tell she was thinking, "You're doomed too!" She did not smile when Trickster tried to ingratiate herself by turning one of her goofy half somersaults.

At our house Trickster once tried to eat a white mop of a dog called Montaña, who belongs to Linda Ann. Through half-closed eyes, Montaña could be mistaken for a powdered-sugar-covered croissant. Since Linda Ann was standing right there, however, I had to hit Trickster a little less softly with the broom than I ordinarily do when she forgets her manners.

Some nights when it is oppressively silent and Mozart is not enough, I read aloud to the three dogs. They love the sound of a human voice and my undivided attention; it reminds me of bedtime storytelling during my own childhood, and that of my sons.

Some mornings it surprises me when I don't have the energy or inclination to get up, brush my teeth, and dress; I want to stay in my cave of a bed forever.

Trickster will have none of this malingering. She plunks her great forepaws on my pillow and nuzzles me until I respond appropriately. Sometimes she will settle for me crooning to her like Celine Dion,

> You are the reason I wake up every day.
> It's you
> It's all because of YOU, Trickster.

If I shove Trickster out the door so that I can return to hibernating, she knows how to cope with this inappropriate behavior too. She gallops down to Casa Fresen, begs a croissant, and carries it back clamped between her iron jaws for me to eat, however forlorn it may look. Talk about man's best friend. It is far above and beyond the call of duty when Trickster sacrifices one of her coveted croissants for the good of a cause other than stuffing her own beautiful face.

It appears that this grief process is going to take me about two years to get through. If I should ever lose my precious Trickster, I brood, it would set me back again. Then my spirits lift. Why torture myself with morbid thoughts when there are croissants and pecan rolls to be eaten, and the irrepressible joy of a free-spirited dog to tap into right this minute?

After brushing my teeth, washing, and dressing, I struggle out to feed the horses. Trickster laughs and barks and nips at their hocks until she has both horses bucking and stampeding about the corral. Unless she is sleeping, there's never a dull moment. Even asleep she often thrashes about in the midst of fantastic dreams, probably of being Super Dog on some planet made entirely of croissants; or else she is growling along with Dion's wild version of "Treat Her Like a Lady. Go! Go!"

I tend to agree with Melanie, who wrote me after dogsitting our half-coyote dog, "You can tell by looking into Trickster's eyes that she is a Wild Child. And you can't expect too much from her."

"Wild Child," I whisper, "I wish you could always be free as the wind and never have to be fenced in . . . or I should say chained up."

No fence can hold her. If it's eight or nine feet high, she simply leaps up, hooks her front paws on top, and works her back legs up and over. I try not to chain her much, except when we're traveling. An avid traveler who loves to ride in cars, Trickster doesn't mind this minor loss of freedom in exchange for expanded horizons.

The main appeal of traveling for her is the increase in personal contacts; invariably, strangers are drawn to her. Trickster is a people person. And she has charisma. Although I love Morgan and Crystal dearly too, they do not have that extra spark that ignites Trickster's personality. As if aware of this, Trickster carries herself with an air. Like one of those regal lions crouched at the entrance of New York's Public Library, head high she stretches out in the middle of Casa Fresen's flagstone entrance waiting for others to pay homage.

Women call Trickster "a sweetheart" or "such a *sweet* dog." Men more often say she's "cool," and are less intimidated by her size. They also pick up on tail-wagging more astutely than most women. Sideways wags mean, "Don't just stand there. Go ahead and *pat* me." Circular wags mean, "I'll have a piece of that croissant, please."

Toni says, "You know, Trickster likes to follow me on hikes. And I love her to pieces. I live on five acres, and I could give her a really good home."

I shake my head slowly. "Thanks, Toni. That is very kind of you. But I'm kind of superstitious about her. There's a lot of Frank in her. He belonged to the Hopi Coyote Clan, you know. His Hopi name was *Kukutema*. It means Always Looking Forward. . . ."

My voice grows too scratchy to finish. Toni pats my hand and says, "I understand."

Before she finally put on weight, some people didn't realize that Trickster's skinniness was due to having a fragmented bullet in her stomach. She was shot by a neighbor the morning of Frank's memorial service.

Thinking she was being mistreated by me, a well-meaning young woman named Autumn later kidnapped her and held her prisoner in the ABOMINABLE SNOWMANsion for five days. She probably kept the poor beast drugged on croissant morsels.

When an informant at last led me to this hideout, Autumn said, "Vera loves living here. She's perfectly happy here, and we feed her well."

More than anything, I was shocked at the sound of Trickster's new name. In a shaken voice I said, "Vera. Vera? W . . . w . . . well, I want Trickster to be happy. Th . . . that's the most important thing. She's had a hard life. Maybe we could sh . . . share her."

Then I burst out crying.

Now Autumn looked shocked. Putting her arms around me, she said, "No, you take her back. I wouldn't think of keeping her. I had no idea she meant so much to you."

"Me neither," I said, choking up again.

After that Trickster stayed home for three whole days. Vera. Imagine calling a coyote dog *Vera*.

It may not have been too difficult to hold Trickster captive, for she *is* a fickle female. She likes to follow hikers and bikers and is perfectly willing to get into strange cars or to stay overnight with a new admirer. She has her share of weaknesses. Veterinarian offices and explosive noises turn her into a quivering mass of jelly. And she is hell on other dogs who try to get near me. Horses and cats bring out her jealous streak too. Most of all she hates other coyotes and puppies.

Trickster was starving to death on Calle Coyote half a block from here when she begged me to take her home. For five days she had been sitting on the front porch of neighbors who resented the fact that she had been dumped in our area. They refused to feed her, one of their children told me.

On one of my daily walks I got this message directly from Trickster when she stood on her hind legs and stretched herself to my full height of five foot nine. With her paws on my shoulders, she spoke directly into my blue eyes through her eloquent topaz eyes. A whole saga of tragedy glinted there from the depth of her being.

"I understand. You can come home with me," I replied after a time.

Shaking with relief, she continued to imprison me with her forepaws for some moments before dropping to all fours and following me home. She hindered our progress by constantly repeating her pleading stance, just in case I had a short memory. Instead of walking or crawling, though, even then she pranced.

At home I told Frank, who did not greet our starving newcomer with open arms, "Dogs take to me. I can't *help* it. If I had an Indian name, I'd like a beautiful one like 'Touch-the-Clouds.' But it would probably turn out to be 'Dog Woman.'"

Talking quickly to divert his displeasure and to entertain him, I rushed on, "When Terry came home after being wounded in Vietnam, we went to this stable in Tucson to rent some horses. We found it deserted. Looking for a stable keeper, I went one way, Terry the other.

"Suddenly I stumbled over seven huge black Belgian shepherds lying inside the shady stable, which, unknown to us, was no longer a public place. Thinking they had to be friendly to mingle with the public, I murmured, 'What beautiful dogs! And what *fine voices*. No wonder they used your relatives as foghorns on the canals of Belgium. Oh, you are very, very good watchdogs.' I patted them all, and they lay back down and went right to sleep, I thought.

"Quite a while later when I returned to my car, Terry lay sprawled on its hood. He was kicking wildly with his size thirteen cowboy boots at these seven big black dogs snapping and baying at him.

"'Where the hell have you been?' he shouted. 'Get these mad dogs off me!'

"After I'd reassured them, they went docilely back to their naps, on the way growling deep in their throats, 'You can catch more dogs with honey than with vinegar.'"

"Rarf! Rarf," Trickster agreed. "Honey!" She licked Frank's hand and turned a captivating half somersault that exposed her skinny white stomach to be patted, a stomach that would grow sleek and well rounded in our home. Her blonde coyote appeal soon got to him, and he grew to love her at least as much as I. Her crazy antics and loving care eased his last lingering illness by frequently pushing it from the forefront of his mind. As with all our dogs, joy far outweighed inevitable grief. They were our family.

That we ever managed to fatten Trickster is no small miracle. Believe me, this girl has seen troubles. First she was taken from her babies and dumped in Arroyo Seco. Then our neighbors starved her. After this, while staying with us she was spayed, wormed, inoculated, and bathed. She had close encounters with bullets, skunks, a porcupine, and burrs in her throat. In Tucson a rattler bit her and an argumentative Doberman chawed her here and there. In Taos a neighbor shot her directly in the stomach, where half a dozen bullet fragments still lie embedded. And Autumn kidnapped her.

With good cause Trickster whimpers, "I have *bad karma*."

"For sure you've outlasted the nine lives of a cat," I say with another shiver of foreboding.

Trickster tosses her head like Scarlett O'Hara and bats her eyelashes. "I'll think about that *tomorrow*," she growls, for our Wild Child lives in the Now.

And now is Sunday, a perfect day at Casa Fresen. The warm sun makes everyone sleepy, and kind. Church bells ring. In the apricot tree rascally sparrows chirp just out of reach, bestowing their calling cards here and there upon careless customers below. Lots of people offer croissant tidbits to bewitching Trickster, pat her, or extend their hands to be licked.

You can read her mind. Men's hands are nice and salty, real salty. But little boys' hands are best of all to lick. Their hands have *everything:* salty dirt, cereal, croissant crumbs, crayon wax, spilled pop, sticky candy, stinky pee, mashed bananas. They have the most *smells* of anyone too. Not as strong as car tires, but more mysterious. Even dogs have to work hard at sorting out all the smell layers of a little boy. Part of him smells soft and earthy like bread dough and Dog Woman. Part smells sharp like men, but not sharp and hard like bad men with guns. And then there are the other parts. Boys are irresistible. As long as they don't have water pistols or popping balloons, or firecrackers that sound like gunshots.

A storyteller sprawls in a rocking chair on the rickety front porch of the Art Lab next door to Casa Fresen. He specializes in telling trickster-coyote tales. "I like the one where Trickster crashes a party and dances wildly until midnight," he says with a lazy Sunday morning yawn.

"'Party's over,' they tell the blonde coyote at the stroke of twelve. 'You have to go home now. Get lost!'

"Disappointed, Trickster trots slowly off toward the River of Parting, her long, shapely legs still twitching to the beat of the mambo.

"To her delight, beside the river she encounters another lively group of revelers who are dancing up a storm. Joyfully, she joins the happy throng. With gay abandon they dance away the night.

"At dawn she is startled to discover that her swaying partners stand rooted in shallow water. Tall and thin with fuzzy brown heads, they are the Cat Tail People. Gravely they bow farewell to their coyote friend."

Our beloved Trickster suddenly is to disappear for good the day two German shepherds are found shot to death down the road. Another dog has its muzzle bound shut with barbed wire. Of all the mental scenarios I have since suffered through, I choose to think of Trickster dancing eternally with the Cat Tail People, her golden eyes alight with love and joy and mischief.

At the River of Parting

Trickster, the party-
girl, dances forever with
the Cat Tail People.

14
Shangri-La

Frank used to wait eagerly for my return from the beauty shop every Tuesday morning. "Tell me all the latest gossip!" he would demand with a grin as soon as I stepped inside our door. Big Rita owns Kachina Beauty Salon, and Stella and Mabel have worked there forever, along with Little Rita, who resembles Rita Hayworth in miniature. A superb dancer, Stella leads most of the marches preceding wedding dances; she knows everything about local brides, grooms, weddings, wedding dances, and divorces. Frank took folk-dancing lessons from her parents, Phil and Lucy Mares, in the late '60s Before Barbara, luckily. I am a terrible dancer; Frank was a born dancer, light on his feet with a great sense of rhythm. But we danced only once, in Mesilla with Keith and Heloise Wilson in an old Billy the Kid hangout. With luck, Frank may not have remembered the experience next morning.

The rest of the beauty operators specialize in news of local deaths, illnesses, recoveries, tragedies, scandals, and amusing incidents. This week a live mouse swimming in the beauty-parlor toilet freaked out Big Rita; now she won't use it for fear the mouse will flush back up. Two horses have been mysteriously shot in their pastures. Our historic blinking light, a major Taos directional signal north of town, has bitten the dust in exchange for a conventional stoplight with not a shred of personality. Where Indians hunted rabbits not too long ago, a supermarket may be built. One thousand people tried to squeeze into tiny Calvary Chapel for the funeral of a man thrown from his pickup on the Ski Valley road. Stella was one of the first to hear of the tragedy.

I am happy to return to the comparative peace of Arroyo Seco, which looks today like Shangri-La, covered with mysterious cloud curtains absent from Taos, a thousand feet lower. Bill Farr scolds from Taos, "*Your* cloud is hiding *our* sun." From El Prado on the north edge of Taos, El Salto Mountain—also called Cuchillo—looks as sharp as Huayna Picchu, the mist-veiled jagged mountain thrusting above Machu Picchu's ruins.

Huayna Picchu was a jungle paradise full of orchids and exotic undergrowth I had never seen before our trip to Peru in 1982. Altars and observatory ruins on top exuded power. After climbing the peak, I wandered slowly back down through this jungled wonderland. Caught up in its enchantment, I didn't realize dark had descended and a gatekeeper was about to lock me out of Machu Picchu for the night. Beside him stood Frank in a tizzy, wringing his hands. A few years later when he listed his view of our twelve "Happiest Moments," I was surprised to see as his eleventh: "That evening when you had climbed the straight-up peak Huayna Picchu across from Machu Picchu and the guard was starting to lock the gate and I was nervously waiting. I thought any moment he'd tell me they'd found a beautiful blonde fallen from the pinnacle. And then you came running and laughing and out of breath up the path just in time to get through the gate."

By the time one reaches Arroyo Seco, El Salto Mountain has changed from a second Huayna Picchu into the soft, rounded rump of what looks to me like a woman lying on her stomach. An adjacent mountain called Vallecitos shapes her upper half and arms, which reach out and touch the legs of her lover, Taos Sacred Mountain. He too lies on his stomach with his head resembling an Easter Island sculpture slanting in the direction of Taos to the west. Light and shadow appear to make him smile or frown, forecasting what is in store for me on a particular day. The two giants are cold lovers now, entombed in ice and snow. But still they touch. Contrary to my belief, Frank thought Taos Sacred Mountain was female, El Salto Mountain male. She was good, he evil. He changed this later to positive and negative, saying he meant only to show their duality. That one is female, one male, is enough to perceive. They are part of one whole, rather than opposites.

The mother of Mabel, the hairdresser who does my hair once a week, was a sister to Elizida Duran next door, Salomé's wife. After Elizida's death, Salomé had his phone disconnected. He has lost touch with most relatives. On one of her rare visits Mabel noticed that Elizida's purse remains on their bedroom dresser; her nightgown and robe hang on the bathroom door.

"Frank's slippers are still under our bed," I say.

"Still!" Mabel shakes her head and purses her lips in disapproval.

In Shangri-La no one is supposed to grow old. Yet here we are alone, growing old next door to one another, Salomé and I, with Amada Quintana aging alone a couple of doors down the opposite way.

It is good we have the lambs to keep us young at heart. They are black and playful. Instead of running, at first they bob jerkily forward and backward, like rocking horses. By three weeks old the five bravest gambol smoothly up and down the inner pasture where they are confined. They could be tiny tots frisking about a school playground. Two puny late arrivals press close to their puffy white mothers, then nurse from them. Two others are napping. White wool patches are beginning to polka-dot the oldest three.

Salomé understands English, speaks a minimum. His white hair is kept short and neat. Usually his teeth are in; sometimes not. His right foot is badly clubbed, turned at a ninety-degree angle toward the left. But still he drives his car, and he attends Holy Trinity Church just often enough so that his absence is not a beauty-parlor issue. His cancer has been in remission for some years.

Seated at a kitchen table with chrome legs, he pours his tobacco into a small white paper square, rolls and lights it, and stares through misty glass panes of a thinly curtained door before him. Mornings and evenings he watches the news on a television set that is mostly as silent as he. He smiles and chuckles, however, whenever he talks—whether about cheerful or dire subjects. He and I visit while Judith Bronner photographs his lambs.

"I tell Arturo, the *mayordomo*," he says with his widest grin, "he have much trouble this summer. Trying to make everyone happy with water for our fields. But no water!" he laughs into the silence around us.

Later, Judith notices three valuable Toby mugs sitting on a shelf above his sink. "I collect Toby mugs too," she says.

Knowing Salomé has no idea what a Toby mug is, I add, "Up there above the sink; aren't those Elizida's cups?"

"Yes," he says with a full turned-up smile matching those on the three mugs. I see why he has kept them, though they are less simple than the rest of his home now. While we see his reflection in them, he sees Elizida, who seldom smiled. They are a positive, therapeutic influence in more ways than one.

On the shelf above my bed sits a Peruvian vessel, a grinning young Moché man's face with a curved spout for a handle. Simply to look at it, consciously or unconsciously, cheers me and causes me to smile a little.

Elizida and Salomé did not marry until the late '50s, when they were well along in years and he was winding down his annual stints of sheepherding in Wyoming. Mabel's mother was matron of honor at their wedding. Both women wore gray suits with pink blouses and pink pillbox hats. They looked very beautiful, Mabel says. Now Mabel's mother has Alzheimer's and tries to beat up everyone with the heavy cast on her broken arm. Sometimes she pulls Mabel's hair. There are worse ways to go than emphysema.

Elizida specialized in baking desserts for restaurants. She was an immaculate housekeeper. She also had a green thumb; their yard was dense with orange tiger lilies, red peonies and white ones, wild sweetpeas in different shades of pink, deep pink climbing roses, phlox to match the pinks, giant maroon dahlias, and a white snowball bush like the ones that grow in Illinois.

At the boundary between her flower garden and their lush green front yard she erected cement blocks as a base for a two-foot-high statue of the Virgin Mary wearing a blue cloak over her flowing white gown. At each side stood a candle. Behind her an American flag fluttered from the curlicued headboard of a brass bed painted white. Standing on our back porch, we could look through our bedroom picture window and across the room through a bank of windows facing Our Lady. She seemed to be hovering at the edge of our room and protecting us too.

The summer before last I asked Salomé, "Where is that beautiful Virgin Mary statue that's always been out here in the yard? I miss it."

"It broke," he said. "Arm broke."

"No one will notice," I said. "I think it brings both you and us good luck. I could glue the parts together, or buy a new one, if you will put it back up."

"No one will notice." He put it back up, and it has stayed there in good weather ever since. I miss it this winter but expect Our Lady back this spring in all her glory, along with Old Glory.

A few nights I don't sleep well and am up and down all night. After one such session, Salomé looks over the fence next morning at me and my swollen eyes and says, "Lots of nights I not sleep after Elizida go. Hard! Hard with no sleep. Hard when they go." He smiles and chuckles, at the same time shaking his head from side to side as though he means this as a serious, heart-to-heart talk. We were in Tucson when Elizida died of cancer. I thought of him then as a stoic sheepherder used to being alone, not as a grieving husband.

The thought of his own grief and of his effort this day chokes me. "Hard," I say.

Salomé's house is a green, L-shaped Hansel-and-Gretel cottage made of adobe. A lived-in kitchen faces El Salto Road; a bedroom and an off-limits parlor face our house. Outer walls are painted pale pale green, and a steep metal roof slopes down close to the ground. Today it is trimmed in front with a perfect fringe of eight-inch-long icicles that I covet for our house. In back a few are twelve inches long. The wood trim is green, including five porch posts, one splintered in two near its base and supported on each side by a leaning adobe brick that Elizida would never have tolerated. Green indoor-outdoor carpeting covers the porch floor. Thick vines shadow the porch in summer beside an emerald-green lawn, giving this the air of a fairytale house tucked in a forest. Our aspen are spreading to Salomé's lawn, and great cottonwoods line his front yard. Behind lies fertile open pasture stretching back to our aspen grove called "the Cathedral," where our land crosses the foot of his.

An intriguing white enamel soup ladle hangs from the back fence next to Salomé's house. Impaling the tip of a post next to it is a large red coffee can, close to two moss-green squares of tin covering window-like apertures at the rear of his house. His tumbledown sheep pens are patched with two rust-colored squares on one roof, a light blue rectangle on another. A turquoise metal window adds another patch of color. Somewhere a green splash gleams through the slanted gray wood, and flashes of bright blue tarp warm his haystacks. Artists love his place almost as much as Salomé does.

He has sold his sheep to Mike Medina, a plumber who continues to pasture them on the old man's land. Medina speaks of selling them altogether; he says they're more trouble than they are worth. This change would be almost as devastating to me as to Salomé. Checking on them throughout the day is his only joy and exercise. The soothing sound of sheep bells is one of the cheapest, most effective therapies available. In bed at night and early in the morning, the soft clang of these bells was Frank's favorite music.

I once "saved" one of two stray black lambs from the back of our property. Fearing they would drown in the rushing water of the *acequia madre*, I tried to lasso them with Morgan's narrow dog leash. Instead of drowning, they leapfrogged back and forth across the mother ditch, baaing in great distress—or in defiance. After a hot, sweaty hour, I finally corralled one at the furthermost boundary of our land. It didn't act cute at all after I picked it up in my arms. It was a wiggling, squirming, kicking mass of quicksilver with mean little heels.

Salomé met us when we reached Calle Coyote and dragged the lamb along the lane by its forefeet until its dangling back hooves bled. I picked it back up after we had passed the Deer Glade, where Frank used to sleep on summer nights, and pushed it through a hole in Salomé's fence.

We were so exhausted that we gave up on personally rescuing the second lost lamb. Salomé drove his flock to the back of his property, and the stupid little thing came tripping right over to them sweet as pie without one bit of help from us.

As a child, Crystal Jongeward played across Calle Coyote from the sheep pens in a wildcat lair she called the National Cat College. Here her orange cat Marmalade was forced to attend school each day in a warren of dense brush, chokecherry and blackberry bushes, aspen and cottonwoods. Crystal transformed it, in her imagination at least, into student dormitories, classrooms, a kitchen, a dining room, and special living quarters for professors.

While clearing this corner of his land a year after Crystal and her parents had moved to Toronto, Mike Medina discovered a family of wildcats in residence. They appeared to have been living there a long time. Apparently Crystal's "professors" had educated them well, for they were never known to have bothered humans. Marmalade disappeared, true, but that could have been an acute case of truancy.

Snowflakes big enough to hang on a Christmas tree bombard us this afternoon. Salomé's older sheep are coated twice as thickly as normal. They look like snow-white Missing Yeti monsters, with nine black lambs tucked into the maw of their stomachs. During the storm Jimmy Morningtalk's buffalo herd hunkers down across the road like hairy yurts. At last they stand and shake themselves, snorting white fire, scattering crystal light. Morgan stands sabled against the white backdrop of a winter portrait. Crystal is a flash of silver fox in the foreground.

A Shangri-La of sparkling Christmas trees seems to murmur, "Here is your March Christmas present, Barbara: hundreds of white Christmas trees to make up for this first Christmas without a tree of your own."

Perhaps the snow is a symbol of Frank as well. For he was Leo the Lion, and in Illinois they say, "March comes in like a lion and goes out like a lamb." If it's Salomé's kind of lamb, the weather will still be kicking up a storm at the end of this month! Nine months since Frank's death, the storm roars in reminder. As if each monthly anniversary date were not already a wrenching Damn First.

The two shelties can't get enough of this cotton-candy snow. They have the same reaction as children everywhere: rolling in it, turning mad circles, jumping, making angel tracks. As soon as I bring them in, they want to go back out. Like a good Navajo mother, I let my children romp in it so they will love snow instead of dreading it. Frances Gillmor writes of snow in *Traders to the Navajos:* "'If you treat it as a friend, it will not seem as cold to you through the long winter,' they said. 'The earth sleeps in winter, and the summer is more beautiful for her rest, even as the day is more beautiful after the night. So we count the winters and not the summers, the nights and not the days. And so the years come and go.'"

"Roar, Lion, Roar!" That was the name of our school song at Lyons Township High School and Junior College in LaGrange, Illinois. Two of Frank's best friends—Chuck Adams and Bob Kostka—went to school there with me. We didn't get to know each other until a quarter of a century later after we had met through Frank. He said a ley line must stretch from Arroyo Seco to the Chicago area. More than one close friend has journeyed here from there. The lion roars now in a complete whiteout with gale winds blowing the snow horizontally. In this howling silence one is attuned to the infinite energy of natural forces. Only our sparrows and juncos sass back the storm. Three gluttonous yellow grosbeaks beleaguer the birdfeeder. In these primitive surroundings, daily distractions are blotted out.

"Our inner mind hears the choir of invisible forces," as sculptor Malvina Hoffman expresses it in her autobiography, *Heads and Tales*. We tune in to the infinite, which results in renewal and a truer perspective of our finite, everyday selves. Achieving this result takes solitude, a certain degree of near primitive silence, and commitment. Too few of us allow ourselves the luxury of "lonely communion."

As the full moon rises over Vallecitos, I stand out in front amidst the close white hush with my arms open to her renewing strength. Laughing stars twinkle back the happiness Frank and I once shared. It is still out there, somewhere. A flurry of chiffon snow sets my heart shimmering with hope again.

Earlier Celestino arrived at sunset to plow my driveway in a universe blossomed pink and apricot. Crystal whirled her most ecstatic dervish circles. It maddened her with joy to have a truck to bark at—her favorite pastime—in her own backyard.

"The snow has pretty much stopped, and the sky is clearing. You won't be a prisoner much longer," he said.

"You don't know how much I appreciate this, Celestino. It seems such a miracle that the year I need help, you suddenly have access to this beautiful vehicle." He is a master at manipulating that plow, especially backward—fascinating to watch.

For years Celestino worked at the molybdenum mine near Questa. When it closed, this whole area suffered severe unemployment. Nevertheless, Celestino felt grateful that Moly Mine had already paid for his home and his children's college educations. Always cheerful in public, Celestino has eyes that sparkle like Saint Nick's. He laughs a lot at his own jokes. He has snared a good retirement job in Taos as a park maintenance man and gets to drive one of their pickups with a snowplow blade attached. He seems content with life, less prone to private, moody spells than he was while working at Moly Mine and raising a family. Despite his job he lives much in the old way: sowing alfalfa, cutting it himself, rais-

ing a few head of cattle, breeding a horse every now and then, hauling and cutting his own wood. A fine mechanic, he always has several junkers in his overflowing backyard to fix up and sell or use. He
bought my '77 Monte Carlo, which we'd taken to Guatemala and
back without even a flat, and drove it with considerable pride until
he sold it at a profit. Frank called him by the intimate nickname of
"Celes." That sounded to me more musical and celestial than his
real name, which does have its own beauty.

As Celestino beamed with pleasure at my compliment about his
plowing, I continued, "I've been meaning to tell you that I thought
the long poem your sister Oclides wrote about your father was excellent. I'm happy they printed it in the Spanish section of the
newspaper, and that her Spanish was easy enough for me to understand."

"Yes, my father was a fine man."

"And he looked exactly like *you*, Celestino, in that photograph
of him on horseback."

"Oh no, my father was a *good-looking* man. He had a very square
jaw, a strong jaw. That dog in his lap had the trick of jumping up
from the ground onto a horse's back, especially when a rider was up
there. The picture was taken by some vacationers in Red River
when Father was herding his flock of sheep over there in the summer. They sent it back from Oklahoma with another picture of the
whole flock and of all the riders on horseback. Yes, my father was a
good-looking man. And smart too."

Frank had not written well of Celestino's parents, the family
thought. Once Mrs. Quintana, her son Bolivar, and Amada came
over, seated themselves in a row on our living room couch, and
complained about this, each in his or her own way. Bolivar gave
Frank hell; Amada shook her head sadly; Mrs. Quintana wept.
Frank became terribly upset at her tears. He thought the world of
her. But he had passed on in a book some unfounded gossip that
two of her relatives are spreading to this day; I myself have heard
them. To Frank it seemed to make Mrs. Quintana more of a fey
person. As for Celestino's father, Frank had known him only late in

life, when Mr. Quintana frequently asked him to buy half pints of whiskey in town on the q.t. Since Frank was buying them for himself too, it didn't seem like any great sin. He neglected, however, to give both Quintanas credit in writing for being educated teachers and hardworking pillars of the Arroyo Seco community. Moreover, Mrs. Quintana had been a Martinez, a direct descendant of the original owners of the Martinez Land Grant, part of which now comprises Arroyo Seco.

The specific area where we live has been called "Quintanaville." Stacked downhill west from us are the homes first of Celestino and then his brother Bolivar; next comes the old homestead of Alicia and José, now occupied by their lonely daughter Amada; then Alicia's nephew Luis Torres's spread is followed by the house of Pablo, a third Quintana brother whose widow, Rose, lives there with her son Felix. In Mrs. Quintana's back pasture stands the home of a granddaughter named Saundra, and farther back a grandson named Robert has a place. Other offspring of Bolivar live nearby.

Once in Tucson I was speeding a bit while rounding a curve on Ruthrauff Road. A former student of mine who had become a police officer stopped us. Frank was impressed that he let me off for old times' sake after we'd rehashed with considerable laughter his school days and noteworthy sports accomplishments. Calling me by my former name as he returned to his car, over his shoulder the officer yelled, "You owe me one, Mrs. Hayes!"

In similar fashion, it seems to me we should say, "We owe you one, Mr. and Mrs. Quintana." Even though Frank did write well of Alicia, mostly. For this reason, here is the gist of Oclides's touching poem in honor of her father, who died of pneumonia one winter after falling during a mild stroke and breaking eight ribs.

Memories of Our Father José María Quintana

He was eighty-two years old when he passed to a better life. On January 28 we suffered his departure. Despite being well cared for, our father José María broke his ribs and death carried him away. José María Quintana was born here in Taos. He was presented to the world on March 9. Soledad and Melquiades welcomed him. He was one of eight from a loving family. His siblings were Cristobal, Pablo, Eliza, and Telesfor. Also there were Virginia and Margarita and Elizardo, the eldest. As a young man he attended college. With ability and skill he studied to be a teacher. In 1916 he joined the Navy. For three years in a row he traveled and sailed. He was a faithful soldier, noble and excellent. He defended his country with the highest patriotism. He was a valiant soldier who knew all Europe. He completed his military service and to his country returned. With much enthusiasm he returned from the war, continuing his task as a schoolteacher. He was a faithful teacher to all his amiable students. He treated them all equally, even those better than he.

While he was teaching, his state changed. One day in November he married Alicia. His destiny, too, changed soon after his marriage. From Alicia's parents he inherited a flock. In the high mountains he passed the summers. Alone with only his flock of sheep, he tended them carefully. He was a humble man, good and friendly. People respected him, but then he was very kind. He was a very religious man, who never abandoned his religion. Because of this, he passed without fear into the other world.

It was a very sad time when our father died. He left behind many friends and a family who loved him. As a war veteran, he was given a beautiful funeral. He went to rest in his grave with military honors. His family cried silently to themselves. With a military salute, he was given a last goodbye. With God and the Virgin Mary rests our father José María, for certain. It has been twenty years, but we haven't forgotten him. He left this world then, our father José María. Death arrives for all, for all are equal. He walked the path he wished; this too is universal.

15
The Itching Foot

To set sail somewhere
is more important than life itself.
                    —Isak Dinesen

In *Don't Push the River*, Barry Stevens advocates going with the flow. It should be so simple. Sometimes you have to shove like hell. I desperately needed our "Happy Moments" list to complete a counseling course and graduate with my counseling master's degree. Our professor thought some of us were kowtowing to our husbands too much and not doing enough risk-taking toward our own self-development, particularly those of us married to successful or well-known men.

Frank had dropped out of college after three years and had a chip on his shoulder about education and teaching. Unhappy about my earning additional degrees, he would repeatedly try to chop me down with such comments as, "Teaching is not creative." The University of Arizona was always "that damn university" and its instructors "those damn professors."

I had completed my own "Happy Moments" list and had asked him to do the same many times. So far, Dr. No had come up with only his standard reply, or silence. Finally, when I was about to leave for California, where my father lay dying, Frank agreed to dictate a "few items."

"Twelve," I reminded him.

"Oh, come now," Frank said. "I couldn't possibly think of more than six."

"Our happiness is a real stumbling block for you, isn't it?"

"I have never believed in publishing my private history and thoughts," Frank replied in his most haughtily leonine manner.

He dictated three, then hedged, "I'll tell you when I felt *unhappy*. It was that time about midnight before we were married when I left you off at Indian Hills Inn. You stood there near the door, waving. All alone. And you'd be gone in the morning. . . ."

"You're not supposed to be thinking of *unhappy* times," I said. "Besides, we'd had a very happy time that evening. Remember? And then while you watched me wave, you backed into that light pole and dented the Tank again!"

Frank laughed and reeled off the other nine "Happy Moments" as if he were the most model husband in history. This exercise brought home to me that successful relationships take work, optimism, and persistence. I wish Frank could know how happy this list makes me today. It is one of the most precious personal gifts he has left me. Both lists vibrate with enduring energy and love.

Frank's Happy Moments Together

1. That evening campfire picnic way back in Oshá Canyon hidden along the original El Camino Real trail.
2. Seeing Machu Picchu for the first time and walking together through the ruins.
3. Discovering the Victorian 1900 Restaurant around the corner from Hotel Bolivar in Lima, Peru, with those two fellows playing the harp and flute, and a native girl dancing.
4. In Veracruz, bursting upon that tremendous display of lights; it was so beautiful to see that plaza after we'd driven

through that decrepit neighborhood on Christmas Eve and were the last ones left on the bus.

5. When you came up to Taos at Easter with your friends and came out alone to the house and said all you wanted to do was rock in our chairs before the fire burning in my Indian fireplace.

6. Our wedding day, December 23—a great day—with Bill tight on champagne and scotch, and I got that way too; and those beautiful banks of poinsettias we had bought on 17th Street.

7. When you telephoned to Taos and said you'd found a little house we could afford in Tucson off the beaten path.

8. When I turned into the driveway of our Tucson house for the first time. I couldn't believe it! We'd bought a *real house!* It wasn't a tin-roofed shack after all, as I had feared.

9. Of course I was always *very* happy when you drove up to Sedona from Tucson. Those were *very happy* times to have you come up there on weekends when I'd been so lonely all week.

10. I was very happy on the day you retired from teaching school. I thought you'd have all the time in the world to write your little children's books. (I was *very unhappy* when you signed up for five courses at the university instead.)

11. That evening when you had climbed the straight-up peak Huayna Picchu across from Machu Picchu and the guard was starting to lock the gate and I was nervously waiting. I thought any moment he'd tell me they'd found a beautiful blonde fallen from the pinnacle. And then you came running and laughing and out of breath up the path just in time to get through the gate. Talk about happy!

12. And, oh yes, my big outdoor party for my eightieth birthday. I dreaded it so much! I hate all those people around. But you just kept right on arranging things. And it turned out to be the most beautiful party I've ever had. Everyone so warm. And friendly. And happy!

Barbara's Happy Moments Together

1. Oh, our wedding day in 1979 at the Tucson house—though we had already lived together there for two years—when everyone was so totally surprised (especially Bill and sharp Judy, who thought she was loaning silver dishes for an important publisher's visit) and we all had so much fun, and champagne with corks popping everywhere; and John Gilchriese drank his first drink in twenty-five years in our honor.

2. Feeling like Mona Lisa the day Mr. Van Driest painted my portrait in 1970 because I thought of you all the while and of coming over to eat white grapes in your bed that night.

3. Watching the Santo Domingo Dance from an adobe rooftop with your brown deer eyes full of my blue eyes and blue-flowered squaw dress.

4. Making love among yellow sunflowers and purple asters beside the overgrown lumber road near Pot Creek.

5. When you finally drove up to our newly purchased little house in Tucson—having never seen it, realized it wasn't a "tin-roofed shack" as expected, and loved it immediately. You thought as we sat later in the junglish backyard that we had lived together in just such a setting in another lifetime, probably in Mexico.

6. Waking you up with my unexpected arrivals and peppy ways late at night the winters of 1974 and 1975 in Sedona.

7. The mockingbird that sang all night outside your apartment window that first winter of 1976 here in Tucson.

8. The perfume you have discovered for me—heavenly Charles of the Ritz.

9. Roasting green chiles with and for you, after Mrs. Quintana taught me how in 1978.

10. Rubbing sexy-smelling good-luck sage on our faces, forever renewing US.

11. That Christmas Eve on the plaza in Veracruz in 1974 when we drove out of the dismal dark into the dazzling white

plaza erupting with silver and red rockets and Christmas-tree lights!

12. Driving together to and from Guatemala in 1979 and shar-ing our *bolillos,* avocados, and papaya from the market with passing natives, plus smelling copal in Chichicastenango!

Frank's voice cracked frequently as he dictated. His voice hardly ever did that, never when he spoke before crowds, only when he felt deep emotion.

I kissed him when his list was finished and said, "See how ther-apeutic this is?"

Miracle of miracles, Dr. No did not say, "No." He grinned and didn't argue at all.

In the mid-'60s Frank's sister, Naomi, and Carl bought land on the west side of Sedona, Arizona, where they built a fine home with lots of glass picture windows and a surrounding sun deck. They lived in it only three years before Naomi died of cancer in 1969; Carl died two years later. Frank lived there part time in the winter of 1974 and all the winter of 1975. I spent my weekends and days off from teaching with him. We had a great time. We would ex-plore ruins, eat at the Owl Restaurant, and glow like Naomi's red enamel woodstove—Frank's "favorite Indian color"—while sipping Amaretto liqueur before bed. Ever after, Frank would raise his eye-brows and grin mischievously whenever we encountered that liqueur again, or mention was made of it.

At Christmas in 1975, I automatically decorated the Sedona house and put up a Christmas tree with lights. To my surprise, Frank grew very emotional over this. It turned out he hadn't had his own tree for many years, possibly since childhood. He couldn't remember the last one he'd had as an adult. I would sit out on the deck sunning and addressing Christmas cards or writing in my journal while he wrote parts of *Mountain Dialogues.* Years later, to my astonishment, he said this view of me on the sun deck had left an indelible picture in his mind. This Christmas I am not yet up to taking the route to California that goes through Sedona.

The fifth item on Frank's list was another surprise. That Easter incident occurred in 1971 when I came up from Tucson with a carload of teachers who wanted to ski. We had left school at 3:30 P.M. and driven straight through, arriving in Taos about 2:30 A.M. To keep our driver awake on the way, I told the story of Rudolfo Anaya's *Bless Me, Última.* Just at the climax, where Última turns into an owl, a gigantic owl hit our right front headlight. It hovered a moment, then flapped against our windshield, and rose into the dark night above us. My friend Susan screamed, and we each felt charged with a thrill of fright or delight. I marvel at the synchronicity, for Rudy, an admirer of Frank's work, was to become a good friend both to us and to our Foundation. He was one of the few men who got as close to Frank as he allowed and yet remained always his own man.

When we arrived at last, I had to wake a night watchman at La Fonda Hotel, where I was staying alone, and have a glass of Greek wine with the hotel owner, Saki Karavas, who had the habit of reading newspapers and magazines until nearly dawn. Frank said Saki was the last true character of Taos, once rife with unique characters. Saki saw himself as the last of the Great Lovers. Hearing about his latest escapades, or fancied escapades, or anticipated escapades, was more entertaining than most movies. In his office Saki displayed D. H. Lawrence's paintings, once considered risqué, as well as photographs of internationally known friends and acquaintances, and gleaming rows of fine shoes shined to perfection. Saki was always too full of hot air to suit me, and I must have seemed too schoolteacherish to him; I was able to get a good night's sleep before heading out to see Frank around 4:00 P.M. I was tired, too, from having to turn in grades before our departure from Tucson.

Frank had a cozy fire going in the corner living-room fireplace, with two old rocking chairs drawn up before it. The house looked rather bare and sad back then in wintertime. Indian rugs were scattered around the floor without any carpeting, and it was drafty. Much of the sparse furniture had seen better days, especially the "talking" couch. I learned later that except for the good pieces from

Mabel Luhan, these were castoffs from Naomi and her daughter, Susie.

"What would you like to do?" Frank asked as I collapsed into a rocker with a broken spoke. "It's so good to have company on a dark day like this!"

"All I want to do for days is sit here in front of this fire and rock!" I said, never dreaming that these would remain memorable words to him. At the time I felt embarrassed about being so tired.

We should have a saying to cover occurrences opposite "The best laid schemes o' mice an' men gang aft a'gley." Perhaps "The unlaid schemes o' mice an' women gang aft aright" would do.

Meeting Frank through Anne Nagle was happenstance. I didn't plan to appeal to Frank by addressing ordinary Christmas cards and rocking in a rickety chair, which incidentally remains the same to this day. Tucson writer Laverne Clark used to say, "We're going to have to think up a plan of action to catch that man for you." But we never did. There was simply my unswerving conviction that he and I would spend the rest of our lives together. And fortuitous happenstances continued.

Once I was hoeing in my garden on July 4 when Frank passed by on his way to a picnic without me. He liked that hoeing bit too. I was not overjoyed myself.

I often wondered why Frank finally decided to take the Big Fourth Step with me. He had his astrologer friend Giovanna Klopp read my horoscope. She preferred one of his other girlfriends. Rather ungraciously she said shortly, "Barbara would be of help to you if you ever got sick." As Frank was never known to be ill at this time, none of us were at all impressed with this little gem. I was decidedly displeased, as a matter of fact. It still rankles. For starters, any rank amateur could see that his sun sign and my rising sign were conjunct to the exact degree, meaning our basic drives were in synch; and any joint project such as the Foundation would succeed because our Mars energy was also in productive correspondence. Yet how accurate Giovanna's curt prediction did turn out to be.

Frank was in seventh heaven when Craig Vincent made it possible for him to visit China for a month in the fall of 1976. Frank always said he had been a mandarin there in another lifetime. In his *Mountain Dialogues* chapter about this visit he wrote, "China gave me a conscious feeling of familiarity, admiration, and an enlarged perspective that greatly enriched my life."

He felt that China's collectivism had crowded out his own individualism, however, and for a time after his return suffered great physiological and psychological distress, the latter manifesting in nightmares. "My bed was so full of people I couldn't turn over. This distressing dream-state showed me how powerfully the psychic influence of a new continent, with its own spirit-of-place, can affect one," he wrote.

To make matters worse, Susie had for some unknown reason rented the Sedona house to others for the winter without consulting Frank. I did not know her yet. For ten years after that he refused to speak to her. She finally sent a tentative card as olive branch in 1986, and I put a stop to his nonsense by inviting her to lunch at my sister's home in California while we were visiting there.

Frank telephoned me from Taos in November of 1976 after he'd recuperated from his China trip. Nonchalantly he said, "I need a nice, roomy, inexpensive apartment in Tucson for the winter."

Now, decent apartments in Tucson were extremely hard to find during the winter at that time. Inexpensive apartments were, and still are, practically nonexistent during this so-called snowbird season. Again, an unplanned event cemented our relationship, for I did miraculously find an apartment that he liked very much, a "roomy, inexpensive apartment" that came complete with a fabulous mockingbird that serenaded us all night long from a mesquite tree near his bedroom window. Rather than annoying Frank, it reminded him of his mandarin days, when he felt that surely a mockingbird had sung in a flowering plum tree outside his palace window. Leos in this lifetime never see themselves as coolies in former lifetimes, you will find.

For the rest of his life we would slow down in passing to see how this small, privately owned apartment complex a block west of 6th and Country Club was carrying its years. Oddly enough, just one mile east on the same road, which changes its name to 5th Street, Janey and he had stayed twenty-five years earlier with her mother in an impressive house still standing. This is another reason I sensed Janey's blessings were with us from the start, though she had been dead for ten years when Frank and I first met. Frank had the lower west apartment in the center of three buildings forming a U shape. It impressed me that he wrote each morning at a long table facing the blank west wall with no windows or view. Light came in over his left shoulder from a picture window facing south.

I wonder if Janey's energy sent me over there with a valentine one evening on my way out of town with some students participating next day in a tennis tournament. As I lightheartedly placed my surprise valentine in his mailbox, who should come running across the yard hand in hand but a strange woman and Frank. At the time this man was seventy-three years old! Age had not withered him at *all*. They'd met at a metaphysical conference in Phoenix where Frank had spoken the previous weekend. Her name was Fischer, she said, and she was living on the Hopi reservation with one of the Sekaquaptewa brothers. Frank was "safe" with her. They "just had a lot in common, metaphysics and Hopiland and all that, you know." My parting with Frank the night before had been such sweet sorrow. Upon my return, his sorrow was considerably less sweet.

I had already learned the crucial lesson that women of all ages throw themselves at well-known men, who respond at all ages. I called these women lion huntresses. One even had the last name of Huntress. Today she is a friend, and I am fond of her poetry. Not so pleasing was the French huntress with hairy armpits who arrived in Taos during the summer of 1974. Her daughter, a circus bareback rider improbably named Nanook, had written to France that Frank would make a perfect husband for her mother. He reserved a room for her at Saki's La Fonda Hotel. One day later she ran out of money, she said. She would have to move in with Frank for two weeks, which she proceeded to do. "What can I do?" he said with his most put-upon, guileless look. She developed the novel habit of walking naked through the pastures and woods to El Salto Waterfall and back. This one was a formidable challenge. But she went her way at last, laden with expensive purchases and leaving behind a memorable Normandy peasant recipe for chicken marengo, "Napoleon's favorite dish."

Twenty-two years later, after I have written these words, Charles Hathaway sends me a copy of Frank's letter of September 3, 1974. In it he refers to she-of-the-hairy-armpits as "a charming middle-aged woman who was an excellent cook" and stayed with him for two weeks. Of more interest to posterity is his news, "My *Mexico Mystique* is at the printers, with galleys due soon. We are all hoping that the book can be released in time to pick up some Christmas sales." Frank also mentions a week-long visit from Susie and returning with her to Sedona for a short visit, then stopping overnight at the Grand Canyon on his return trip to Taos. He does not mention that he would be spending much of the winter with an Amaretto-sipping schoolteacher without hairy armpits. As I've said, one always wonders what tipped the scales.

Our trip to Veracruz on Mexico's east coast over Christmas of 1974 had been another big step forward in our relationship. Betty Burkhalter thought up this inspired idea. I had lived in her parents' Rinconada cottage south of here for two summers, with Frank visiting me frequently. She and I were of an age, with similar interests. I kept extensive, effusive records of these summer joys and pursuits that are best left buried in dusty boxes festooned with rat droppings. Suffice it to say here that we met Betty and her lawyer friend Don on Christmas Eve in Veracruz after a dismal drive through a dark barrio district as our bus dropped off other passengers who had come in on the same plane with us.

Suddenly Frank and I burst upon the main plaza; red-and-white lights and white buildings dazzled our eyes. A glowing

Christmas tree sparkled two stories high. Silver and red rockets exploded with joy. Strangers laughed and hugged. Marimba music sparked dancing and singing. At midnight we drank tequila with salt and slices of lime and ate heaps of pink shrimp and *huachinango Veracruzaño*—red snapper smothered in chile sauce. Much later we hugged Betty and Don, kissed newfound *compadres*, and floated off to bed on Cloud *Nueve*.

Next day Frank lost his wallet at the beach. Otherwise, unceasing marimba music and love of Mexico kept us in right rhythm. We rented a car and drove up past coffee *fincas* and women washing laundry in streams, through a fragrant flower world to Emperor Maximilian's favorite towns of Fortín de las Flores and Orizaba. With sad "La Paloma" echoing in our ears, our eyes feasted upon tiled roofs sheltering roses, hot-pink azaleas, orchids, gardenias, red marigolds, and a riot of tropical flowers unfamiliar to us gringos. Glistening with its eternal flame of snow, Orizaba Peak reminded us that the body of legendary Quetzalcoatl is said to have been consumed by divine fire upon this sacred spot, his spirit mounting through the universe as a peacock. Xochipilli, Aztec flower god, and his mate, Flowered Quetzal Feather, danced with us as Betty and I flung exuberant flowers to the heavens.

Four years earlier Frank had set out alone, shortly after we had established a mutual commitment, to spend six months in Mexico researching *Mexico Mystique* on a Rockefeller Grant that had been unexpectedly offered him. Much of the time he spent in Mexico City, particularly at the magnificent National Museum of Anthropology and Archaeology in Chapultepec Park. At Christmas-time he met Ann Merrill in Oaxaca and Lesley Brown in Mitla, as arranged before our affair began. I imagined him consistently in surroundings with a more scholarly bent, but have always believed "what you don't know won't hurt you." His letters sounded devoted. And patience has its rewards. (It took considerable patience with this man.) Together, nine years later we were to cover this same ground, and much more.

Prior to our month-long drive to Guatemala and back in 1979, we had spent Christmas of 1976 and part of January in Alamos near Mexico's west coast. My sadness on Valentine's Day of 1996 was due partly to the awareness that our friends Art and Susan Bachrach were leaving that day for a visit to Alamos and La Aduana. It brought back vivid memories of another in our series of unforgettable "honeymoons." I do not want to return just now, yet "I am a part of all that I have met," as Tennyson put it. And "all that I have met" does help to strengthen me at this time of testing, more than it saddens.

Mario and Isabelle Larrinaga owned and had designed the lovely Alamos house, garden, and guesthouse where we stayed. They offered to sell the entire place to us for $45,000, furnished, the same price we soon were to pay for our unfurnished Tucson home, which had none of its elegance. Strangely enough, though a beautiful colonial town to visit, Alamos has no vibrancy or sense of creativity crackling in the air. With regret, we turned down their offer for this reason.

At the end of the eighteenth century, Alamos was a silver capital of the world with a population of thirty thousand persons. Rich deposits of gold and silver were developed, and magnificent homes sprang up along streets shaded with graceful cottonwoods. The city declined when silver prices dropped, but it is now a national colonial monument and has been restored by wealthy persons whose main occupation when we were there was partying. For years afterward Frank was embarrassed that we'd taken a large bottle of kahlua to a New Year's Eve party at a vast hacienda with five stocked bars, a dozen strolling waiters, and half a dozen musicians circulating through a seemingly endless array of rooms. His impoverished background sometimes brought him up short in surprising ways, including being impressed for a time with some wealthy person, such as Mabel Luhan. Then he would regain his bearings and proceed along an independent path free of that materialistic influence.

The Larrinagas' guesthouse was impressive enough for us. We could have made do with this beauty of a building if we hadn't had the whole place to ourselves, including awesome grounds and gardens with five colors of bougainvillea massed among the usual plethora of exotic blooms. And a gardener named Plutarco to care for them. Plutarco had a thing about tall, blonde, blue-eyed gringas and wanted to make beautiful music in the guesthouse while Frank was writing in the main house. Plutarco brought his own favorite music and planned to teach me all the local dances, and perhaps more. I forestalled his intentions by taking clothing to his children and meeting his wife. Plutarco's favorite saying was, *"No es problema."* He soon realized this gringa was a *problema* and settled back down to his gardening while glancing at me reproachfully with smoldering dark eyes.

For Christmas Frank surprised me with a cut-glass crystal decanter that he'd brought all the way from Tucson without my knowledge. This pleased him inordinately. And I treasured his decanter just as much until Ann Merrill, of all people, broke it some years later. I've always thought it was an unconscious purging of some of the understandable feelings she had kept buried. I still have its crystal stopper.

La Aduana, a nearby ghost town, deeply moved Frank, for he had stayed there in the '30s when traveling through Sierra Madre country on muleback and had never expected to see it again. At La Aduana in another century had risen and fallen the great smelters where silver ingots were cast. Time has stood still here. Pigs still root along dusty streets. A cactus grows out of one ruined wall of the old church where a vision of the Virgin Mary is said to have pointed out a rich lode of silver. A few years after our visit, Frank had his first hip replacement, necessitated by the klutzy mule that had fallen with him underneath it on his original trip through these parts. A native woman had submerged Frank's hip in mud until he felt able to go on—for another half century.

After our visit to Alamos, the catchphrase that always brought smiles to our lips was Plutarco's *"No es problema."* It has the same effect on me today. And it was the perfect slogan for our relationship with all Mexico. People would say, "Aren't you afraid of the soldiers lurking along roadsides there?" No. We went our way and they went their lurking ways. Betty Burkhalter would say, "Aren't you afraid of the fish here? Maybe it's not fresh. Maybe we'll get sick." We ate the same fish. She got sick. We did not get sick. We didn't expect to get sick. Customs officers neglected to check our car and trunk. We often said we could have smuggled dead bodies in and out or become king and queen of drug-smuggling had we been of that persuasion. We tried to speak the language and won friends happy to correct our laughable mistakes. We shared our food along the way and ate in unfashionable places at unfashionably early hours. Traveling in Mexico just never was a *problema*. We were home again.

At home, in Tucson or Taos, like most couples we had our disagreements. When traveling, in spirit we were kids on a lark. We refused to travel in groups, generally planned our own itinerary as we went along, moved at our own leisurely pace, and thus were free from stress. Frank's one eccentricity was his lack of interest in ruins, the very ruins about which he had written so well. This I had not expected. A powerful ruin rekindles my energy with every visit; identification grows ever deeper. Once Frank had visited and written about a ruin, he usually refused to return. He sat in a waiting taxi, for instance, during my first visit to the pyramids of Teotihuacán in 1979. It was a long wait. Visiting ruins by myself was sometimes lonely, yet such experiences were probably all the more powerful for the solitude.

We shunned tourist traps such as Mazatlán. What a shock that was to us both during our 1979 trip! Teachers and students alike had made it sound like the garden spot of Mexico, a regular Eden, a "must" I had to see. Frank had last been there in the '30s, when *one* hotel existed on its great horseshoe-shaped bay. Now it was packed wall to wall with hotels, body to body with suntanning tourists.

We fled south from the state of Sinaloa into tropical Nayarit past stately palms, through emerald canyons of ebony and brooding mangrove swamps crusted white with oysters to the ghosts of

San Blas, to peace and quiet and the tantalizing aroma of *bolillos* in a tiny, fragrant bakery near the sea. What of those pesky no-see-um gnats and mosquitoes, scourge of the Spaniards who had built the ancient fort on the hill above us and died of malaria? *No es problema.* It was February, of course, when such pests were not in residence. Worn reds, greens, blues, and yellows of small fishing boats soothed our eyes as silken sand and a symphony of waves lulled us to sleep. Mazatlán had lost the most fundamental part of old Mexico, its siesta time. San Blas had not yet awakened from siesta. But the clock was ticking.

Frank believed it was good luck and good common sense to travel in Mexico without a gun or camera. I took along a camera but used it discreetly, except in Chichicastenango, Guatemala, where the explosion of color has inured natives to photography. Saki Karavas repeatedly quoted and misquoted Frank's own favorite story from his earliest trip to Sierra Madre country. The wisdom of his simple traveling habits was illustrated best to him when a bandit chieftain and his men surrounded Frank's campfire one night. Frank stirred up his fire and offered coffee and a cigarette to the *jefe.*

Explaining his presence in Mexico after his visitor had so requested, Frank said, "I like your country. I want to see it."

The bandit kicked a canvas bag full of Mexican silver pesos. "What's this?"

"This is the money I need to travel in Mexico," Frank said.

Then, Frank recalls in *Mountain Dialogues,* "The *Jefe* stood up, the firelight reflecting a sheen from the silver mountings on the gear of his black stallion. '*Pase.* As long as you're in my territory, I'll see you're not molested.'"

With ghosts of the past riding on winds of change, we turned inland, skirting smoggy Guadalajara but stumbling upon its ugly extension Tlaquepaque, a picturesque country town when Frank had originally visited it on the Day of the Dead. One writer calls it now "the chamber-of-ceramic-horrors of Mexico." Lake Chapala was a happy change, and historically important to me because of my interest in Frieda Lawrence, who spent some time here with her husband. Moreover, at Lake Chapala nearly half a century before our current trip, Frank had met by chance poet Witter Bynner and his lover Bob Hunt. Hunt had snapped Frank's photo as he looked pensively out their hotel window toward the lake. Over sixty years later this photograph hung above Frank's head at his death, the youth and the elder come full circle in a fulfilled life.

Bynner's remembrances of the Lawrences were valuable to me in my research on women married to successful men. Much of the time Bynner was sympathetic toward Frieda and all the guff she endured from her husband. For instance, at Lake Chapala, as she nodded over a book, Bynner asked, "Is Frieda reading or asleep?"

D. H. Lawrence replied, "With Frieda, it's the same thing."

Another time he stamped on one of her paintings because the "perspective was wrong." Frieda broke a plate over Lawrence's head after he said women had no souls and couldn't love. On occasion I myself have felt the urge to take a page out of her book and toss a plate or two at Frank. Exasperated with Mabel Luhan, a persistent lion huntress, Frieda once told her, "Try it then yourself, living with a genius, see what it is like and how easy it is." In certain ways Frieda served as both a positive and a negative role model for me. We were part of the same sisterhood. I felt happy to visit Lake Chapala, where she had been mostly happy, sometimes mad and sad. When her husband insisted that they leave, Frieda sobbed, "I like Chapala! I *like* Chapala!"

The names of our stopping places were pure music and magic: cobblestoned Ajijic; Tzintzuntzan, the Tarascan place of hummingbirds and ancient olive trees; Pátzcuaro, the "place of delights" and long most Indian of modern Mexico.

To me, Pátzcuaro was still old and quaint with sixteenth-century church bells tolling across the street from our room and butterfly nets skimming the lake below town. It saddened me for his sake that Frank could no longer climb the bell tower, as he had in 1940 beside Mabel Luhan when they attended the First Inter-American Conference on Indian Life here with her husband, Tony. Frank saw change even then; crowds and politics also jarred his view, along with the town's inevitable growth. But much of what we saw in 1979 mirrored Frank's description in *Masked Gods* of his first visit to Pátzcuaro in 1930, with the exceptions of blue aprons and remoteness: "There it was. Blue pine mountains surrounding a blue lake. Tiny white villages with red-brown roofs. Tarascan Indians swarming the great ancient plazas, the men in brown *serapes* bordered with red, the women in full, pleated, red skirts, and blue aprons. All set in red Indian earth under a turquoise sky, with white clouds unraveling overhead. As beautiful and poignant as any remote spot on earth."

Some fiesta or celebration was constantly igniting color in this innately rainbowed land, a contrast to more somber Peru.

On we sped toward the beckoning heights of Sleeping Woman and Smoking Mirror—Izta and Popo—into the City of Insane Drivers, Mexico City itself, where the Géneve Hotel in the Zona Rosa was booked solid. We stayed instead at Victor White's favorite María Cristina and imagined him writing his novels in its intimate courtyard, pressing rose petals to accompany his trademark blue gentians in letters to friends and fancied loves. So much to see, so much to return to. A year here would not be enough in which to absorb everything. Even to an inveterate museumgoer, the National Anthropology Museum was exceptional. It alone made the smog and traffic worthwhile, to say nothing of Teotihuacán.

We moved to the Majestic Hotel facing the Zócolo in order to consume addictive *mole de guajalote*—turkey in chocolate chile sauce—at their rooftop restaurant, where we ran into Rosa and Bob Ellis from Taos. Expatriates are never far.

Across the Zócolo, we visited the powerful Diego Rivera murals. Frank had begun *The Yogi of Cockroach Court* with Rivera's tribute to Mexico's peons; it was signed with the famed artist's obscure pseudonym "Hexotziquense."

Frank writes in *Masked Gods* of visiting one night long ago "a drab and murky *cantina* just off the Zócolo." Later he and his friends "pushed back our benches and staggered out of the smoke-filled *cantina* to yell a little drunkenly, '*Toston!*'—('Taxi!')—under

clear stars sparkling in the midnight black." It is good to see this serious young man kicking up his heels, to catch revealing glimpses
of his carefully guarded "private history." It is good, too, to have
been part of his odyssey.

On to Cuernavaca, aglow with pastel houses umbrellaed by
trees and tropical blossoms. Here Frank had twice accompanied
Mabel and Tony, hit the bars regularly with his imposing Indian
friend wearing a red chief's blanket, and accidentally humiliated
Tony by laughing when his chair collapsed, sending him sprawling
on the floor.

It came to me that a girlfriend in my fifth grade class came from
a family with two Mexican-style mansions, one in Oswego, Illinois,
the other in Cuernavaca. Her parents took me once to an ice-
skating show in Chicago, forty miles from home. Miss Campbell,
our fifth grade teacher, had us decorate our classroom in the style
and vivid hues of Mexico, where she vacationed annually. We filled
tires with dirt and plants and painted their outer rims with zigzags
of wild reds and oranges, purples and greens. And we hung posters
of Mexico on our classroom walls, just as Frank did on his walls.
Cuernavaca was a favorite of Miss Campbell's too. When she came
to dinner at our house, she smoked cigarettes with my mother in
our bathroom. She was the most avant-garde teacher our farming
community had ever seen. It was said by older people that
Montezuma's Revenge would surely strike her dead in heathenish
Mexico one summer. Layered memories, early influences, and perhaps influences from another lifetime continued to surface during
this long trip with Frank. I wondered if Miss Campbell had become
a bag lady in Cuernavaca, or joined the nunnery at Tzintzuntzan.

16
Soledad at the Wheel

Ralph Meyers, Frank's Taos trader friend, long ago wrote to Frank, "Everything is OK here, but the March doldrums are on us again. The dirty old town is swamped in mud and bad tempers." Taos is that way still in March, especially if one is trying to mush one's way through the grief process, like a sled-dog husky mired in deep snow—or a morass of mud.

This morning little Carmen, who cleans for me, cannot reach the top of our tall handmade chest of drawers. Wearing reading glasses, I interrupt my typing to dust it for her. At the same time I dust a small dark wooden statue sitting on top that was Marcia Gaiter's pride and joy before her death. My glasses magnify a name printed in tiny letters at its base: "*Soledad de Oaxaca.*" I am catapulted instantly out of my Taos doldrums and transported on the magic carpet of the mind to Oaxaca, *the* most favorite of all our favorite places in Mexico. With Guatemala and Peru, Oaxaca occupied the warmest spot in our hearts.

Surely the Virgin of Solitude was with us as I drove toward Oaxaca from the north over the Sierra Madre. In congested or strange places Frank left the driving to me, or we would have needed *all* the Troops. He was a tense driver and preferred sightseeing as a passenger during most of this long journey. Before our trip Chicagoan Father Peter Powell, an expert on Cheyenne Indians, had exclaimed with approval, "Barbara's a Chicago driver! A driver with the highest skills, yet always at ease behind the wheel." Coming from a man whom he admired, Frank treasured this compliment as much as I did and relied upon Father Powell's judgment.

Then, unexpectedly, the unfamiliar mountain road before us curved into a tight hairpin turn to the left after a straightaway stretch had lulled me into increasing our speed. I suddenly found myself inside the car as my usual smaller being. Simultaneously, I hovered outside the car as my greater self. I could see—can still see—the right rear wheel lift into empty space off the edge of the road. As I stepped hard on the gas and yanked the steering wheel left, seemingly with direction, my larger self outside saw the entire rear end flipping across empty space with only a sheer drop below. The accelerated forward momentum and the firm hold of our front tires on the highway carried us just far enough for the back tires to hit the edge of the road with a wrenching thud and continue forward, firmly gripping cement. Afterward, my smaller being began shaking, not from fear of the close call to myself, but from fear of Frank's demise and the effect his loss would have had on a following anxious for his words urging us toward a permanent state of higher consciousness. This feeling of a need to protect him for the world often bore down heavily upon me.

Thanks to my higher self and Soledad, we were given another sixteen years of his wisdom. One might wonder if similar powers protected my friend Linda Ann and me two weeks ago as she panicked at sight of an approaching school bus while driving to town down narrow, icy El Salto Road. Jamming on her brakes, she fishtailed the car's back end into the bus, leaving our front end perched at the edge of a steep arroyo. We walked away unscathed from her badly damaged car. "In my opinion," Linda Ann said, "Frank was with us." Of course. He now is one with Soledad and the rest of the Troops. The more we acknowledge these energies, the more strongly they vibrate.

Marcia's small *Soledad de Oaxaca* statue wears a black cloak patterned with gold flowers, leaves, and crosses. A Byzantine gold crown topped with a cross sits on her head, backed by a halo of the same style. A gold ruff with dangling tassel frames her face. The patron saint of Oaxaca city and state, her celebrated counterpart is locked in a glass-and-gold enclosure at the *Sanctuario de la Soledad* in Oaxaca. Robed in black velvet, the larger version is a jeweled queen with an outsize pearl planted in the center of her forehead like a third eye. According to legend, this statue of Soledad arrived in a box on the back of a mysterious thirteenth mule that had somehow mixed in with a muleteer's string of twelve pack animals. On the spot of the present sanctuary, the intruder dropped dead. A note indicated that the statue on its back was "Our Lady of Solitude at the Foot of the Cross." In Mexico she is said to possess miraculous powers of healing.

Referring to the golden age of the seventeenth century, Wilder and Breitenback state in *Santos: The Religious Folk Art of New Mexico*, "Our Lady of Solitude is one of the profoundest manifestations of Spanish mysticism during the Golden Age. However, the spirit of loneliness is not confined to this subject alone, but is rather the expression of a mental attitude which pervaded the whole age, and which has left its imprint on Spanish religious art and poetry alike."

As is so often true with local *santo* art, New Mexico has a slightly different view of Soledad. It explains why she has spoken to me today. Here she usually wears a plain black robe and represents the Virgin as archetypal crone mourning for her husband and son. Widowed and childless, she is the patron saint of women living alone. Soledad's black cloak seems to isolate her in loneliness and sorrow. It represents the nun-like garment said to have been worn by Mary after the deaths of Joseph and Jesus. She broods over her loss, yet her pyramid-shaped cloak emphasizes that her spirit soars ever upward. She looks calm, accepting, uplifted. Locally, she was an important part of Penitente ritual emphasizing crucifixion, death, and mourning. We should have used their appeal to help

Maria of the Snows out of purgatory, for Penitentes prayed to Our Lady of Solitude,

> Your power is so great
> Against the wicked Satan
> That you save the souls
> From eternal fire. . . .

> If to Purgatory our colleagues go,
> We pray you, Oh Mary,
> That you immediately save them.

It's the tiny daily miracles we tend to overlook that delight me. Who needs "Joseph" or "Michael" channeling through one in an unconscious hypnotic state when ordinary dusting or a visiting dog bring to light the knowledge one seeks? I'm slumped despondently in the guest room on a twin bed with a visiting cockapoo named Brindle after ransacking our bookshelves and unpacked boxes in vain for my copy of William Anderson's book *Green Man*.

"Can't you help me find *Green Man?*" I ask the cockapoo. "I'm worn out from looking."

Brindle yawns and stretches her head up against the headboard bookshelves with her right ear flicking spasmodically against *Green Man*.

I am looking for tree information. Between my hands the book pops open instead to a photograph of a Black Virgin wearing a pyramid-shaped cloak and a cross-tipped crown exactly like Soledad's. She is the Black Virgin of Notre-Dame d'Espoir in Dijon, France. She and the other Black Virgins must be another manifestation of Soledad. Anderson writes of the Black Virgin's numinous calm and independence, "She is the manifestation of a level of being and experience infinitely beyond human failings and sufferings and it is, perhaps, precisely because she possesses this freedom from misery that she is able to comfort and to bless through her presence. The atmosphere she generates is the evidence that there is, in truth, a level of peace that is attainable and is full of suc-cour for human griefs and hope."

Marcia Gaiter kept her Soledad statue on a fireplace mantel below a gilt portrait of a Hungarian Black Virgin, perhaps not by chance. Anderson traces the Black Virgin back to Egyptian Isis mourning her dead lover Osiris; several churches where Black Virgins have been venerated were built on sites sacred to Isis. Black Virgins were connected with miracles. Many times, Anderson states, they "first revealed themselves in trees as though, in another form of transference from an older religion to a new faith, she is-sued from the tree cults of the past."

Marcia painted for Frank and me a sparkling variation of *Nuestra Señora de la Soledad*. She wears the typical Byzantine crown and cross livened with soft yellow, blue, green, and a few dots of bright red. Her face is framed in a light yellow ruff with matching tassel. Her pyramid-shaped cloak is tinted warm shades of turquoise, pale blue, and pink and worn over a white lace robe. A quirk of a smile lingers about her lips. The cerise of her features matches the background color of this unusual *santo*. Our cerise-and-turquoise Soledad reminds me much more fervently than tra-ditional renditions that mourning need not be all darkness and gloom and negativity.

Yet my other vivid memory of that wicked mountain route above Oaxaca is of a burro with tears dripping down its cheeks as it stood close to a burro companion lying dead in the road.

The blue of Marcia's Soledad cloak is the blue of Oaxaca, the trumpeted light blue of jacaranda blossoms carpeting Alameda León, our own private plaza outside the immensely tall windows and French doors of Monte Albán, the old bishop's palace, where we stayed on the second floor. Its history appealed to the regal and ascetic sides of Frank's nature. And I could even imagine myself be-stowing papal blessings upon crowds massed beneath our ancient stone balcony.

The first thing Frank did when we arrived at a new room was lay out his comb, brush, shaver, pajamas, and slippers. The first thing I did was make our room homey with fresh flowers and fruit, a *serape* flung over a chair for color, a bright scarf over another, perhaps on the dresser a carving or a piece of pottery purchased along the way. Some years after I had been doing this without a thought, Frank said, "I like it that you always brighten up a place right away and make it cozy. Mabel Luhan had the same knack of putting her stamp on a place wherever she went."

It's a good thing I didn't mind living with ghosts. They were always there to haunt me. In fact, I sought them out by checking out the old Hotel Francia a few doors down from us, where D. H. Lawrence, Frieda, and our friend Dorothy Brett had stayed. Brett described their huge, bare, cool rooms here in *Lawrence and Brett: A Friendship.* Our room at the Monte Albán was huge and cool but comfortably furnished with massive beds, dressers, and a Spanish colonial armoire, my favorite piece of furniture. More interesting ghosts hung around our place too, what with the bishop and all. I would not have cared to have the spirit of that devil Lawrence hanging out in our room or on our balcony. As Bynner said, the man reminded him of "a bad baby masquerading as a good Mephistopheles." The Francia had seen better days by the time we got there. A photo in Brett's book gives the feeling of how it once was. Frieda and her husband are sitting on the *portal* in fancy rocking chairs looking right at home. The caption refers only to "Lawrence" sitting there. At times Frieda was a ghost in her own lifetime.

Thoughts of her came to me after visiting the nearby ruins of Monte Albán, some dating back to the fifth century B.C. I felt powerfully attuned to this site, particularly the observatory, ballcourt, and famous Tomb Seven, which I accidentally stumbled upon. The remarkable treasure of gold jewelry, turquoise, jade, crystal, pearls, and alabaster originally found here is on display in the Oaxaca City museum. Some pieces I had already seen at Mexico City's National Museum. I came back to our room from these ruins trailing centuries of energy and beauty about me. Frank was not pleased with the transformation. He had written that the Monte Albán ruins weren't all that impressive, and he would have liked that judgment to be definitive for me too. When it didn't work this way, he would fall silent, take up his reading, and refuse to listen to my impressions or to speak at all.

This was a new spin on Frieda's experiences with her husband. When she said Shelley's "Ode to a Skylark" struck her as "false," Lawrence interrupted, "You are showing off; you don't know anything about it."

In her book, Brett tells of the three of them cantering together near Taos. Frieda exclaimed, "Oh, it's wonderful; wonderful to feel [my horse's] great thighs moving, to feel his powerful legs!"

Lawrence called back from his horse, "Rubbish, Frieda! Don't talk like that. You have been reading my books: you don't feel anything of the sort!"

"Yes, I do," Frieda tried to argue, but Lawrence had galloped off and couldn't hear her.

These charismatic men have a lethal way of chopping people down. Their negative remarks are twice as cutting because one expects bigger things of them. When Lawrence could not make a success of a tryst in bed with Brett, for example, he dismissed her with the succinct words, "Your boobs are all wrong." Two years older than he, Brett was very deaf and at that time possessed something of an inferiority complex connected with her deafness on top of what she perceived as her homeliness—to say nothing of her breasts.

Frank was a saint compared to ill-tempered Lawrence, but his negative words could carry the same sting. This point comes out in Charles Hathaway's memories of Frank, written when Charles was ninety-three. He still remembered one of the most hurtful. "I had worked many times to make a pancake batter stand up real thick and puffy," Charles recalls. "Frank said, 'I do not want to ever have to eat any more of your fat pancakes!'" This on top of telling Charles's brilliant wife that she'd "always be a scrubwoman"! Charles writes, "While in Frank's later years he radiated a very gentle nature, earlier he could be caustic and critical. . . . Even though in one of Frank's books he depicts me as a boy who went to prison and in another book describes my mother in very unglowing terms, we always forgave old lovable Frank."

Poor Charles. I've got news for you, dear man: to his dying day Frank could be caustic and critical. But then, all firstborns who assume their legitimate role are inclined to be caustic and critical. Being a firstborn myself, I know. At least Charles was spared the silent treatment.

Frank did indeed hate "fat pancakes." At home he labored to make exquisitely thin, dollar-sized pancakes. They were too labor intensive for most restaurants to serve. He was therefore perpetually frustrated in his odyssey to find perfect pancakes while we were on the road. During this visit we ate breakfast each morning in the bishop's dining room. Throughout our years together, breakfast remained the most important meal of our day; it was the one meal Frank never tired of cooking. Breakfast sent our spirits soaring and our energy percolating, and we never had to worry about high cholesterol, for ours was low. This was fortunate since we ate *huevos rancheros* about four mornings a week when traveling south of the border. At home five mornings of the week we ate chunky oatmeal made of steel-cut oats.

Papaya with lime juice was a must as many times a day as we could get it in Mexico. Here it was the size of a small watermelon and orange or pink-orange in color. The pepcid in this sweet fruit of the gods was an added bonus in keeping our stomachs settled. More often than not, therefore, our Mexican breakfasts consisted of egg concoctions, papayas with slices of lime, *bolillos* or *pan dulces*, and hot milk in coffee strong enough to make our hair stand on end. The hot cereal *quinoa* was a welcome change when available, or *atole* in places that made it the consistency of cornmeal mush instead of thin enough to drink. Pancakes we kept trying, fully expecting them to be as terrible as they usually were. Hope springs eternal.

Like most tourists we were careful to drink only bottled water. In the evenings before dinner we would have one or two drinks, our favorite being vodka martinis on the rocks with olives. We never got sick from this medicinal drink, as we chose to consider it, but it gave us pause mornings in Veracruz to see the daily delivery of ice plunked down in large blocks directly onto the street in front of our hotel.

Dinner usually consisted of papaya and some kind of fresh fish five nights a week, as we never tired of it. Being a chocaholic, Frank went for chocolate desserts while I ate my way through the *flan*, or caramel-covered custard, of every state in Mexico. Today I consider myself a *flan* connoisseur. It is a light dessert to specialize in and never gets boring; every restaurant makes it a different consistency. Holey and chunky is good. Smooth, bland, and congealed is *baaaad*.

We attended folk dances in a green courtyard of our hotel, absorbed the rococo splendor of Santo Domingo Church, promenaded under arched *portales* surrounding an ornate bandstand in central Plaza de Armas with the sound of marches and anthems gentled by great shade trees through which nightly concerts wafted toward us. Built in 1486, Oaxaca is an ancient town with mellow buildings like the sixteenth-century cathedral, famous for its facade and great wooden clock, located directly across from us on the south side of our small blue-flowered plaza. We stopped by Pension Suiza on Calzada Madero, where back in 1970 Frank and his harem of two had drunk evening cocktails on the rooftop while watching writhing "dragon" clouds, as Ann Merrill called them; and we ran into Ed Bewley and his Taos party eating dinner on a *portal* near our hotel. Oaxaca's marketplace was a classic mosaic of color, cacophony, and chaos, with unbelievable fresh tropical flowers, brilliant native costumes, and horrendous masses of flies shrouding exposed raw meat, a typical sight that did not deter us from our shopping.

At Santa Maria de Tule we sensed the ghost of Cortes resting in the shade of a two-thousand-year-old cypress 160 feet in circumference. And at Teotitlán del Valle in the country we bought a black-and-white Zapotec rug and were made welcome in a red-flowered hacienda bustling with family weavers, laughing women

170

grinding corn on *metates*, naked children, haughty chickens and roosters, even a pet pig.

"I feel so touched, and saddened, to see these places one last time," Frank would say.

"You always say that," I would cheer him. "And we always come back! Just like California. Every single time we've crossed that desert, you have said it was for the last time."

He smiled. He once told a close friend, "Barbara is cheery and laughs a lot and is fun to be with." I suppose that is really what tipped the scales.

But there comes a day when one is not able to go back. Then even the cheery feel saddened and touched at the thought of what once was so casually taken for granted. No one can take away the memories, though, and vibrant memories of Oaxaca live on in a small statue of Soledad, speak out from a black-and-white Zapotec rug with one corner now frayed by a hungry coydog.

Our memories of the next stop down the road were not so treasured. Ahead of time Frank had told me, "It is said the most beautiful women in all Mexico are to be found in Tehuántepec."

The women we encountered here were fat, ugly, and bellicose. None of them wore the beautifully fluted face ruff with matching white pleated skirt ruffle that Frieda Kahlo cherished and frequently wore. The thin mattresses on our cots were hard and crawling with cockroaches and bedbugs. Frank slept soundly, as usual. I sat up all night in a straight-backed wooden chair under a single bare lightbulb dangling from the dirty ceiling as scurrying creatures rustled about in shaded corners of our filthy room. In retrospect, striking out just once on such an extensive, unplanned trip was the best of batting averages. At the time I did not have this benign overview to sustain me through the endless hours.

At San Cristobal de las Casas we tagged along with some architecture students from the States to appreciate more fully its old Spanish colonial buildings. Soon we broke away to visit Indian Market and to gawk at the wonderful Zinacatecans wearing sandals, shorts under brief tunics, and flat straw hats rainbowed with ribbon streamers; these were men's hats designed to attract women. We saw the greatest variety and quantity of vivid Indian costumes in colorful Las Casas, though it was difficult to tell whether their hats were working or not.

Nonetheless, I felt put out with Frank for not taking me to meet Gertrude Blom, widow of archaeologist Franz Blom, and to stay at her famous compound Na-Bolom, as he had done nine years earlier. In *Of Time and Change* he calls it "the most unusual guest house in town." It was actually more of a research center and last bastion of civilization. Frank writes circumspectly of Trudi ruling Na-Bolom with "dictatorial aplomb," "shouting and cursing" in several languages, presiding at the head of the dinner table, and assuming the role of "Great White Goddess of the Lacandones."

Trudi, now dead, did a great deal for the needy Lacandon Indians. But Frank could not bear what he called her "Germanness." His unacknowledged shadow side caused him trouble when it came to races whose people tended to act domineering at times, particularly if the women acted this way. When I tried to interview him about Frieda Lawrence, he said irritably, "I *told* you. Frieda was a German housewife. Just a *German housewife*. That's *all*."

In Las Casas he told me, with his elbow jumping in a spasm of annoyance, "I cannot endure another meal with Trudi Blom *pre-sid-ing* over the dinner table. That woman! With her *strong will*."

Despite my annoyance with him, I burst out laughing. He had used exactly the same words in connection with Billie Blair, I reminded him, a non-German former editor of the *Taos News* who had gone on to direct an affiliated Santa Fe newspaper. Thirty-five years earlier Frank had been editor of the same Taos paper, for as long as he could stand it. Of Billie he had said, "That woman! With her *strong will*. Making friends with all the right people. Going along with the establishment's views on all the major issues. No wonder they've promoted her to president of the board."

Most often this issue was not a laughing matter. It infuriated me one Christmas, when I had hung up the phone after wishing my two best therapist friends a happy holiday, to be hit with Frank's waspish words: "I think it is so *strange* for an American girl to have a *German* and a *Jew* as her best friends." Being called a "girl" was not enough to soothe me that day.

It did not set well, either, when at Hopiland I met the wife of Oswald Fredericks, Frank's Hopi interpreter for *The Book of the Hopi*, and Frank said, "That *willful* woman. Now she wants to be called Brown Bear because he is White Bear! She deserves every word I wrote about her in *Pumpkin Seed Point*."

Coincidentally, another great man of strong will—D. H. Lawrence—wrote a short piece about Mabel Luhan titled "The Wilful Woman." And he wrote his sister-in-law, "Everything in America goes by *will*. A great negative *will* seems to be turned against all spontaneous life—there seems to be no *feeling* at all." He was still smarting about Mabel *willing* him, as she put it, to come to Taos, which he had his regrets about doing.

At least I have Frank's memories of Na-Bolom, meaning "at the sign of the jaguar," if not my own experience. Apparently, willful jaguars and Leo lions do not get on well together.

In a meditative vision at a David Carson workshop, I saw myself as a huge black bear rearing back on its hind legs beside sacred Blue Lake near the peak of Taos Mountain. Claws of my raised front paws were extended in a fierce, aggressive manner. David and I agreed that this vision signaled a stance I might have to assume more often for the future good of my cause, the Frank Waters Foundation, rather than my usual mother-bear stance. Lion and mother-bear persons do get on well. Our Taos lion would not have taken to this fierce, rampant bear at Blue Lake, though. I can hear him roaring, "That black bear! With her *strong will*."

Inside, our Taos house is a living museum of our journeys together and of Frank's journey through life. On the side of our refrigerator in Tucson hangs his poster of Mexico that Marcia Gaiter duplicated for our Taos refrigerator. Another magic carpet, it instantly brings alive a volcano exploding fireworks like the plaza in Veracruz on Christmas Eve; the famed cathedral on the north side of Mexico City's Zócolo not far from the Majestic; folk dancers; a bullfighter;

the most beautiful woman in Mexico in her lacy ruffled Tehuántepec finery; Mexico's golds, oranges, reds, blues, greens, and purples; the Pyramid of the Sun at Teotihuacán; the Sierra Madre.

In our living room on the back of Frank's chair rests a tasseled chieftain's headdress from the cloud country of Guatemala with mountains, sun, moon, and stars embroidered in vermilion, fuchsia, tangerine, turquoise, and royal blue. My typewriter cover is a rich red weaving with three blue fish, a blue llama and a brown one, and three native women doing their cooking, spinning, and weaving upon a reed island floating twelve thousand feet above sea level on Lake Titicaca. Over our bed is thrown a thick Peruvian blanket woven in grays and blacks. And on our bedroom windowsill is a wooden mother llama and her offspring; they come from another island near Puno where we saw a wild llama with fierce untamed eyes, eyes that drew us into the frightening primeval depths of the collective unconscious.

To afford these treasures, I did not go to Canada when Frank, Rudy Anaya, and Tony Hillerman journeyed there together to speak. It was a hard decision for me to make, but the right one. In those days one never thought of grieving, or of the healing effect of certain souvenir tangibles linked with treasured intangibles.

An extra bonus were Hillerman's words written in 1998, partially as a result of this trip. On the occasion of his being awarded a Frank Waters writing award in Colorado Springs, Tony wrote the awards committee, "Being considered a worthy follower of Frank Waters means a lot to me. He was a great man as well as a great writer, and a genuine friend of the Hopis and all the other Pueblo People. I had the good fortune some years ago to spend some time with Frank in Canada, during which we rented a car and drove down the St. Lawrence to Quebec and I learned something of the great-hearted kindness of the man behind those books. He's a hero of mine."

When I thanked Tony for these words, he added, "Frank was the *best man* I ever knew, and he was the last of the good, old-fashioned *gentlemen*. He was also very lucky to have found you."

Frank's own vivid words are of course a big help in bringing back sensate memories of him and of special places we visited together. In a single paragraph from *Mountain Dialogues*, Frank brings alive Chichicastenango, and all tourist Guatemala:

> Its immense plaza is crowded with thousands of Indians from the mountains and hamlets, carrying on their bent backs loads of fruit and vegetables, firewood, clay pottery, textiles, even pine tables and chairs. All wear their native dress, whose variations designate their own villages. From the steps of the great church of Santo Tomás rise clouds of copal smoke, the sweet-smelling resin which the people burn to accompany their prayers. And inside, the bare interior is filled with more barefoot worshippers kneeling on a floor strewn with wildflower and rose petals, burning candles and more copal.

Of Peru and Bolivia Frank wrote nothing, for he suffered from altitude sickness during most of our visit and never absorbed these countries enough for them to come out his fingertips as words. Perhaps he would have had trouble writing about Machu Picchu at any time. The tourist comfort at Hotel Bolivar and awe of the treasures ensconced in Lima's museums are not overly difficult to capture, nor is the stone-carved antiquity of Cuzco, the picturesque quality of a Pisac market day, the royal sacredness of the Valley of Kings, the lifelessness of the prehistoric Tiahuanaco valley, the upside-downness of Orion at La Paz, that magnificent hole in the ground. But to me Machu Picchu was a world of the priestess and always will be, despite the discrediting today of Bingham's theory.

Hiram Bingham, modern discoverer of this site, found more than one hundred human remains in burial caves here; most were skeletons of women. He theorized that they were holy women, called *mamacunas*, or "Virgins of the Sun," and trained originally at Cuzco's Temple of the Sun. If these female energies prevailed here, it can be expected that sensitive women at a later date would most easily attune themselves to lasting vibrations of their "sisters."

Machu Picchu seemed to me a state of mind where time ceased to exist. It remains such an enigma that its primary function has not been established; it could have been religious or agricultural, various experts now say; it probably was not military. One person's knowledgeable guess concerning its background is as valid as another's.

It is interesting to test one's initial sensations at major sites here without knowing their speculated function and modern names. The Funerary Rock is sure to elicit immediate chills, along with the Condor Stone, without knowing that the latter is designated by one authority as the "awesome sacrificial condor stone." At first encounter with the elegant six-foot-high pillar tapering upward from a curving stepped base, energy pulsates from the "Hitching Post of the Sun," or *intihuatana,* a solar observatory. It seems natural that Bingham would call stunning walls curved into a tower the "sun temple" of Machu Picchu. The Sacred Rock shaped like the mountain behind it fills one with a vast sense of oneness between man and nature. Humanity's allegiance to nature suffuses this enchanted site. The Urubamba River curving like a sacred necklace below; the Vilcambamba Mountains to the west; crouching Huayna Picchu pawing at the saddle of Machu Picchu; tame llamas; white bridal veils of mist; sun, moon, and star tiaras; the remnants of ancient native man; man the discoverer and traveler; all are one.

We had come looking for the sun, myself and the sun worshiper. He wrote in *Masked Gods* of "the Sun Father who lives in Heaven, manifest[ing] itself as the infinitely expanding radiance which imbues all things with life." He had traced sun worship through Indian religions; now he wanted to follow it back to the Incas and earlier, possibly to Tiahuanaco, the "City of the Dead" thirteen thousand feet above sea level where stands to this day the monolithic Gateway of the Sun. Sight unseen, using information gathered from other sources, Frank described its lintel as "thirteen and a half feet long, seven feet wide and a foot and a half thick . . . one of the finest specimens of stone cutting in the world." It was that, but Bolivian authorities have removed the ruin's essential mystique with poor reconstruction and very high fencing so that except for the gateway we sensed only coldness and imprisonment rather than a melding of humankind and nature. Still, one felt impressed with the dressing of stone slabs weighing up to one hundred tons, fitted into four main structures and a number of minor units scattered over about one-sixth of a square mile.

Combined with lack of oxygen, the bleak vista of the altiplano here subdued Frank's enthusiasm for a time. His preparation for this trip had sapped his strength too. After all, he was eighty when we set out. Our friend Alan Kishbaugh had warned him, "The way you're hobbling with that bad hip, you'll never make it around Machu Picchu's ruins. You'd better listen to your doctor and get a hip replacement if your heart is really set on going."

Frank therefore submitted to his first hip operation in 1980. Eight years later he had a second hip replacement after the first gave way. It's hard to tell, but he might have lived another half-dozen years without this energy depletion. Yet he couldn't have borne the pain much longer. Despite his indomitable will to go on, his energy imperceptibly began to ebb after that first operation.

It surprised me that Frank suffered from altitude sickness even at Machu Picchu. It is not much higher than our home in Arroyo Seco, lower than Taos Ski Valley, where we attended concerts and ate dinner from time to time. It was his habit anywhere to take an afternoon nap. Now he took one or two morning naps as well, giving me more time to scout about on my own. By evening he felt well and sociable and interested in my explorations since he hadn't set his Seal of Interpretation upon these ruins.

I had gathered the courage to plan and conduct our own Peru trip from Marj Allen, an old girlfriend of Frank's who had worked with him for the Atomic Energy Commission at Los Alamos and Las Vegas back in the '50s. She had saved her Las Vegas winnings to pay for a historic home in Santa Fe, of which she was justifiably proud. Marj was five or ten years younger than Frank. At first glance she looked like a little old white-haired lady when I knew her, but she had continued to travel all over Mexico alone or with her mother. In the late '70s Marj planned a trip to Peru and went there by herself, as her mother was dead. Our friend had a marvelous time. Sad to say, after safely traveling the world by herself, she was murdered in her own home by a drug addict. To carry on her spirit, we acquired her couch, a matching chair, and some silverware for one of our Foundation studios.

Marj gave me much helpful advice, such as staying on that small island with wild llamas not far from Puno. At twelve thousand feet above sea level, it featured some interesting hiking and a brand-new hotel. At this altitude most visitors experience queasiness. Beaten Coca-Cola, ginger ale, or coca-leaf tea was enough to settle my stomach. Frank stayed in bed much of the time but never complained, unlike the Ugly American it was our misfortune to meet here. What was he *doing* here, we wondered? A middle-aged man with a reserved wife, he shivered dramatically and swore up a storm. "This goddamned hotel isn't like the ones back home," he would shout. "Christ, where's the *heat?*"

What makes a site sacred? Members of one of our writing workshops decided the individual or groups of humans make a site sacred through their own beliefs. This could be true of the man-made Nazca lines, if they are indeed sacred. But it seems that there is more to it than simply human invention. For instance, the Sacred Rock at Machu Picchu lined up in miniature with the similarly shaped mountain behind it feels as if it has been eternally imbued with some of that mountain's vast energy. In certain spots, vegetation, natural objects, air currents, sun, water, or other elements appear to come together in an alchemical transformation that renders them more powerful than in other untouched locations. Then the human element is added to the equation, the sensitivity to pick up on this different energy and internalize it. Machu Picchu is one of the great isolated, primordial spots of the world where one can tune in to the innate energy of nature combined with a pervasive human reverence.

Mayans called this force of energy *k'ulel.* It is the soul force imbuing all things. They sensed it in all the important basics of the world: sacred mountains, mountain peaks and bases, springs, caves, ritualistic objects, and humans. They thought one could share the freed *k'ulel* of the departed. All fundamental interactions occurred between the *k'ulel* of things, they believed.

Ann Merrill says some outdoor spots have such a negative feeling about them that she is totally unproductive as an artist and has to move somewhere more stimulating to her creativity. In her paintings she roughs in an undercoat while on location. Later she details in the "alive" places of energy, the *k'ulel*. She compares this technique to ultrared photographs that pinpoint hot spots of energy.

Machu Picchu is one great mass of these energy hot spots, called *huacas* in Peru. Arthur Schneider, an old friend of Frank's, is finishing a book that focuses on a stone animal *huaca* he believes is key to past worship at this site. Cuzco itself is laid out in the shape of a great puma, and puma-shaped stones—or any incorporated shape of an animal—make a *huaca* more powerful with the animal's component strength.

We visited sacred *huaca* springs, especially Tambo Machay, that had the same numinous feeling as our stream at home. Once you wake up to *huacas*, you become aware that they are everywhere. The outdoor surroundings of our Taos home remind me of the universality of the sacred *huacas* of Peru. Our own private land, to say nothing of places like the Grand Canyon, is a mass of energy hot spots: our Sacred Aspen Grove and the Cathedral, the oak tree, my meditation tree, the Shaggy Mane mushroom patch, an aged fallen cottonwood, the rushing *acequia madre*, our wilderness picnic grove, Frank's stone walk, the boulders in our lower pasture, and Frank's monument boulder. *Huacas* located not far from our property are El Salto waterfall, and the mountain of which it is a part, as well as Taos Sacred Mountain with Blue Lake at its heart.

Like others, I am a priestess of sorts when I attend our *huacas* and nurture them with my own energy so that others can draw upon the enhanced *huaca* energy and thus become part of a greater whole. I attended the white sun worshiper, a *viracocha* or creator.

Now that he has set out across the waves after teaching us, I am carrying on here. We all must carry on in our own ways, but as he taught us. There is no single inheritor of his mantle, no one who will walk in his footsteps. He was his own man, had his own genius, his own *k'ulel*. Nevertheless, we can follow his example, absorb his milieu, his philosophy, some of his *k'ulel*, then synthesize them with our own particular *k'ulel* in preparation for the "Coming Sixth World of Consciousness," as Frank called it.

17
The Third Fate

One must pay dearly for immortality:
one has to die several times while still alive.
   —Friedrich Nietzsche

For some reason in the fall of 1968, while recuperating from foot surgery, I read a biography of D. H. Lawrence that mentioned the wonder and "curious otherness" of Taos. None of our family ever had heard of the place. A few weeks later, after my divorce from my first husband became final, I said farewell to the fertile plains of Illinois and headed for my brother's home in Tucson, via New Mexico. It took me one and a half years to reach Tucson. Instead I took a teaching job in Taos, and the strange mountain village turned out to be all I had intuitively known it would be for my spiritual growth. It possessed a soul that vibrated on the same emotional level as mine, and it did not spit me out, as it is apt to do to people. Taos was blue and gold that autumn, as it once had been for Lawrence, and lavender with wild asters.

My traveling companion, an aristocratic gray Afghan named Sheba, did not complain about visiting the Lawrence ranch first thing. What she did object to was our flat tire afterward. At that time the dirt road winding up to Lawrence's old Kiowa Ranch fifteen hundred feet higher than Taos was rough with potholes and rocks. Once there, Sheba was as jubilant as I over the pungent odor of cedar and pine, the sheltered log cabin where we felt sure the author had created his masterpieces, and the shrine to a lost love. The wind soughed, "Welcome home." It seemed we had made this pilgrimage before, Sheba and I. Perhaps we had been among Lawrence's women in another lifetime. Al Bierce, the ranch caretaker, seemed to think so.

When we returned to the main highway, it was he who came to comfort me. Sheba took off like a shot as I stepped out of my Chevy Monte Carlo to identify a peculiar whistling sound, like a jet preparing to land on top of our car. Shrewd and intuitive, she wasn't fooled for an instant. She knew immediately that we had a flat tire, and she knew very well that neither of us at that time had the slightest idea how to change it.

Bierce changed it after I ran out of breath during a fruitless dog chase and hobbled back on aching feet to my car. Four road-construction men in a pickup pursued Sheba, still cantering down the highway in a glorious bid for freedom. Tears trickled down my face as I sobbed, "It's all Lawrence's fault! I wouldn't *be* here if it weren't for him. How could he do this to me?"

Al put his arm around me, patted my shoulder, and said, "There, there, honey. Lawrence always was hard on his women."

Sheba shed a tear for all captive women when she returned. But it would be some time before we realized just how hard Lawrence had been on his women. Or that it was more likely the spirit of his widow, Frieda, buried near his ashes at the ranch above us, who had called me to Taos—not he. I could not know then that Taos would be the home of my heart for the rest of my life, never losing its fascination. Or that I would follow in Frieda's footsteps and marry a writer with some of the same talent and tendencies as her husband. At least she had to put up with only a Virgo during this marriage, not a Leo.

When I was to speak before a Taos literary group in 1996, a young woman artist who'd heard I would make mention of Frieda Lawrence said, "What does that dead old woman mean to me? She doesn't speak to me in any way." The artist also may have been thinking, "What that *living* old woman has to say means nothing to me either." I felt that this artist was not too smart if she hadn't heard of role models and mentoring.

Although Frieda had died before I arrived in Taos, she is still very much a role model for me. My niece once called me a "nomad of life"; Frieda saw herself as a nomad. Her writings and writings by others about her teach me by example what to do and what not to do. Even her mistakes are helpful. She followed her heart and intuition. She learned. She grew. She laughed and enjoyed. She endured much of what I have endured in milder forms. She stayed the course. Most important, her dedication to Lawrence's work and reputation after her husband's death serve as my primary example. She spent the rest of her life defending his writing and promoting it. A sizable portion of the successful efforts to promote and to enhance his reputation were hers. Her business sense turned out to be sound, her investments good. I hope that after my death I may somehow be a positive role model for another woman or two in the same manner as the departed spirit of Frieda is for me.

As I encounter discouragement from time to time in writing this book, I think of Frieda writing *Not I, But The Wind.* "Listen," I lecture myself, "you know a lot more about writing a book than she did; you've already done more writing than she. Frieda had to feel discouraged frequently. She wrote a most interesting book anyway. And it was well received. Now, you just *do* it, as Frieda did. Quit stalling around and making up excuses."

Frieda met David Herbert Lawrence in 1912 at her home in Nottingham, England, before he became infamous for writing *Lady Chatterley's Lover* and famous for producing a substantial body of literature increasingly esteemed today. When they met, Frieda had been married to a professor named Ernest Weekley for thirteen years and cherished their three children. Born in 1879, she was six years older than Lawrence, who was then twenty-six with only eighteen more years to live. The robust, free-spirited woman was proud of having been born a von Richthoven; her cousin would carry that aristocratic family name to fame during World War I as the German flying ace popularly called the "Red Baron." She had some upper-class inclinations, which she called "my High and Mightiness." Lawrence, son of a coal miner, later referred to this as her "God Almightiness." Yet her father had not been a financial success, and her husband earned a modest salary teaching language at Nottingham's University College.

Frieda viewed herself and Lawrence basically as two simple persons needing little but each other. She would run away with him; they would thrive on uninhibited sex, love, and the companionship she lacked with Weekley. Her mother called Frieda a throwback to the primal; Lawrence advocated this return to the primal. Frieda's overall view prior to meeting Lawrence partially mirrored that of the early-twentieth-century German movement that advocated replacement of the existing patriarchal society with a new version of an older matriarchal order.

During her marriage to Weekley her affair with Freudian psychoanalyst Otto Gross had put her on the fringe of this romantic rebellion, sometimes called the erotic movement, in which rebels turned from the newer scientific, mechanistic, rational gods to older emotional gods of primitive cultures and myths emphasizing feminine instinct, intuition, and sexual freedom. The latter supposedly would make obsolete such existing corruptions as jealousy, possessiveness, self-denial, and self-sacrifice. A woman's role in the free-love aspect of this movement was to consider herself "religiously called to take many lovers and bear many children without submitting to a husband/father/master."

Luckily, Frieda's strong intuition and common sense kept her from running off with Gross, who died a miserable death as a drug addict. Still, some of Gross's ideas about sex-psychology were markedly similar to those held by Lawrence, with whom Frieda did run off and who spent the rest of his life trying to tap into the vitality of primitive cultures. The ideas picked up from Gross, and Frieda's adaptations of them, forged facets of personality that made her unique to Lawrence and well suited to his literary purposes. Along with these characteristics, her Teutonic vitality and that of her extended family provided him with a treasure trove of material to be fictionalized that was not available to his English peers. He had struck a rich vein of ore right in his own backyard; it is easily traced in his subsequent literature.

In *Journey with Genius* Witter Bynner writes that Frieda told him, "He quotes me all the time in his books. He may quote me just to attack me, but he quotes me and often what he quotes from me is attacking what he himself says and in the book he lets me have the best of it." Frieda claimed she wrote "female bits" in Lawrence's work. And she acted out scenes to show him what the female reaction had been or might be to specific incidents, real and fictional. In addition to all this, she served as critic—always outspoken, often astute. Like other women at every period of his life, Frieda functioned as a sounding board for Lawrence's creativity.

Chauvinistic males and others appear to have fostered the "just a German housewife" view of Frieda to keep her assets and complexity out of sight. After more careful and objective study of the Lawrence literary canon, some later critics have recognized her true influence upon her husband's literature. Like that of other seemingly insignificant women in his life, her influence was considerable, though seldom acknowledged publicly by the Great Man himself.

In his biography of Lawrence, Richard Aldington agrees with Frieda that her husband presented her with a "new world" but stresses that it was due to her that Lawrence had a new world to give. It should be added that her good care kept the man in this world longer than expected, in itself no small contribution. Martin Green, one of her husband's biographers, states, "Of what Frieda meant to Lawrence, all his work subsequent to 1912 bears witness." Claiming that Lawrence owed much of his greatness to Frieda,

Green adds that she saved the famed writer from "artistic as well as sexual impotence."

His male-female duality caused Lawrence much inner conflict; some critics believe his feminine side overbalanced his masculine in this unconscious battle between his two natures. Frieda encouraged him to use his so-called feminine traits such as instinct, intuition, emotion, and sensitivity as assets in his writing. Many in his generation tended to categorize these traits differently than persons today such as Robert Bly and Sam Keen, who see less of a dichotomy. In his last novel Lawrence did attempt to breach this sharp division with a chauvinistic amalgamation of all traits for the male, but not for the female.

Frieda made a particularly important contribution to their liaison when she led Lawrence to *experience* an original relationship free from convention rather than merely to learn vicariously about the new theories of eroticism and sex-psychology that interested them. Frieda was a catalyst who set free Lawrence's energies.

"It was given to me to make him flower," she wrote Brett.

Lawrence himself said to Mabel, "Frieda is the freest woman I have ever known."

In later years Brett recalled that Lawrence had told her he stayed with Frieda because "she was the only woman who could *make* him feel like a *man*."

Unfortunately, in practice his theories did not embrace equality for women. During one of his more intense patriarchal periods, for instance, he wrote novelist and poet Catherine Carswell that men should take precedence over women. "I do think men must go ahead absolutely in front of their women, without turning round to ask for permission or approval from their women. Consequently the women must follow as it were unquestioningly. I can't help it, I believe this. Frieda doesn't. Hence our fight."

Like Frank Waters, Lawrence desired one hundred percent of his wife's love and devotion. Frieda divorced Weekley in the spring of 1914; two months later she and Lawrence married. Using the third person, Frieda wrote in her second book, which was published five years after her death, "In a sovereign way he took her for himself; she was his and he would never let her go again while he lived; he would kill her rather. She liked it. He wanted her, he needed her, and that was bliss."

This pairing was bliss for a time. She added that "nothing else mattered." But one thing did: she desperately missed her children. Lawrence never comprehended the depth of her grief over separating from them. She told Mabel Luhan that her loneliness for her children was like "a terrible hunger." She had thought her ex-husband would turn all three children over to her for raising after a year or so of trying it on his own. He never relented. And Lawrence the master would brook no rivals; he demanded her single-minded attention. He must be her child, son, lover, and resident genius.

Lawrence continued his boycott of her children until the last years of his life. When Frieda's grown daughter came to visit her mother in Spotorno, Italy, he still showed resentment. In her first book Frieda recalled that he burst out at Barbara during dinner, "Don't you imagine your mother loves you."

With this, he flung a glassful of red wine in his wife's face.

Barbara jumped up and blazed at him, "My mother is too good for you, much too good; it's like pearls thrown to the swine."

Sobbing, Frieda left the room.

Barbara asked Lawrence, "Don't you care at all for her?"

"It's indecent to ask," he replied, chiseling away at Frieda as ever. "Haven't I just helped her with her rotten painting?"

When Frieda arranged for a ten-year-old Italian boy's operation, Lawrence sneered in a letter to his mother-in-law, "You've heard how Frieda wants to act *Sancta Santisima*, she's really St. Frieda, butter doesn't melt in her mouth: because, of course, she has taken a Bandelli child to the hospital." This reminds me of Frank sarcastically calling me the *"Patrona"* whenever I helped someone. "You really *enjoy* playing the *Patrona*, don't you?" he would say.

Huge amounts of Frieda's energy were given to or taken by her husband, to his benefit. Yet she told Witter Bynner, "He never mentions how closely I watch his health and how usefully I take care of him."

Life severely tested this sheltered woman, who claimed she had not had the slightest idea how to turn on the gas to heat tea water on the servants' day off during her first marriage. "Being born and reborn is no joke," she wrote in her first book, "and being born into your own intrinsic self, that separates and singles you out from all the rest—it's a painful process."

She was to tell Brett, "I am not used to playing second fiddle. Always at home I played first fiddle."

The contrast could be terrifying. Frieda wrote at a time when Lawrence was infatuated with a titled Englishwoman, "I am powerless and a Hun, and a nobody."

Her considerate farewell to Mrs. George Bernard Shaw during a visit after Lawrence's death highlights the familiar feeling some women experience of being the best-kept secret in their marriages. She made a point of singling out Mrs. Shaw and saying with her usual fervor, "I am so glad to meet you."

"She opened her eyes wide," Frieda wrote in her book. "'Me, they always want to meet Shaw.'

"I laughed: 'I also have been a writer's wife. I know.'"

It took Frieda a long time to acknowledge Lawrence's Great Man self. In a letter, she wrote, "If the day came, which God forbid, that I should see Lawrence as the 'great man,' he would be a dead thing to me and it would bore me. Greatness is a thing of the outer world, where I indeed am nothing and don't want to be any more! So I grant you that in the world of men Lawrence is and I am not! But that world is nothing to me, there's a deeper one, where life itself flows, there I am at home! And the outer world isn't my affair!"

It behooves a woman in an intimate relationship with a successful man to acknowledge his Great Man self at certain times, even if she generally sees him as simply—or not so simply—a *man*. If his partner backs off and lets him have his moments in the sun without hanging on to his coattails, the couple experiences less tension over the inevitable. During these times the tricky part for the woman is to avoid feeling as if she is "nothing," or as if "I am *not!*" At no other time is she more estranged from her mate than during his Great Man period. "Estranged" is an apt word, for he does indeed become a total stranger. During this manifestation the king deigns to share his throne and throne room with *no one.* She must learn to accept and to cope positively with this phenomenon. It is good practice for dealing with a similar major challenge, his Great Guru self. In most cases, both are passing but recurring selves with which to reckon.

Frieda wrote the same man, S. S. Koteliansky, "You see I am also his wife on this earth, the wife to the *man* as distinguished from the *artist;* to that latter I would always submit but, you see, some things I just *know* and he doesn't." I can identify with this too. Each fall in the '70s I returned to Tucson with confidence to teach school after reminding Frank, "You'll wake up one of these days. We are destined to be married. You'll wake up."

Searching for a healing climate for Lawrence's tuberculosis and a revitalizing setting in which he could write, the couple trailed restlessly back and forth between Italy, Germany, England, Scotland, India, Ceylon, Australia, New Zealand, Tahiti, the United States, Mexico, Spain, and France, where Lawrence was to die in 1930. He seemed to have been seeking a golden time and place where he could exist eternally in a world of right-brain creativity, a mythic primitive world where Pan would happily pipe his magic forever free from man's mechanistic left-brain world.

Along the way he was drawn to Taos by his idealism and by one of those "lion huntresses" who invariably and relentlessly pursue talented married men and try to snare them as their own. For years Lawrence had longed to begin a unique social existence where persons judged good and decent from birth, instead of bad and sinful, would live in harmony creating a communistic community that would lead to a new moral world. Mabel Dodge Sterne, a wealthy patroness of the arts, urged him to come and live in one of her Taos guest houses making up "Mabeltown"—as Lawrence later called it.

Here she would inspire the great man to write the Great American Novel about two great undiscovered American souls: that of the Indian, rooted in his sacred land surrounding her home, and that of herself, star of the proposed bestseller.

Born in 1879 like Frieda, Mabel was about to marry her fourth husband, a Taos Indian named Tony Lujan; she would change the spelling of this last name for only herself to "Luhan" after their marriage so that it seemed less ethnic. Her written descriptions of the Taos Indians and the rugged, untouched beauty of their land made northern New Mexico seem to Lawrence like the perfect setting for his utopia, which he called Rananim. In 1922 the Lawrences arrived in Taos with no money but great expectations.

Their financial condition improved, along with Lawrence's health. He abandoned his social dream after garnering only one disciple to inhabit Rananim. Another huntress, more timid but even more tenacious than Mabel, she would cause Frieda many a headache and temper tantrum. Dorothy Brett was an aspiring English artist whose main claims to fame were a viscount father and a dance in her youth with Winston Churchill. Also, she informed Lawrence after he had chided her about her supposed rudeness toward Mabel, she had been famous at the Slade art school for her "good manners" and her "ellipses."

"*Ellipses*," Frieda laughed. "What are ellipses?"

Lawrence said dryly, and cruelly, "I never knew you ever had been famous anywhere."

Brett's method of lionhunting was to tag along everywhere after Lawrence like an adoring sheep, helping him out whenever she could. Convinced that only she truly comprehended and shared her idol's spirituality, she attempted without much success to be all things to him. Frieda felt threatened and exasperated when Brett through thick and thin "stuck to her lollipop of imagined spiritual communion": "Her adoration for Lawrence seemed a silly old habit. 'Brett,' I said, 'I detest your adoration for Lawrence, only one thing I would detest more, and that is if you adored me.'"

Two years older than Lawrence, Brett typed many of his manuscripts. She was to gain fame for her subjective, mystical paintings of Indian dance and ritual; she also painted her idol as Christ and as Pan. Yet he criticized her art mercilessly at times. He frequently called her "dumb" to her face and wrote to his mother-in-law, "The Brett is a little simple but harmless, and likes to help."

Lawrence possessed a natural flair for painting and strove to bring alive his amateur art works. He never bragged about his writing talent, but his view of his own artistic merit was chauvinistic and inflated.

"Look at my Teepee and the Indians. Aren't they much better than yours?" Brett recalled him asking her during a typical painting excursion.

"I don't know," she replied. "Mine are good too."

"Not as good as mine. I never think your things are as good as mine. There is something vital you leave out. Some spark. Don't you think so?"

"Yes," she answered "meekly," knowing that argument was "no good, and too often disastrous."

More accurately, Frank Waters wrote in *Of Time and Change*, "Brett's pictorial record of traditional Indian life will always remind us who have known Indians of that spiritual essence, common to us all, which is forever immune to the worldly encroachments of the changing aspects of modern society."

At the beginning of Brett's memoir is a photograph of the women she called "Lawrence's Three Fates" when she painted them later. Each wears her own version of a Cheshire-cat smile in the photo. On the left broods Mabel Dodge Sterne Luhan, her dark hair chopped off in a short pageboy with bangs almost touching her eyebrows, her eyes appearing inwardly closed and indecipherable like the rest of her face. She could well symbolize the shadow side of humanity. In fact, biographer Martin Green states that "she stood for the unconscious." Lawrence once called her "a cooing raven of ill-omen." He frequently called her "little black buffalo."

Seated in the middle, Frieda gazes straight into the camera. Chin high, cigarette dangling from the left corner of her mouth, hair blowing free in the breeze, she seems to represent the physical conscious self. She looks open and Teutonic.

On the right, Brett's short hair is bound back with a folded scarf banded Indian fashion about her forehead. One eye is shadowed while the other looks almost directly into the camera, as if she alone acknowledges and can live with her duality. Lawrence on his better days felt there was "something of a touchstone about her—that shows up things."

Brett outlived the other two by reaching age ninety-three. Mabel might have lived longer than eighty-three years had not the shadows of alcohol misuse and senility darkened her last years. Frieda's robust heart would give out first at age seventy-seven. It is interesting that the longest-lived was the only one who never married. Life may be safer and easier for those who worship from afar.

The cover on the second edition of her book features Brett's painting of these "Three Fates." She reveals more about them by portraying the three women in the same position as in the photo but gathered around a table at Kiowa Ranch on Lobo Mountain. Mabel and Frieda wear dresses, Brett her favorite long dark pants. Mabel appears about to begin writing; Frieda's crossed hands rest calmly on a manuscript. On the right Brett sits typing, one eye still shadowed, her white hair flying upward as if electrified by the language in Lawrence's manuscript before her. Her vivid orange blouse blends with the intensity of Lawrence's orange-red hair and beard as he writes outdoors. Glimpsed through an open door behind Frieda and Brett, he sits leaning against a tree, as was his custom when writing. Dressed in a shirt colored spiritual blue to match his blue eyes and to blend with the mauve halo circling his head, he looks like a saint.

By this time, below his rusty brush of a mustache Lawrence had grown the familiar pointed beard seen in most of his photographs and paintings. While his shock of hair had darkened to golden brown, his beard was still tawny. His great dome of a head and forehead overhung deep-set eyes, flamed with blue, widely spaced. His skull tapered downward in a triangle, accentuating his burnished beard, creating the image of an inverted pyramid glowing from deep within with vibrant intensity and intellectual power. Frieda's daughter Barbara observed, "He seemed beyond being human and ordinary, and I felt at once that he was more like an element—say a rock or rushing water."

Frank had this same charisma.

Lawrence's slim, straight legs gave an appearance of tallness in spite of his stooped shoulders. He was described as quick and sure in his movements; Brett thought he seemed at times so light on his feet as to float above the earth. Like Hemingway, he believed in living life "all the way up."

All three Fates penned their subjective "my-turn" views, as should every woman so inclined. Mabel's more intellectual, uptight book about her role in their *ménage á quatre* was titled *Lorenzo in Taos* (in Italy Frieda and others had called her husband this equivalent of "Lawrence"). Since Mabel had given Kiowa Ranch to the Lawrences, she was potentially the biggest thorn in their flesh. They repaid her with the original manuscript of *Sons and Lovers*, which today is almost priceless. None too wisely, she passed it on to her psychiatrist in partial payment of a bill. With her money, connections, and intellect, Mabel seemed to be all things Lawrence needed. Or so she thought. He actually was more into the Doormat Type whom he could bully, like Frieda and Brett. Mabel was too willful and independent, too strong, too much like himself.

Frieda's book *Not I, But The Wind* was the warmest memoir. Brett's *Lawrence and Brett: A Friendship* was the freest, most sensitive, and painterly, a portrait in itself. Unfortunately, she tended to make Frieda seem like a giant slug who did nothing but cook and lie around in bed all day smoking cigarettes, which impression Brett probably passed on to others while living with the couple, and later. Not overly clean herself, Brett was unimpressed with the huge washings Frieda regularly did by hand in a tub with scrubboard and brush.

Life continued to be challenging for Frieda. Mabel told her point-blank that she was wrong for Lawrence; their benefactress was his true kindred spirit, and she should have him. Frieda blew her top. Not without cause did Taos Indians call her "Angry Winter." Mabel backed off and sought refuge in that old adage, "The pen is mightier than the sword." Biographers quote her Lawrence memoirs with caution. One calls them "pathological" and "neurotic reminiscences." Another considers them an unreliable reference to be avoided as much as possible. It is believed that Frieda hastily wrote her own first book after reading Mabel's acid words prior to publication of her manuscript. As Frieda intuited and wrote her, "You didn't want a *relationship* with either Lawrence or me, you only want people in your *power.*"

"Slings and arrows" issued from others whom Frieda saw as envious of her for being married to Lawrence instead of them possessing him—as if anyone could. Koteliansky told her she should separate from the great man; she wasn't good enough for him. The couple's mutual "friend" Aldous Huxley, in referring to her so-called stupidity, said Frieda convinced him that Buddha had been right in making stupidity one of the deadly sins. It remained for Witter Bynner to write of the "lion-chasers and neurotic women, who tried to disparage Frieda and to attract him [Lawrence] by substituting their ambitions and vanities for her fond, amused, understanding, creative patience."

It surprised me that Frieda used the same term as I in referring to the female of this species. "Oh dear," she wrote, "we were asked to lunch by a few lion huntresses and the human being in me felt only insulted." Rather than naming them or discussing their infinite variety, it is best simply to dismiss them from mind and print. They are cast in the classic mold of the lion huntress who much later touched Indian activist and writer Vine Deloria with one finger and breathed, "It's almost like touching God!"

Coping with Lawrence was a full-time job without outsiders complicating matters. One wonders if his long illness affected his brain. Besides "ordinary" incidents like breaking records over

Frieda's head and smashing dishes or her paintings, he "sometimes went over the edge of sanity." She wrote in her second book, "I was many times frightened but never the last bit of me. Once, I remember he had worked himself up and his hands were on my throat and he was pressing me against the wall and ground out: 'I am the master, I am the master.' I said: 'Is that all? You can be master as much as you like, I don't care.' His hands dropped away, he looked at me in astonishment and was all right."

Instinctively, Frieda had changed her customary move in one of the many games this volatile couple played. Instead of fighting back, which she had come to do more often as she absorbed more and more of her husband's frenetic intensity, she had surrendered. She had unexpectedly taken the wind out of his sails by changing tactics in midstream, a good lesson for all of us involved in challenging relationships. The unexpected packs a wallop. As Adlerian therapist Oscar Christensen expresses it more uniquely, Frieda "took the sail out of [Lawrence's] wind" with this new ploy. Her mate was stalemated; he had no further obstruction to push around.

Lawrence's impotence after 1926 destroyed his ability to experience the uninhibited male-female relationship he advocated in theory. Frieda, on the other hand, remained healthy and robust as ever while carrying on more than one affair. Mabel called her "the mother of orgasm." Her husband's biographers have called her amoral, and worse. Yet people in the Lawrences' circle, in Brett's, and in Mabel's often led freewheeling sex lives. Mabel revealed in her autobiographies that she had indulged in numerous extramarital affairs. Frieda's continued health, and even that of their plants and animals, may have been more upsetting to Lawrence than her so-called amorality. His change from a feminine philosophy to a belligerently patriarchal stance, as in the just-described incident, could have been in part an unconscious retaliation against her continued health, sexual activity, and candid opposition to some of his views. His jealous nature did not help matters.

Despite his all-knowing genius, Lawrence still wondered on his deathbed, "Why, oh why did we quarrel so much?"

Frieda retorted, "Such as we were, violent creatures, how could we help it?"

One has to admire the lionhearted old girl for enduring. She was a Leo, whose motto is "I will," with the emphasis usually on the pronoun "I." In the imagination Frieda can be heard gritting her teeth and vowing during their rougher times, "I will survive this marriage. I *will*."

All Lawrentian scholars agree that Lawrence had an oedipal side to his personality; they merely quibble about whether he got over it or not. Most likely it began in 1902, when pneumonia took his brother's life and almost took his. The ailing survivor received his mother's total attention. Vicariously, she pinned her hopes on Lawrence's future success. Later he would see his mother, Lydia, in other women. Frieda observed, "His mother, though dead, seemed so alive and there still to him." Once Frieda "got fed up" and wrote a piece partially titled "His Mother's Darling" that aroused her husband's ire.

An obsession with mother often causes in the son a male-female ambivalence that he may find alarming, particularly if he does not have a strong male role model at hand. A male aggressiveness can manifest in an attempt to override unconscious fear of parental incest with the female and subsequent castration as punishment. Instead of competing unfavorably with Lydia's role, as she had at first, Frieda wound up *being* the mother and consciously accepting that role herself after her husband became impotent, if not sooner. A fancied incestuous aspect to their relationship may have helped to hold his impotence at bay for a time.

Frieda verified that she saw herself in at least a variation of the mother role when she wrote, "I think a man is born twice: first his mother bears him, then he has to be reborn from the woman he loves."

This final combination role of mother, manager, and caregiver is a difficult one after the seemingly richer roles one has earlier experienced. Nevertheless, richness and closeness do exist in this final stage. Carrying it off with grace is important. This Frieda did at the end of her relationship with Lawrence.

Her multifaceted personality and contributions have merited thorough analysis. Yet until recently only two books were devoted in large part to her life, as opposed to more than one thousand books dealing with her husband's work. I had written a fifty-page analysis of her life with Lawrence in another of my manuscripts when Janet Byrne's excellent biography *A Genius for Living* suddenly appeared. It delights me that even Byrne's title gives Frieda deserved credit, to say nothing of the author's thorough research.

Despite Frieda's doormat periods, like many of us she did fight the good fight: the right to remain *beside* one's man, not five paces behind. She suffered, but refused to view her life as a tragedy. Instead she asserted her happy nature. At times she rebelled, withdrawing into her own world away from her husband's domination. Although he took some of the backbone out of her, Frieda endured Lawrence. At the end of his life, her husband exhibited grudging admiration for her battle to remain equal and independent.

Frieda's words echo in my mind as they enhance the lasting glow in my own heart: "I am old and alone now but the glow of his world makes one feel rich."

18
More Fates

His friend John Gilchriese once said, "Frank was always crazy about attractive women." When they went to bars together, John drank while Frank danced with women and drank. On a tape with Lois Rudnik, Frank repeatedly speaks of the "luscious babes" he danced with at a Harlem nightclub while Tony Lujan played a drum and sang during several of their nights out on the town. On a short-term basis Frank was fascinated with Oriental or Eurasian women, and dark-eyed Mexicans. This most likely was a taste he acquired in Mexicali when he first was on his own in his midtwenties. Such women had the passion to carry encounters.

He frequently became infatuated with women, but he did not sustain these relationships. He may not have cared to, for most of his life. It was most often a love-them-and-leave-them sort of thing. Tom Lyon in analyzing Frank's work wrote that he obviously was "equipped with a fine, wild receptivity to beauty." This applied to women as well as to nature.

In Las Vegas, Nevada, Frank and I stayed at a motel-casino called Sam's Town when he was to give a speech at the university. Our first night there we decided to play blackjack since I have a lot of card sense and as a child spent long hours playing what my grandmother called "21"—the same game.

"First we have to find the *right* girl," Frank said. "I will choose her."

"I prefer a man dealer," I demurred. "Besides, how do we recognize the 'right' girl?" He had piqued my curiosity. He was not sober; I was curious about what he would do in this state *and* about what was the "right" girl for a seventy-nine-year-old man.

"I know," Frank replied with a smug half grin. "I know the type that appeals to me."

We drifted around the tables with Frank looking the female dealers up and down as if he were buying one for the night. At last he chose the most beautiful and enigmatic-looking Oriental. Her eyes seemed to flash more than those of the others. She was *right*.

Frank, who had no card sense whatever, soon lost all his money along with all his other sense. He sat there staring into this woman's eyes, flashing her what he considered his sexy, intimate smile, his thumbs tucked into the front pockets of his frontier pants in a stance he assumed when he wished to look very masculine and cool. He most often stood this way around groups of men with whom he did not feel completely confident. He pulled out all the stops for this prime-rib special of the night. She didn't give him the time of day. But it put him back in fantasy to a time when this same type *had* given him the time of day.

I felt somewhat appeased by winning back all Frank's lost money, and more. In retrospect, however, I felt bad. I could have kicked myself for going along like a little sheep with his fantasy. I should have insisted on choosing one of those good-looking hunks of men as our dealer! It was extremely disheartening to see these Leo love spasms occur in an old, "enlightened" man. We did not gamble again. A gambler friend of Frank's once tried to teach him to deal cards. The dealer finally gave up, saying in despair, "You just don't have the hands for it, Frank." I don't think he had the *sense* for it.

Edward James, said to be an illegitimate son of King Edward VII, wrote in his diary of visiting Taos about 1940 and meeting "the tall and graceful and snake-brown eyed" Frank Waters. John Lowe,

James's biographer elaborates, "Edward had lost his secretary, Anna De Goguel, to the 'snake-brown eyed' writer, Frank Waters, who had fallen in love with Anna and wrote Edward a long letter on 2 September, imploring him to be unselfish and to release her so that they could get married."

Before Lowe's book came out, I had learned about this affair while cataloging our books in 1980. One quite passionate book inscription concerned Anna. At the time I asked, "Who was this Anna?"

"Oh, she was just someone I once fell madly in love with for a time," he said.

"What happened? Why didn't you get married?" I persisted.

"Well, the whole thing blew over in a couple of weeks. We drifted apart. I think she went back to New York. I actually grew more fascinated with her *mother;* she and I remained friends for many years."

The cataloged file cards I made for each of our books are a treasure lode for biographers since I also copied inscriptions on them and what Frank had to tell me about the book, author, or inscription—if he was in the right mood that day.

While cataloging Winnie Dean's *Jefferson: Queen of the Cypress,* I found out more about Lois Moseley, who was married to Frank for a year in 1944. I'd read the concerned letter Tony Lujan had supposedly dictated to his wife, Mabel, urging Frank not to marry Lois because they were ill suited. It seemed really to have been written by Mabel, who'd probably had a brief affair with Frank a few years earlier. Men did not usually escape unscathed from Mabel, to say nothing of women. Lois taught voice lessons and was connected with musical and theatrical people such as Kitty Carlisle, who once came to visit Frank. He had told me Lois and he broke up shortly after their marriage in New York and that he had moved into his own apartment.

As I was doing the file cards, he added, "I was going to set a novel in Jefferson, Texas, Lois's hometown near Shreveport. Then we had a big spat just before the wedding was to take place and decided to call it off. But our well-meaning best man patched things up briefly enough for us to make the mistake of going through with the wedding ceremony. Lois went along with me to Jefferson to do my research work. She stayed there only a week or so, though, before going back to her job in New York. And I came on out here to Taos."

We still have brochures that Frank gathered in Jefferson; the unfulfilled project must have remained in his mind, as did his guilt feelings about the failure of this first marriage. In his old age he wrote Lois a letter of apology for his failings. It came back stamped "address unknown."

To my surprise, in 1996 I learned that Lois was still alive and living in New York again after spending some years in Dallas. She is now in her nineties and suffers from postpolio syndrome. She has kept the name Lois Waters all these years. Yet she said over the telephone, "Living with Frank Waters was *hell*. I don't even want to think about it. He's the only man I ever knew who couldn't carry his own empty coffee cup out to the kitchen."

She added, "I told the same thing to a fan of Frank's at a cocktail party in Dallas when he asked me, 'How could you have divorced a man who writes so sensitively, intelligently, and beautifully?' 'Because he was hell to *live* with,' I said."

A friend of hers from Dallas told me, "Lois herself would not be an easy person to live with." Lois also told her friends cock-and-bull stories about Frank writing Franklin Roosevelt's speeches and Eleanor Roosevelt telling them just to come on over and stay in the White House whenever they were in town since their own apartments were so cramped and small. Lois claimed they often did this to escape Frank's small apartment in Washington, D.C., and hers in New York. Frank Waters Slept Here? I doubt it. To him FDR was such a major hero that we never would have heard the end of Frank's White House stories had either myth been true.

For the file card on one of Theodor Reik's books, Frank commented, "This is the man Janey went to in New York—every day for two months. Didn't do her a *damn* bit of good. He stopped up here once. But we didn't hit it off too well. He was so ooo-l-l-l-d. And so set in his ways about Freud."

When I'd confronted Frank about lying to me in regard to his divorce from Janey, his second wife, he had hedged, "Well, it wasn't *really* a divorce. Reik thought it would help her for us to separate a while and then get back together. But she died." I have explained that they actually separated, then divorced, and Janey remarried before her death in 1960. Frank married Rose the following year.

On a file card for Tom Lyon's book *Frank Waters* is Frank's statement that he and Rose, his third wife, had divorced in 1963. Tom placed the divorce in 1965. "So it isn't accurate to say you were married only a few months," I persisted.

"Well, we *lived together* only a short time," Frank said. "The rest was in name only." He often began an answer with a long drawn-out "well" to give him more stalling time. He was patient with my calm questions that had a biographical emphasis rather than an accusatory one.

One book inscription is written by Ann Merrill, who gave Henriette Mertz's *Wine Dark Sea* and some other book to Frank. It says, "To *Francisco de Aguas* with love on this Christmas of 1968." Her inserted card in the other book reads, "To Frankie—with love from Ann—I didn't sign it—so you can give it away if you don't like it. Merry, Merry." Little did she know a New Girl had just come to town.

In March 1996 I asked Bob Bonney if the Frank Waters Foundation, represented by me, could make a slide presentation in conjunction with the Millicent Rogers Museum, for which he was education coordinator. He thought this was a "great idea" but suggested I expand the concept into a tripart series. We were to meet at 1:30 P.M. a week later to discuss my "plan." While eating breakfast at Northtown Restaurant three hours before our second meeting, I suddenly remembered my assignment. First would be the slide presentation of photos of our land accompanied by Frank's words from *Mountain Dialogues*. Third would be a panel of literary experts discussing his work. My working titles so far were "Frank Waters: The Man and His Land"; "————"; "Frank Waters: The Works." How could I fill the gap?

It dawned on me over a second cup of strong black coffee. The women! "Frank Waters: The Women" would be the second in our series of three. We would pray it didn't turn out to be "Frank Waters: The Fireworks"! Just like Lawrence, I realized, Frank in his later years had suffered Three Fates: Rose Woodell, Ann Merrill, and myself. We were all three still here mentally and physically. We had mellowed enough to get along, possibly. Each of us needed to speak her piece while she could, and before it grew irremediably distorted. For some reason Fate had destined us to cross Frank's path and become part of his life. I wondered what he had needed from each of us. What had we contributed to him? And what had he contributed to our development? I knew for me he had provided the *environment* in which to grow if I so chose, especially spiritually and psychologically. And his daily schedule set a superb example of *disciplined* writing. For him I had emphasized relationship, and my strong background in English had helped in partnership as his own gifts of writing and memory waned.

The museum director, David McFadden, had been about to turn down this project, I learned that afternoon when Bob and I met with McFadden, program director Vicente Martinez, and a museum librarian. Everything changed after they'd heard the new "plan."

"We've got a winner here!" Bob said.

"In Taos this is bound to go over big," Vicente agreed. "But we don't have room for it in our schedule until November."

"That's all right," I said. "I'm not rushing into things these days. And the other two women know nothing about this bright idea yet."

"That's *your* problem!" the three men chorused.

In parting McFadden congratulated me. "You've obviously put a lot of thought into this."

"Why, y . . . y . . . yes. Yes, indeed!"

Ann agreed over the phone both to participate in the second of the series and to join Rose and me at lunch next day. I knew Rose less well but suspected she would be more reticent about participating and not overly enthusiastic about Ann's presence at lunch. I therefore simply invited her to lunch. A few months earlier I'd sent Rose a poem Frank had written about her. She had sent me a thank-you note asking me to be her friend.

After a slow start, with Rose arriving fifteen minutes late and obviously taken aback by Ann's presence, the lunch turned out to be wonderfully cathartic. We all looked sharp: Ann in a straight salmon-colored dress with brown boots; Rose in a forest-green shirt and tight green pants with a loose red overblouse and brown boots; myself in a long purple skirt, matching overblouse, and dress-length deep purple vest with dark green shoes.

It stunned me to learn Rose's birthday is three days after mine. She is Libra with Cancer rising; I am Libra with Cancer moon. Ann's sun is in Cancer. Frank had four planets in Cancer and always had been drawn to Cancers. I got along with his girlfriends because of my Cancer moon. I hadn't expected a Libra connection.

At the end of our luncheon I said, "I think Frank is watching over us because he feels sorry for all the trouble he caused the three of us! Too bad we didn't have a hidden tape recorder here today. Then we could simply play it and *really* give them their money's worth in November."

They laughed, a little nervously. We would never completely trust each other. No one had brought a recorder, however.

Earlier, over my plate of Southwestern meatloaf, I had told Rose, "We need to do this partly to set old stories straight for future biographers. For instance, both Ted DeGrazia, the Tucson artist, and Frank have repeated the same story to me about you throwing that Thanksgiving turkey at Frank, but I've never heard your version of what happened."

"You surely haven't! But you printed it anyway—all wrong—in your chapter for that book *Frank Waters: Man and Mystic*."

"I don't remember including that story," I said, blushing. "The piece was about interpreting Frank's dreams."

"Yes, I know it was, but you included that incident too. Barbara Sherman showed me the chapter. It wasn't a turkey. And it wasn't Thanksgiving. It was Christmas Day of 1963. We'd opened our presents at my house, and Frank hadn't gotten me a Christmas present. This was a blow. Then he had rushed right off with that agent of his I never liked."

"Bart Fles?"

"Right. Terrible man. They spent *all Christmas Day* watching the Deer Dance and I don't know what all."

Frank said she'd accused him of having a homosexual affair with Fles, but this hardly seemed the time to press the issue. The three of us Fates were on a simpatico roll.

"By the time they got back to my house, our company already had arrived, and I was entertaining them alone. I was busy making drinks in the kitchen when Frank walked in. Everything came together and overwhelmed me. The way he had ruined the whole day for me—no Christmas present, not being there even on *Christmas Day*, not helping. Well, I took this bottle of Scotch I'd been holding, and I lifted it over Frank's head and began pouring, and I poured until the *whole thing* was empty," Rose said with her slight Texas drawl but impeccable manner.

"He was gasping and choking—it probably could have blinded him for life, but I wasn't worrying about that then—and his clothes were soaking wet, of course. He went tearing through the house past our guests, to get some dry clothes, you know. They didn't know *what* had happened."

"That's probably how different stories got started," I said. "Wasn't there something about a broken windshield too?" Ann had claimed Rose shattered it with a hammer.

"Yes. Yes, there was. I went outside to get into my car and leave. And there sat Frank's car. I thought to myself, now, here's something that still needs attending to. So I picked up this log. And I lifted it high above the windshield. Just then my daughter Mindy came running out of the house and she shouted, 'Mother! Don't do th—' Right *then* is when this big old log came smashing down on his windshield. She was too late!

"Later I passed Frank on the road driving with his head stuck way out the open car window beside him. Trying to see, you know. It did look rather dangerous. But kind of humorous at the same time, the way his head was stretched out so far sideways to the left."

Andrew Dasburg, a noted Taos artist present at this incident, ate dinner afterward at Taos Inn with Bart Fles. Feeling "contrite and embarrassed," Frank joined them.

Bart Fles, whose wife had recently deserted him, shrugged. "You're no different from the rest of us, Frank. It happens to us all."

Dasburg added, "Wine and women! You and I've had no luck with either of them, Frank."

In his last manuscript, Frank changed Andrew's quotation from the way he usually quoted Andrew to read, "Wives and women! I've had no luck with either of them." This way only Andrew's failings were recorded. Frank's "turkey incident" also was somewhat different from Rose's.

As we entered the house, Rose, inordinately jealous of all my friends, hurled at me the cocktail shaker. Before I could recover from this surprising welcome, she rushed to the oven, removed the browned turkey, and flung it on the floor. She then dashed outside the house and threw stones through the windshield of my car in the driveway. What an exhibition, what a mess it was! Broken glass and spilled liquor over the living room, turkey and dressing spread over the kitchen floor! Dasburg and Fles fled to the Taos Inn, where they ate their Thanksgiving dinner.

After more than thirty years of this story being represented from only a male point of view—particularly that of a novelist—Rose's version seemed a blow struck for all downtrodden women.

And trod upon we did appear to have felt in the past, we three Fates at our notable luncheon.

I said to Rose, "When you sat next to me and my friends at Jacquelina's Restaurant this summer, you said you'd written your own version of the barranca trip to Tarahumara country. It was far different from Frank's. That might be perfect to speak about in the lecture series."

"Yes. I wrote it up, all right. It tells a lot more about all the *dangers*. We could have died there. He didn't put those parts in *Pumpkin Seed Point*. I tried to keep it as humorous as possible, though. I wrote up my version without Frank knowing about it and sent it off. He was there when it came back. There's nothing wrong with rejection slips. He had plenty of rejections himself. But he sure was mad about me writing something.

"'What's *this?*' he said, holding up my article.

"'It's my version of our trip to Tarahumara country. I should be able to have my say too.'

"'*I'm* the writer in this family,' Frank said, flinging my manuscript across the room onto the floor like it was trash."

"See? That's the I-centeredness of his Leo sun and Aries moon," I said. "It took him a long, long time to realize there are *two* I's in a relationship, and the key pronoun is *we*, not *I*. A few years ago his niece said to me, 'I have always felt that Frank took from those closest to him more than he *gave*.'"

"Oh, he had an Aries moon?" Rose said, as if her attention had been sidetracked. "I didn't realize that. They're the infants of the zodiac."

"They're also aggressive," I said. In my opinion, Frank disliked aggressive people because they reflected his own unacknowledged shadow side. This hidden side made him passive-aggressive, and it usually came out only at home. No one realized it existed unless they spent a lot of time with him. When I pointed this out once to Dr. Charles Adams, he said coldly, "We don't *know* that Frank Waters. We know only the Frank Waters glimpsed in his books."

You could tell he didn't want to hear another word about the real Frank Waters. It's like the woman who told me, "I'm in the midst of reading his magical *Pumpkin Seed Point.* And you tell me Frank Waters likes to eat *corned beef* and *cabbage.* In a place called the *Iron Mask.* Spare me any more details that might send me crashing to earth." I guess I was supposed to say he lived on ambrosia, honey, and nectar like the rest of the Olympian gods.

"I think Frank was just plain narcissistic," Ann said in her deep, rich voice. "He was just like my first husband, a doctor. Frank's mistress was his writing. Dave's was his career, his fancy car, and his golf game. They put everything into these things and had nothing left for relationships. Frank put all his sexuality and sensuality into his writing. Then he expected the woman he was going with to sustain the sexual aspect, to carry the sexual impetus of their so-called relationship.

"And he didn't want any responsibility for kids, or anyone else, really. He was good with kids if he wasn't responsible for them. He was good with animals too. Once he went out in a rainstorm to bring in a horse for my nephew to ride. He remembers that to this day. Frank had no responsibility for raising my kids, so he liked them. And they kidded him out of his bad moods and teased him a lot and were playful with him. He used to say about Lolly, his favorite and the most sensitive, 'She can read my mind; I don't even need to talk to her.' He'd come over to dinner wrung out from reliving all that old family stuff while piecing together *Pike's Peak* out of his trilogy. He was drinking too much, carrying around those little pint bottles. We picked him up better than any alcohol and put him back together again. I think we brought *joy* back into his life."

"He hated my kids," Rose interrupted. "Said they were spoiled. Maybe they were. But he could at least have been decent to them and given them the time of day. I guess he did kind of get to like Mindy."

"He liked Mindy very much," I said. "You know fame and other people falling all over him had their effect on Frank too. When Caitlin Thomas was married to Dylan Thomas, she said, 'With all that flattery and adulation he seemed to forget my existence altogether.' On a smaller scale Frank used to act that way toward me whenever he gave a speech, or sometimes at a person's house. He would act like that at John Manchester's house, for instance."

"Of course. John flattered him unmercifully," Ann said. "He would give these *grand* dinners with Frank as the star attraction. John hated me. Once he narrowed his eyes and said with pure *venom* in his voice, 'I'm the biggest threat you have.' Around John, Frank would often act just like him. Frank could be so *snotty.*"

"Yes, he could be," I said. I see that same word connected with him in my own journals. "And his poor-boy complex made him vulnerable to anyone who acted *grand*—like Mabel Luhan or John. John treated me somewhat the same as you, Ann—only more gingerly."

"Really? He was always pretty nice to me," Rose said, smoothing back stray strands of her long, bright-red hair. "I will say I was not ready for another marriage when I met Frank. I'd just come from a physically abusive marriage to an alcoholic. The problem with Frank was so much of the time he made me feel *invisible*. Like on our 'honeymoon' trip to Tarahumara country. He didn't treat me like a bride at all. He ignored me. Or he got mad at me."

"I think only a therapist could live with Frank for a long time," I said. "It took so much *work* to get through to him."

Ann agreed. "Yes, he never wanted to get down to the real nitty-gritty and discuss an issue. He'd close everything off with his favorite phrase, 'We won't go into that.'"

"God, yes! *'We won't go into that.'* And *'I wouldn't do that if I were you.'* And *'No'.* Those were his three favorite sayings. I called him Dr. No. And I told him God wasn't going to let him go until he learned about *relationships.* 'He's going to see to it that you finally get it *straight* this time around,' I'd say. This kind of tickled Frank and made him laugh. I really believe, though, that fouled-up relationships were part of his negative karma from other lifetimes and that this still needs perfecting in another lifetime."

As I paused to sip my wine, Ann interrupted, "You know, this all reminds me of a play I'm reading for my drama class. It's Arthur

Miller's *After the Fall*. He wrote it after Marilyn Monroe's death, and it's just what we've been talking about—a man struggling with failed relationships, and awareness. He's afraid he can't love. And he makes all his women—except his mother—feel uninteresting and ashamed of themselves and invisible, as if they don't exist."

"Sounds familiar. I'll reread it," I promised. "It's important that we make our own contributions known while we can. Hero-worshipers can be so obtuse. Like this person who came into our home and said, 'I assume *Frank* hangs all the art work.'

"'Why would he?' I said. '*I* hang all our paintings.'"

Rose said, "I know exactly what you mean. During our marriage I kept my house and Frank kept his. People would come into my house while he was there, and they'd compliment *him* on its beauty, and he would accept the compliment for *himself*, never acknowledging me at all."

I nodded vigorously. "Just the other day someone said to me, 'I suppose Frank sold his papers to the University of New Mexico himself and made all the arrangements with them for the Frank Waters Room there, and all.'

"'No, he didn't,' I said so bluntly the man blinked. 'I did.'

"And then I went into this whole song-and-dance that everyone should *know* by now. Several times before his death I had to remind *Frank*, as a matter of fact. He got to thinking it was a good idea for him to have done all this stuff, including starting the Foundation, which he pooh-poohed like the rest of my ideas, at *first*. Luckily, I have the documentation. One of the main things I've learned from this marriage to a successful man is that she who sits around like a little mouse waiting for her due never receives it. But what I'm most interested in is the *history* part. We need to straighten out and spread the *truth* while we still can, whether it's about the houses Frank really lived in and slept in or the state of his shadow or contributions to his success or the movie star he was said to have married but didn't."

"Right on!" Ann exclaimed, half raising her fist in an enthusiastic gesture.

The irony of all my wasted breath was that at this very moment she still thought Frank had rewritten *The Woman at Otowi Crossing* because of knowing her! Ann had met him in the summer of 1966 after he returned from teaching a course at Colorado State University. He had sent the manuscript off before he met her and had signed a contract with Swallow Press on May 5. It was published on October 29, 1966, when he barely knew her. But he did sign her book "To a woman at another crossing." Terry Tanner's bibliography of Frank's works has excellent documentation for such dates, as well as many fine letters from Frank to publishers and agents that show the endless battles he fought for acceptance of his work. It proves Rose's point about rejections too, for it substantiates that *Otowi* alone was rejected by John Farrar; McGraw-Hill; Knopf; Little, Brown; Viking; Doubleday; Holt, Rinehart and Winston; William Morrow; and others. When Frank did revise the book in the mid-'80s, he expanded upon the male scientist's character, not that of the female protagonist.

Once in print it became a perennial favorite and, as detailed elsewhere here, was presented in 1995 as an opera in St. Louis. Movie rights have been sold to a Santa Fe producer. Already it has more than fulfilled Frank's hope "that the novel will go down easily, like a sugar pill, so that its implicit meanings will dissolve and begin to work. In other words, that the book will not be immediately exhausted but take hold of the imagination."

In this same letter, written to Alan Swallow April 7, 1966, Frank explains himself better than his Three Fates could possibly hope to do. "We all live two lives, separated by the psychical Iron Curtain that makes us all schizophrenic, but they meet and blend in our daily actions as plain people."

The minds of writers, and perhaps all creative persons, tend to get stuck on the far side behind this Iron Curtain. Frank certainly was there much of the time. White Bear's wife thought Frank had "crazy spells" while living on the Hopi Reservation. Then he was not a "plain" person. He was on the far side. Susie said he "had the habit of not being there for you when you needed him," such as at her mother's burial when it went awry. Frank had already left. He was on the far side. He was not as often as most a "plain" person on the near side. This could be a problem for those close to him. The glory and the wonder are that we have all his matchless books and insights from the far side.

A second Ann-created myth is her claim that "socially Frank wanted me to become another Mabel Dodge Luhan for him." In reality, Frank had already had his fill of the social life *and* the likes of Mabel. Moreover, he thought Ann and Mabel were very different persons.

"Ann came here from California thinking she could fill Mabel's shoes," he said, "but those were big shoes to fill—too big. Not even by moving into Mabel's husband's house could Ann pull this one off."

Over coffee Rose said to me, "I can't understand why you don't feel hostile toward us. It seems so strange that you've brought us together."

"Isn't this often a Libra's role? You should know, being a Libra yourself."

"Why, yes, yes it is," she replied in surprise.

"You others smoothed the way for me. Like Janey picking apples with Frank to make a living after they'd 'gone broke'—and baking all those apple pies when she didn't turn out to be a good apple-picker. *I* couldn't have done it. They would have hated my apple-picking *and* my pies." I laughed. "Fortunately, by the time I came along Frank had *had* it with picking apples."

"You don't know what a load this conversation has taken off my mind," Rose continued. "Sometimes I've felt so guilty, like the failure of our marriage must have been all my fault. It amazes me to learn that you both had problems with Frank, even though Ann never married him. It wasn't just me! It's such a *relief.*"

"It's good grief therapy for me too. You're asking for trouble when you place a departed one on an altar and only *worship* him. That's not how it was, especially if you regarded him as a *man* rather than as an idol right from the start. Everything was not per-

212

fect, and I make myself twice as much grief if I mistakenly remember it that way," I said.

Rose agreed. "I saw him as a man too."

"*Most* of the time I did," Ann said. "When I got uptight and into trouble was when I didn't."

"It won't be hard to speak in this lecture series if we speak truly from our hearts. It won't be all good that we say, of course."

"That's a big relief to me," Ann said.

"But it won't be all bad. Most of it won't be about the bad parts. We can fill in with reading about Lawrence's 'Three Fates,' from Frank's unpublished manuscript, and from mine if we need to. Frank was put on our paths—and vice versa—for a reason. *That's* what we want to emphasize. When I spoke in Boulder this past February, his helpful spirit was much present, strengthening me when I needed it. Besides providing me with an environment for growth during our years together, Frank's presence consistently gave me this spiritual and mental and physical strengthening. It is the ultimate gift that continues past his so-called death.

"To repeat a toast you once made, Ann: 'Here's to the man who brought us together!'"

19
If I Were You

She is a very together person
if you don't count
the missing parts
the notches in his gun
the holes in her heart.
— Diana Huntress

Struggling for *we* awareness is usually hardest for men, including those in therapy. It is easier for a woman to learn *I* awareness than for a man to learn *we* awareness, for we live today in a basically I-centered culture. A male most often separates early from the feminine to become a masculine *I*, whereas a female continues to bond with her feminine parent or the feminine without stigma, thus forging a *we* from the start. Each sex plays games that correspond to its own orientation. He wants to play *I*. She wants to play *we*. I wanted to play "The Family Game." Frank wanted to play "Follow Your Leader or He'll Scalp You."

One aspect of this difference in perspective could be glimpsed in a *National Geographic* interview with artist Andrew Wyeth. "Do you think I'm selfish?" he asked his longtime model Helga Testorf.

"Yes," she replied, "but you call it love."

The so-called games get more complicated when I am you, in my perspective, or you are I. How different my autobiography would be if I had let Frank's eight little words "I wouldn't do that if I were you" stifle me and keep me low woman on our totem pole.

"I'm thinking of taking a sabbatical from teaching to get a master's degree in journalism," I told him in 1977.

"I wouldn't do that if I were you," said Frank. "Journalism is so noncreative, just like teaching."

"Hemingway said it was a big help to one's writing *if* you got out in time. And you were a journalist for a time at the old *Taos News*."

"You know what I think of Hemingway."

"I'd like to get a second master's degree, this time in counseling," I said in 1985.

"I wouldn't do that if I were you."

"Now that I'm retired and have my degree in counseling, of course I want to start my own practice," I told him in 1988.

"I wouldn't do that if I were you. You've got enough to do around this house."

Like a stuck record I continued to remind him, "You are *not* I." It went in one deaf ear and out the other.

Others benefited when I ignored this limiting litany.

"I'm thinking of buying Arnold an electric lawn mower to get him started in the lawn mowing business," I said one summer. "He can repay me."

"You like to play the *Patrona*, don't you? I wouldn't do that. I wouldn't get involved with our Spanish neighbors this way."

"I think the Bay Foundation will come through with some money for Joseph Concha's project if I write the grant for him," I said another summer. "He doesn't have the faintest idea how to go about it."

"I wouldn't get involved with the Pueblo this way if I were you." And he didn't. But ever after Joseph gave Frank full credit for obtaining this money grant.

Later on I said, "I'm going to call your niece and arrange a luncheon to get you two back together again. Ten years of not speaking to your only close relative is enough."

"I wouldn't do that."

"I feel that I can sell your papers and letters to a more appropriate university and for more money than John Gilchriese is arranging. We'll still pay him a commission, and it will be larger," I said in another inspired moment.

"I wouldn't do that if I were you."

In retrospect the "games" can seem amusing. Yet tiredness overwhelms me when I see how much energy we expended on them. They are one thing I am relieved to be without. One of Frank's favorites was that old Indian moccasin game called "Scare the Shit Out of Barbara." This game ended while I was studying such tactics in my counseling courses. Frank had long been in the habit of sneaking up behind me when my mind was occupied elsewhere. It scared the living daylights out of me to have him speak straight into my ear unexpectedly.

One morning as I daydreamed while washing breakfast dishes, he yelled in a piercing tone that seemed to shatter my eardrums, *"Have you seen my black pencil anywhere?"* I used these charcoal pencils on my eyebrows; when he couldn't find his, there was only one culprit.

My arms flew up out of the soapy water. White bubbly soap drops scattered over the kitchen window above the sink, across the curtains, and down my arms. Shaking, I turned to face him.

"Oh, sorry," he said with a self-satisfied look on his face. "I thought you heard me coming."

"How can I possibly hear you coming when you deliberately make no sound? I've asked you repeatedly not to scare me like this. When you aren't *trying* to do this, I can always hear your footsteps or cane. When you sneak up like a moccasined Indian, it really frightens me."

To my surprise, a big smile beamed across Frank's face as if he were inordinately pleased with himself. This was such an unexpected reaction that I stared deeply into his eyes, my own growing larger and full of enlightenment.

"To you that's a compliment, isn't it? Why, it must be your Indian heritage!" I exclaimed in wonder, as if a lightbulb had turned on in my head. "You're *proud* of being able to sneak up behind me with the same skill used by your Cheyenne Indian ancestors. This is the only way today that you can demonstrate this ancient skill!"

Amazingly, Frank flushed with embarrassment and broke eye contact. Talk about taking the sail out of his wind! Now that I knew what Frank was up to and why, the game held no reward for him. He never played it again. Interestingly enough, one of his fans dismissed this play as "instinct, not a deliberate game."

The grocery store was the setting for one of Frank's more obvious passive-aggressive encounters, or "games." The stuff of movies, I called it "The Kill-Barbara-with-a-Shopping-Cart Caper." We were standing in Safeway at the checkout counter, where our empty metal shopping cart behind me was supposed to be shunted off to the left. Instead, from behind, Frank pushed it straight ahead at me as I stood writing a check to pay for our groceries. He hit me with the cart, making it difficult for him to proceed. Nevertheless, he kept on shoving with all his puny strength.

"Frank! You're hitting me. Stop!" By this time he had shoved me past the counter, where my checkbook and purse lay abandoned.

"Stop, Frank! You're running me down!"

"You're running over your wife, sir," said the checker.

"What's the matter with you?" I protested after he finally stopped. "You could see what you were doing, and feel it too."

"Well, yes, I could. But I thought we should get this cart through to the front of the store right away."

"He's just a fun-loving guy at heart," I reassured the clerk while checking out my bones.

Brushing off my suede suit, I muttered to Frank, "You need a lifetime course in how to treat a wife properly."

"Oh, you're off on *that* tangent again," he replied, throwing the ball back into my court.

Often I have to laugh when reading in my journal of the tricks that made up the "Waters Treatment," as Ann Merrill called Frank's psychological abuse. Yet I always recognized it when I saw or heard it. Recording events in a journal gives one more time and perspective to evaluate whether or not a situation calls for corrective action. If we aren't aware of circumstances threatening to our mental well-being, we won't find necessary solutions. And the abuser will grow more abusive with time. Here is a definition to keep in mind: "A woman is being abused if she is belittled, verbally attacked, encouraged into dependency, discriminated against, lied to, cheated on, or discouraged in any way from growing into her full capabilities as a woman and a human being."

One can live with "no" and work around it. Not to be tolerated is "I wouldn't do that." By definition this phrase constitutes psychological abuse. As one way of halting such abuse, Betty Newlon, one of my counseling professors, advocated saying in a controlled tone of voice, "That is not an appropriate remark." Frieda Lawrence could have used this saying, which stood me in good stead; speaking of her husband, she told a friend, "In our lives when we are with other people, he makes me absurd and makes me ashamed. He does not mean the things he says, like no decent woman in England having anything to do with me, but he says them and I don't know what to do about it. If I answer him, it's worse. If I don't answer him, that's bad too but it's the best I can do. So I sit and stare at him like a silly dummy and people think that what he says is true or that I have no feelings, that I'm just a dumb beast as some of them say."

On the long drive to Taos late one May I gave myself a figurative pat on the back for using this "inappropriate remark" ploy at the right time instead of wishing later that I had said it. As we said our farewells to the Gilchrieses in Tucson, Frank told John and June, "I'll be working hard on my writing all summer."

"Don't you do too much this summer, Barbara," cautioned June. "Take it easy for a change. You work too hard taking care of Frank."

Frank snapped, "Oh, she'll waste the summer again on all her usual *worthless projects.*"

For once I had the presence of mind to intone at the right time and place, "I do not consider that an appropriate remark."

In a composed voice I then went into a brief summary of my worthwhile projects. John interrupted with his booming laugh: "Enough, enough! Stop picking on the poor girl, Frank. You had better appreciate what you've got. You've never had it so good."

Burnie, my Tucson hairdresser, said once, "Don't tell me you two old farts are still playing the same games the rest of us play."

Yes, Burnie, while I hadn't thought of us in exactly those terms, to name just half a dozen we played "Pounce on Mousey," "Kick the Wife—Accidentally on Purpose," "Cough," "Gaslight," "Knock-Knock," and "Little Sir Echo." In the first, a Lawrence favorite, he says a dress was black if she says it was white. Everything is contradicted or dismissed. One quickly learns to line up one's documentation ducks in a tight row. The second game title speaks for itself. "Cough" is wiping out her statements altogether with intrusive coughing, faked strangulation, or mad rolling of the eyeballs. To gaslight is to drive a wife crazy by waking her from a sound sleep with a bright light shone directly into her face or by peremptorily turning off the lights and heat while she's reading. "Knock-Knock" is devaluing her creative efforts and privacy by interrupting her continually in her work space. "Little Sir Echo" is negation by making a partner's statements one's own. If she says, "This rain is terrible; it has killed all the rhubarb in the state," he will announce right after her, "Say, I hear the rain killed all the rhubarb in New Mexico."

Then there is the "Game of Silence," in which I at first participated with a will. Frank would fall silent after stating, "We won't go into that." And I would do the same, thinking, "I can outsilence anyone." To his regret, I came to realize silence is counterproductive to establishing a sound relationship.

Like Lawrence with Frieda, Frank resented the love I felt for my two sons. He too wanted to isolate his wife for himself. While I didn't get wine flung in my face, the following incident recorded in my journal on October 12, 1986, made me feel at the end as if I had mud in my eye. Movie star Leslie Ann Warren had optioned *The Woman at Otowi Crossing*. Later she let the option lapse, and the movie rights were sold to someone else. Judy is my daughter-in-law.

Over the phone I learned today that Judy and Bill have seen Leslie Ann Warren in lots of movies. We had never heard of her. Judy acted upset because I hadn't told her Warren has optioned one of Frank's books and will visit us on Sunday. Judy's shocked that I'm serving egg salad sandwiches to a movie star! Frank overheard our conversation and blew his stack. When Bill called all excited right after this, Frank really hit the ceiling.

"I don't want you telling people *my* private business!" he ranted.

"Your private business is mine," I said.

"It is not," he said.

"And my private business is eventually my son's in this case, since you have no direct heirs," I continued. "I miss not seeing Bill more often. You won't travel across town to see them, and you make them feel unwelcome here."

Frank replied, "You can go visit Bill by yourself any time you care to."

The upshot was that Judy and Bill came over to meet Leslie Ann Warren on Sunday, Judy's birthday. Frank was polite but noncommunicative. They seemed tense, with Judy talking nonstop until our guests arrived. She said she and Bill felt nervous about Frank. I said not to worry.

Then Leslie Ann arrived with her friends. She looked remarkably young and beautiful with her hair swept high in a ponytail effect. She has a nervous habit of wisping it continually around her face. Long earrings of turquoise and ivory dangled above her turquoise cutoff sweater and outsize beige pants. She acted totally down-to-earth, and giggled as she autographed Judy's birthday card from us. With Bill's camera, her friends snapped photographs of Bill, Judy, and Leslie Ann together. Soon Bill and Judy dashed off to a birthday brunch.

At dinner, when Frank and I were alone, we agreed that it had been a perfect day. I added, "The best part was having Bill and Judy over briefly, since family means so much to me."

Frank said, "It's enough to say it was a good day. Let's leave it at that."

Again, it is important to remember all of how it was. It wasn't just Adam and Eve in Paradise. In *To Heal Again* is a lovely painting of a grieving woman climbing a long zigzagging flight of stairs. This is the Trail of Grief. Several of these stairs to be recognized and surmounted are the negative ways we were.

"The awareness of sameness is friendship; the awareness of difference is love," said W. H. Auden.

If Frank had been on a deathbed and asked why we'd had our conflicts, paraphrasing Frieda Lawrence I would have answered him, "Such as we were, creatures striving to find our own unique Selves within a relationship, how could we help it?"

20
"Like Bogie and Bacall"

It is easy to detail the faults, the failings, the lapses. But one can scarcely bring alive for others the chemistry, the stimulation, the love, the always being there for each other. Looking forward each morning to the day's blessings, joy, and excitement. To sleeping together each night.

"I *miss* you," Frank would say. "I just don't sleep well when you're not here beside me."

"Ha! That will be the day—when *you* don't sleep like a log."

"I mean it. There's a big difference when you're away. And besides that, my feet get cold!" Then he'd laugh that rolling, half-smothered chuckle and hug me.

Even after ten months, it takes courage to list all that is gone, for we very nearly had it all, as it says in the song, like Bogie and Bacall. The warmth. The knowingness from past lives. The words of appreciation. Just enough fame for Frank so it didn't "destroy" him, as he feared it might. The acts, such as asking Ann Merrill to buy my birthday present when he couldn't get out of the house. And she did it for love of him. "Bless her heart," as Frank liked to say about people. And confiding in her, "I'm terribly worried. I don't know what will happen to Barbara after I'm gone." Ann had the good sense to remind him that I have always been my own woman, and frequently on my own.

Our sharing: books, birdwatching and feeding, learning, travel, eating out, picnicking, friends, money, philosophies, land, love of nature, animals, writing. Our sameness. Our needed differences. Our solitariness. Our respect for each other. Our clinging to each other, for there never would be enough time, with our late start. The sensuality. Working together creatively. Daring together. Cooking, suffering, and laughing together. Frank's curiosity, intellect, gentleness, kindness, kind as his great brown Deer Eyes. His generosity: he of all people saying to me and other amateurs, "If only *I* could write like that." Moreover, unlike many men, he never complained about paying a bill!

The stability. The completion. The balance. Most of all the contentment.

My three regrets loom large: I could not save him at the end; I was not with him sooner before the end; I was not at my best with the final bladder failure–diaper routine, and he said, "Your tongue is sometimes sharp, but your hands are always gentle." This last failure I will take to my grave, like a typical firstborn.

The Jungian idea of marriage is that one projects outwardly to a soulmate one's need for completion of inadequate feminine or masculine traits opposite one's birth sex. Then one must fall out of love with this projection and in love again with the real person. We perfected this in our own version of an "alchemical" marriage by merely holding our love in suspension as we made the difficult transition to reality, then falling in love all over again with the real *becoming* person each of us had married; this reunion in turn united us with the world—and beyond.

Andrew Elkins expresses a variation of this concept in a recent issue of *Western American Literature* when he writes, "Loving is a way of life one establishes by first recognizing one's self nakedly, which enables one to know the other, which initiates one into a loving relationship with the world. . . . Love, again, is a complex union of opposites which are really harmonized and whose union marries both to the world."

When I asked a young writer named Andrew if he had an "alchemical" marriage, he said, "Oh, you mean the turning-shit-into-gold marriage? Maybe we're already gold."

From the start Frank and I together were "already gold," with only a comparatively small amount of residue yet to be converted. Not being there day in and day out for the twenty-five years of our relationship, reading about the troublesome parts writ large, it may be hard for others to believe we nearly had it all.

Marcia Keegan said after his death, "In looking back at photographs I took of Frank over more than a quarter of a century, I suddenly realized that the years with you were his happiest! He glowed then; he was full of laughter, always smiling."

These words of Peggy Pond Church give me some comfort too:

> Nothing seems lost—light's changes, wind-swept silence,
> the arid land reflecting the shape of water.
> I gather pebbles feeling your quiet presence
> companion me still in all we loved together.

How much there is to tell him. I crave the *telling*. The sharing of conversation with my husband again, the teasing things, the little things. I'd like to tell him that I've bought more of those blue-and-white dishes he loved to eat from in the Danish Konditori on Gènoa Street in Mexico City's Zona Rosa during his 1970 stay; most of our old ones are cracked by now. And I bought new red geraniums for our bathroom, as I have each spring because it brought him so much delight. His two shamrock plants continue to thrive and flower white with rebirth as they have for decades. Frank does "companion me still in all we loved together."

I'd like to tell him about waxing the flagstone kitchen floor on my hands and knees, upon which I now strap large kneepads made for working men. Frank would laugh at the sight of knock-kneed me.

224

And he would love the million-dollar sheen. While waxing, I can feel his pride in laying this beautiful flagstone back in the '50s. Jimmy Morningtalk told me the other day that he and Patrocinio Barela, the local wood-carving genius, helped Frank and Janey do the oxblood guest-room floor. I'd known that Barela had carved the posts between our kitchen and living room, but not the rest he had done.

Imogene Bolls, our Foundation vice president, wants me to tape such information, for this whole house is a living museum. Frank even kept the turquoise-colored fish plates made by Angie, Frieda Lawrence's lover and third husband; this delights me. Every item has a story. Taping is quite a responsibility, but I am game. That I have begun to care enough to wax a floor again is an encouraging sign.

He would be happy to know that our house is especially protective and healing right now. I need our numerous mandalas: Frank's Cheyenne warshield above our bed, the snake uroborus carved on a cupboard door in our bathroom, hanging Indian baskets with the sacred maze motif of emergence, Indian pottery bowls, Carolyn Jongeward's tapestry weaving, *Alchemy II*, of a squared circle, our white bedspread afloat with lotus-like mandalas, the big cottonwood drum that Tony Reyna calls an "Indian piano." Just as helpful are the feathers, gourd rattles, peyote fans, kachinas, *santos*, and feathered Hopi *paho* sticks. Valencio Garcia's wood and reed crosses ward off evil, as does the small century-old cross nailed outdoors to the window frame of our old bathroom window. How can our Foundation go wrong? How can I not recover?

I'd like to tell him that protective entities still hover about, such as Star Road Gomez—or Strawberry Jim Suazo. Star Road's large framed photograph is the one hanging in the hallway outside our old bathroom. His black-and-white-striped blanket folds Taos Indian fashion low across his forehead, down around his face, across his right cheek and the edge of his mouth. It shadows his left eye, the intuitive side. He has sensuous full lips and a broken but imposing nose, and between his eyes a deep cleft courses straight up into a blanket fold.

His hypnotic eyes are *alive*. Immense pupils follow one in and out of the guest room, to the right or to the left. Stop to stare directly at him and he stares boldly back, his gaze penetrating to one's soul.

Ten years ago John Rainer told me this was a photo of Star Road Gomez, father of Tony Gomez. A few years later Tony Reyna and Jimmy Morningtalk said he was Strawberry Jim Suazo, who had sold strawberries. Though both names are special, for a time "Star Road" appealed to me most. I started calling a neighbor's friendly horse with a lovely white blaze on its forehead "Star Road." And I gave that name to a black death horse with a white blaze that I drew in memory of my friend Diane Stockman. Frank said, "When my time comes, I would like to go on a horse like that."

A strange thing happened not too long ago. Star Road caught my eye as I left our old bathroom. Instead of piercing me with his eyes, as is his custom, he stared with alarm into the guest room on his right. His face seemed to grow heavy with fear. Following his gaze, I walked all the way into the room. Once I was inside, the soft hum of a breaker switch hidden behind the charcoal drawing of mountains sketched by Nicolai Fechin warned me that something was overloading our electricity circuits in the oldest part of the house. Yet no lights were on. I smelled a wisp of smoke. The smell went away, returned, went away.

A few hours later repairmen discovered a short in the electricity line buried inside our adobe wall. Faulty old wiring had worn through. They replaced it and installed a more up-to-date circuit-breaker box. We were spared a tragedy, thanks to alert Star Road Gomez, or perhaps Strawberry Jim.

It might be more appropriate to begin thinking of this guardian as Strawberry Jim Suazo, for Suazo's relatives claim he is the real "man who killed the deer," not Doroteo Frank Samora. This seems to be true, in a sense. Frank Waters thought of the deerslayer as Samora, yet Suazo did the actual shooting of the deer in 1937. One of his two companions, Samora, resisted arrest and did not tell the whole truth about the incident. Strawberry Jim admitted his guilt, and through the influence of prominent local Anglos, he served no time in jail. In 1940 District Judge Taylor of Clayton sentenced Samora to one year in the state penitentiary. It's hard for some non-writers to comprehend that in fiction one character is often a composite of several persons, and an incident can be adjusted to illustrate theme. Thus Martiniano in *Deer* is a composite of at least three real persons involved in the same problem.

Since most persons have not read *Conversations with Frank Waters*, they don't realize Frank did the same thing with Maria in *People of the Valley*. He would have been surprised to hear the "theory," as I did recently, that Mrs. Quintana—whom Frank was not to meet until some years after writing this book—was the inspiration for Maria. In *Conversations* he affirms that Maria is a composite of at least three persons he'd known earlier.

People make up these "theories" without a bit of research. The Placita house in El Prado where Frank wrote much of *People of the Valley* is today a bed-and-breakfast called Hacienda del Sol. The picture window beside his writing-table space now faces a fence hiding a fast-food LotaBurger store that occupies the lawn where Susie learned to ride Tony Lujan's horse. The b-and-b owners were telling guests that Mabel Luhan had lived here and slept in a bedroom *they* built decades after her death! I told them how their house had been a squalid three-room adobe in the late '30s. Mabel never deigned to set foot in it, let alone sleep there. In exchange for rent Frank made it livable, cleaned up the grounds, and trimmed trees. This he did until Myron Brinig bought the place from Mabel. Brinig wrote a dozen novels, some bestsellers; one, *The Sisters*, became a hit movie starring Bette Davis and Errol Flynn in 1938. The truth makes a better story than "Mabel slept here," but these latecomers were settling for a puny myth instead.

Likewise, at the Laughing Horse bed-and-breakfast nearby, owners claimed a bogus '60s bathtub was the "sarcophagus" tub Frank describes in *Otowi*. He actually had used the famous old tub while renting this place from Spud Johnson in the '30s; it has made its way into his novel, and now into local mythology. Similarly, they called Spud's cubbyhole for printing equipment his "bedroom." Again history has been revised. Frank and Spud slept in the living room, the main room for everything.

It makes my hair stand on end to think of what people will be concocting after the last of us Hawkeyes are gone. It would be best then not to vent one's wrath as a ghost; today's bed-and-breakfast owners are actively *seeking* colorful ghosts, even inventing them if necessary—as is the case at Andrew Dasburg's old place. Wouldn't Andrew be furious! Or amused, possibly. But I for one shall drive anyone *mad* who tries to make our home into a bed-and-breakfast, over my dead body.

For dedicated biographers and to discourage mythmakers, I've compiled a list of eleven places Frank occupied in the Taos area. Somewhere he did the same for his Los Angeles living spaces. Here, it begins with Spud's place, followed by what is now Hacienda del Sol. Next came his two stays in the Tony House garage studio at the edge of Mabel and Tony's property. With Janey in 1947 Frank lived in the upstairs middle apartment at the Harwood Library on LeDoux Street, and on Lobo Mountain in the "Tower Beyond Tragedy." They later rented Ralph Meyers's house on the curve approaching Los Cordovas east of the stream on the north side of the road. Our upside-down, backward barn door with the sunburst came from there. Frank went to California when Janey went to Tucson in 1947; upon his return in 1949 he moved into Nicolai Fechin's studio. Eya, Fechin's daughter, remembers Janey as being there with Frank; he denied this. She may have visited him there; her horse was pastured where Fechin Inn stands today. Frank next lived part time in Rose Woodell's house on Brooks Street during the early '60s; the rest of the time he lived here in our Arroyo Seco house, where he'd been living on and off since the early '50s. After splitting up with Rose, for a time in winter he moved into a rooming house and stayed there in a room above what is now the Apple Tree Restaurant on Bent Street.

No wonder Frank was ready to set a spell by the time I came along. At the Frank Waters conference in Boulder, his old friend Joe Gordon said in his speech, "In my opinion the search for a sense of place is one of the most persistent and compelling themes in Frank Waters's work, and I would add in his life."

I wish Frank could know that here in Arroyo Seco, where he found his "landscape of the heart," as Joe expressed it, our first writer's studio will be ready for May occupancy. We are going forward in our own creative fashion. When he worried about me in front of Ann, Frank may have pictured me as a penniless Baby Doe Tabor driven nutty as a fruitcake by living alone in a shack. "Hang on to the Matchless!" her formerly rich husband had said about his mine. And so she froze to death there on Fryer Hill outside Leadville. Frank and Naomi took her fresh oranges from California a month before her death. I am not Baby Doe. Like her, nonetheless, I shall hang on to our matchless home and land here in Arroyo Seco. It is my salvation, especially this spring. Janey loved this place too. Perhaps the positive spirits of us all are helping to make it the sanctuary it is today, a living "landscape of the heart" for many.

Most of all I wish Frank could know that the opera made of his book *The Woman at Otowi Crossing* was a smash hit at the St. Louis Opera in June 1995, just twelve days after he left us. He wanted so much to be there, and came so heartbreakingly close. The agony of his absence still tears at my insides. Going there without him was the second-hardest task I shall ever have to perform, second after saying good-bye. He was there in St. Louis, I suspect. And they gave him a standing ovation. But it wasn't the same. Sitting next to me on the plane out of Albuquerque was a man who had lived in tiny Mora, New Mexico, in the '30s when Frank did. This bizarre coincidence was as comforting as anything could be, which it was probably meant to be—reminding me of Frank's closeness in spirit.

How he would have loved that opera! Frank said from the start that it would be a hit. The dramatic two-act presentation, Stephen Paulus's rippling music, Joan Vail Thorne's poetic libretto, and the antlered deer chorus had to stir the universe. Frank's seven deer were present at the beginning, middle, and end, a fitting completion cycle for both opera and man. Although Helen wore a baggy housedress and sloppy moccasins—not at all what Edith Warner wore in photographs—and Jack in Act One looked as different from most Southwestern men as Donald Trump, the lead voices of Sheri Greenawald and Kimm Julian were outstanding. Greenawald in particular did a superb job of consistently reaching the high notes she had requested from Stephen for a role that kept her singing in nearly every scene.

The *Santa Fe Reporter* affirmed the opera's success when its reviewer wrote, "The lavish production at the intimate Loretto-Hilton Center strung together striking scenes of outer, melodramatic conflict with inner, mystical visions, drawing the audience into a dramatic musical vortex."

Now we are agitating for the opera to come to Santa Fe, where it belongs, as it is set nearby at Los Alamos. Much of my grief was transformed during my pilgrimage to share in another woman's spiritual journey, as envisioned by the man I love. The opera, and book, should help other troubled women as well.

A month before Frank's death I bought a long black dress, oddly enough, to wear to this gala summer opening.

He would have enjoyed Palm Sunday this year, or at least hearing about how the old Arroyo Seco church looks. It was as much a historic occasion as a religious one. Miraculously, the church is suddenly being reborn this spring. One hundred and sixty-two years old, *La Santísima Trinidad* wears a new rust-red Easter bonnet—a metal roof—after workers hauled away 150 tons of dirt from the old rooftop. They also removed eight dump-truck loads of pigeon droppings. A community dinner and raffle helped to provide roofing funds, which were augmented by private funds. Young volunteers on spring break from northern New Mexico schools helped remove debris and chipped away at the cracked outer coating of inwardly sound adobe walls. Every weekend locals volunteer for cleanup duty. By late summer, the doors of the renovated church should be open for masses, weddings, and passion plays.

One of the most interested restoration participants is Trudy Knox Healy, who with her husband Ed, donated $10,000 to our own Frank Waters Foundation. Her great-grandfather José de Gracia Gonzales was the *santero* who painted the priceless altar backdrop, or reredos, here at *La Santísima Trinidad*. He also painted an altar screen at Las Trampas Church and the lovely one at Santa Barbara Church in Rodarte, among others. The latter is a classic, with its division into nine paintings, like the one in Arroyo Seco, rounded off at the top with cupids and flowers. With it goes the dedication, "In adoration by the slaves of Saint Barbara, this altar screen was completed on December 2, 1871 under the directorship of Fr. Ramon Medina."

Gonzales lived near Las Trampas for eighteen years. One of only sixteen *santeros* who painted in this area, he worked primarily between 1850 and 1871 but lived until 1901. Tradition has it that the impoverished local parish paid him for his work with a thirteen-year-old child from Mora named Atochita. For some time the terrified child bride, wrapped in a Rio Grande blanket, slept under their bed. That Trudy is here today attests to the fact that Atochita did eventually come out from under the bed. Trudy still has her Rio Grande blanket.

Our artist friend Marcia Gaiter lived across the street from the José de Gracia Church in Las Trampas. It appears to have been named after Gonzales, whose name is engraved on a plaque at its entrance. Our most prized painting done by Marcia is a version of the church's reredos. It was a joy to take Marcia back just a year and a half before her death to see her old friends in Las Trampas while she was staying with us to celebrate Frank's ninetieth birthday.

Trickster and I walk down to Arroyo Seco's old church in time for the blessing of the palms. I had attended a few religious plays here around 1969, but church services have not been conducted inside for over thirty years. Tying Trickster to the fence, which is about as much traditional religion as she can take, I sidle into the church and lean against its staunch walls with other pilgrims of the spirit. There are no chairs to sit on. I wear a checked lumberjack-type jacket, blue denim skirt, and black hiking shoes. All our Hispanic neighbors are dressed to the teeth. This is important to them. Acting nonchalant about clothing at such a sacrosanct time is disrespectful. Unless one is suffering from grief dementia.

Delia Varos, who used to do Frank's laundry when he lived alone, hugs me tightly. He thought much of her, with good cause. She is wearing a soft lavender dress and high heels; other women wear white suits, white-and-red suits, or blue suits. A group of shiny-faced boys stands next to me, almost splitting their sides with suppressed laughter when Father Vincent begins lecturing about asses. He eases into it quite gracefully, however, and defuses their laughter prior to biblical mention of these most excellent beasts of burden.

Afterward I stop off at the aging, half-sunken Penitente cemetery down the road from us. Dating generally from the early '20s, many of the cemetery's wooden crosses are now broken, bent, or destroyed. Dented plastic water bottles once used as flower holders lie scattered about amidst strewn plastic flowers and a rusted paint can. Trampled in the dust, one warped wooden cross arm reads cryptically, "Irene." Half of the Taos blue wooden picket fence surrounding the grave of Adolfo Quintana—"1889–1931: Rest in Peace"—has been smashed to the earth, probably by sheep and cattle that have left their calling cards. The marshy land too has taken its toll by canting remains at crazy angles.

On the other hand, Joe and Esmiria Duran's four headstones are still lovingly surrounded with green indoor-outdoor carpeting and a wrought-iron fence entwined with pink plastic roses. Several other headstones endure. The names on them are a soothing litany: Lagarda Garcia; Rosendo Fernandez and Nabor Martinez, both World War I veterans; Fabriciano Garcia; and Apolonita Garcia. The Old Ones come alive again with their headstone tributes: Maria Duran, "She Was the Sunshine of Our Home," and Maria

Eufemia Coca, who died in 1971 but oddly enough has four of the exact same words on her headstone that appear on Frank's monument boulder in our aspen grove: "We Will Meet Again."

The possibility intrigues me that one of her relatives may have consciously chosen these words from *The Man Who Killed the Deer*, and I may have been subconsciously drawn to choose these words from *Deer* for Frank's monument because of knowing this graveyard so well.

A chorale of meadow larks, lowing cattle, and sheep bells hymn Maria Eufemia's promise as caretaker Alex Montaño drives up to lecture me for trespassing. After learning I'm a "local," not a "destructive Anglo tourist," he grows hospitable and shares a touching anecdote. In 1992, when Penitentes were cleaning the grounds of their *morada* here, they decided to burn the cemetery's dry weeds nearest the meeting hall. Their fire erupted out of control and swept the entire cemetery. None of the wooden crosses and none of the headstones, not even the white marble ones, were burned or smudged, Montaño claims.

I find peace in this neglected cemetery, ringed now with fancy Anglo homes but surmounted by frosted mountains beneath layered turquoise and permeated with the lingering, meadowed fragrance of bygone days. My heart leaps up to Frank and to his own promise: "We will meet again. As equal parts of one great life." Then we will indeed have it all.

21
Lizard Woman

The Cocopah Indians say Lizard Woman covered the earth with beauty. From rock she made the grass and flowers, bushes and trees and mountains, valleys, and sand. All was covered with mist. God asked Spider to spin away this mist so He could see the beauty Lizard Woman had wrought. Spider spun the mists into clouds with hanging ribbons. Some clouds dropped to earth, spread apart, and became lakes, rivers, and seas. God looked at this shining new world and was pleased. It would be a perfect place for the humans, beasts, and birds He would create to inhabit it.

When God came down to earth, he found Lizard Woman curled in a circle around a mountain, her tail drooping down into a rocky canyon. She ignored God, for she was tired, hot, and cross. He commanded her, "Get busy and make this ugly spot beautiful at once!"

Lizard Woman scowled. She had a mind of her own. "This land is fine for me the way it is. I want this for my own spot," she said. "Just leave me alone. I've had a hard day!"

God was angry. Yet in as kindly a voice as he could muster, he said, "You have made a Paradise. For this I thank you. As your reward, this horrible spot shall be the Land of the Lizard Woman, just as it is. Here you must stay. Never shall you leave. And never shall it be as beautiful as the rest of the shining world. Here you shall have with you neither beast nor bird, grass, flowers, nor trees."

Back to the stars then God went, to cool off and to watch over the earth to this good day.

Frank began his first book when he was twenty-four after a horseback journey to Baja, a precursor to his long trip through the Sierra Madre a few years later. It was originally titled *The Lizard Woman*. His publishers changed its name to *Fever Pitch*, a title Frank disliked. He was grateful for his first publishing break and went along with them, once; he never allowed this to happen again. And he felt vindicated when Paul Foreman reissued the book in 1984 under its original title. This new edition was poorly executed, but it kept another book in print, which was always Frank's main concern and reward. Now some of Paul's friends plan to make a movie of *The Lizard Woman*. She endures.

Frank liked Paul and had confidence in him for a time. Reprinting this book, however, was not something Frank at first intended to let happen. He wrote later, "The book was my immature first novel, betraying faults I was hesitant to see exposed. This is false pride, of course; one is reluctant to admit early ignorance and ineptitude, as if a writer miraculously falls heir to competence in his craft without any preparation at all."

It took considerable discussion between Frank and me for the reprint to come about. I had begun typing his manuscripts after 1976, advanced to editing more and more, and ended by adjusting parts of *Brave Are My People* in 1993 when Frank's health was precarious. Having taught English grammar, literature, and creative writing for many years in addition to working on my own articles and unpublished manuscripts, I was qualified to do this work, both of us felt. Before teaching I had been an administrator at Union Carbide's Chicago computer center, so Frank's business battles fell on my shoulders too. From the start I had not wanted *Brave Are My People* to go to Clear Light Publishing in Santa Fe. We were to have our regrets that it did when they repeatedly failed to pay royalties and eventually went bankrupt. Likewise, Clear Light surely regretted having to deal with such a blunt person as myself. Whenever Frank wanted the boat rocked, suddenly *I* had free rein to rock it. He thought *Brave Are My People* was not his finest work but wanted it to see light of day after years of lying neglected in a file drawer. Frank wrote in my copy of this 1993 book about lives of famous Indian leaders, "Dear Barbara—Congratulations for this, your first book. It is really yours. Your work largely molded it, from the first manuscript, through the many proofs, to this beautiful format. I look for more books, including one on Don Burro, to follow it. Love—Frank."

His thoughtful inscription made me feel more sad than glad.

Back in 1983 it had seemed to me that an introduction to *The Lizard Woman* explaining what Frank currently perceived as its weaknesses would prove invaluable to young writers, to say nothing of biographers. Charles Adams agreed. And Frank finally did write an excellent foreword, as always, to this new edition. Despite its shoddy appearance, it is now a collector's item.

It embarrassed Frank in later years that as part of its framework he had created a functional narrator similar to one present in Joseph Conrad's writing, a weak device that the movie script of *The Lizard Woman* eliminates. The youthful author may not have consciously realized whom he was copying, for he had done a large amount of varied reading already, although his interest in classic literature was less than one would expect.

He claimed in later years that he avoided reading reviews of his work if possible, for he tended to brood about negative comments concerning him or his books. In 1985 he began rewriting *The Woman at Otowi Crossing*, for example, after Tom Lyon and others had criticized his weak development of the scientist character Edmund Gaylord. A revised edition appeared twenty years after the book had first been published. Frank also believed he himself should never criticize anything he had written. He considered his work a gift for which he should be forever grateful.

Despite some youthful hyperbole, he could always be proud of his fine descriptions in *The Lizard Woman*. When I read him the best parts to illustrate why this book should be reprinted, he marveled, "God! Did I write that?"

Frank really was not a narcissist, one who is completely ruled by his ego. Much of his ego was a sham and a shield erected to protect himself from the vicissitudes that beset writers and constantly hack away at their self-esteem. It was like whistling in the dark.

The words of writer Lawrence Powell's wife, Faye, often come to mind. When I interviewed her, she said, "Of course a writer has to have his ego—*lots* of it. He has to get his own way all the time.

"I have always been a shadow and an also-ran. I never had a career. I should have. But by the time I felt rebellious, it was too late to cry over spilt milk. I guess a happy old age is my reward. I would advise every woman to fight for a career."

One got the feeling that her ego had been given to her husband to buttress an incomplete ego of his own. It was as much of a sham or false front as Frank's, whose ego had been damaged by poverty as a youth. The ego was there, yes, but it was not as strong as it was made to appear.

In public most persons saw only the modest side of Frank. They thought this was his human side. I believe this public image was closer to his cosmic refined side and that only women close to him knew the human side. As D. H. Lawrence had sought a synthesis of spiritual and sexual love in both his work and life, Frank tried to combine the transforming cosmic experience and the human in his work and life, with varying success. His first book set up this recurring theme as well as a protagonist's process of psychically refining himself or herself. Clarissa Pinkola Estés writes, in the magazine *Magical Blend*, "Creativity is less the creating of things, but *much more* so the ability and tenacity to consistently use the tests, the trials and triumphs of one's life over many years' time, in order to become oneself, a true and living work of art."

Frank strove to do this, as do most of us, it is hoped. An interesting set of letters written in 1988 shows Rose Woodell, Frank, and me on our paths of becoming. Rose later said she wrote her letter because it upset her when Frank would no longer speak to her in public, as he had at first after their divorce. She may have been involved in another process too. And I feared there might be suicidal undertones in her note of urgency.

9/18/88
Dear Frank,

I feel this great urgency to make peace between [us] before another day passes.

Though I confess I am in the dark about what has caused your displeasure, I ask your forgiveness. Where I am now in my consciousness I must do this.

My granddaughter and I made a pilgrimage to Cripple Creek in July. That area is certainly a place of power. As I walked down the main street, I had a vision of a shy little boy holding his grandfather's hand, caught up in the excitement of the gold camp.

You cast a long shadow, Frank, and I believe you came here as a Teacher. Thank you for sharing a part of your life with me and my family.

God bless,

Rose

September 26, 1988
Dear Rose:

I would have answered your letter sooner, but we have just returned from Colorado Springs where I had to make two talks at Colorado College last Thursday and Friday.

I appreciate very much the warmth and spontaneity of your letter which as you say springs out of your unconscious. But please don't feel, even unconsciously, that I entertain any ill will toward you for any reason. Or feel, yourself, any guilt for anything.

And for goodness sake don't regard me as a teacher. I'm only, like you, a student learning the first lessons in the school of human relationships. We both have made some mistakes and have learned much from them, so must regard the time we spent together as a rewarding experience. For you and all your children

238

I have warm feelings of friendship and will always wish you the best.

I didn't get up to Cripple Creek, but am glad you remembered me up there. Now don't remember the past with any pain or displeasure. Feel at peace with yourself. It's the best we all can do in these days when all the world is in such turmoil. Peace and cheers.

All best,

Frank

September 26, 1988

Dear Rose:

I have been meaning to talk to you for my research, which you may have read concerns the effects on a woman's self-esteem of being married to a man considered successful in his field. I also think it's important, when you feel up to it, that some record be made of your perception of those years spent with Frank.

Now he has shared your letter with me although I am not sharing this with him. Frank is not an easy man to live with and never will be. His Leo sun self and shadow Aries moon have too often overruled his basic Cancer nature, if you're into astrology at all. What this boils down to is that he most often tends to be selfish for *himself* in personal relationships. I would imagine that you were not selfish enough for *yourself* during most of this relationship.

But you must have made an important contribution to his stifled sexual side, which he still never has adequately developed. His Leo egoism and Aries masculinity have kept him from being concerned enough or for long about how a woman feels. It also took getting a degree in psychotherapy for me to recognize his numerous subtle put-downs and not so subtle ones. You probably did not recognize even half of them, as I didn't at first. I've begun to commit the sacrilege of pointing them out to him now, however, and he can't help but see there's room for improvement with his record: four wives and several girlfriends.

According to Ann Pratt, my former landlady, you voiced the final "displeasure"—not he. He asked ("begged") you in her presence to get back together again but you declined. Therefore, it seems strange to me that you feel he was displeased with you. In a sense, this was a positive development of your own because *you* were being selfish for *yourself.* (He has always been cordial to you in public and never privately speaks badly of you.)

In a speech Frank gave Friday he said, "As a Westerner brought up on the belief of male supremacy, I did not acknowledge the influence of women. A woman's proper place was in the bedroom and the kitchen, and I was taught to repress any display of the feminine qualities of love, tenderness and compassion in my dual nature. It just wasn't manly." (Those are Cancer qualities, where four or five of his planets lie.) Then he went on to say Barbara is "patiently unlocking these qualities" in him and expanding his "inner perspective and spiritual growth." I think he was just putting on a show by saying that last stuff because I'm very *impatiently* T-R-Y-I-N-G. And it's frustrating even now.

I feel sorry for those of you who went before me, especially Janey. But also I am appreciative, for Frank's sake as well as mine, of what you others *did* accomplish.

And you, Rose, should feel very proud of that—never apologetic.

Barbara W.

Oddly enough, Frank and I wrote our letters on my birthday. Rose must have received them on her birthday, September 29. The ways of the gods are indeed mysterious.

Three big boulders in Frank's forward path were his shadow, his anima, and his mother complex. With four planets in Cancer, it may not have been possible to rise above the latter. Frank didn't have many big dreams in his old age. He considered important the three that I wrote up in *Frank Waters: Man and Mystic.* Here is the second:

The Struggle

As Frank enters a room, a woman rises from the right side of a bed situated ahead of him and to his left. Although she says no one else is in the room with her, Frank notices the bedclothes on the left side of the bed are heaped as if covering a figure. He reaches in with his left hand and feels a man's neck. Frank tries to choke him with one hand and deflect the man's revolver with his other hand. He does not know whether this shadow man will try to kill himself, or Frank, or the woman, who does nothing but stand aside passively. During their struggle the gun goes off and the man is killed, shot through the heart. Frank wants to run out and find the shadow man's accomplice or to run away. Instead, he decides, "I will accept full responsibility, call the police and wait until they arrive."

The symbols neck, heart, bed, and gun signal that this dream has much to do with a struggle over sexuality. Weapons are counterparts of the particular monsters with which we struggle. Two men are struggling in bed, not a man and a woman. At first the man in control is standing over the powerful hidden man, the shadow. Not wanting to embarrass Frank, in my interpretation I slid in only one sentence concerning this problem: "Conscience, masculinity, femininity, and sexuality continue to stew in a cauldron of doubt laced with guilt." The ideal for sexual orientation would be for one to go one's own individual way without judgment from others. How helpful to the psyche it would have been for society had we hewn to this ideal. How much simpler it would have been for a man in particular to go his feminine way, if he so desired, and to be in a couple with another man without stigma. In *Yellow Woman and a Beauty of Spirit* Leslie Silko states that in the old days at her home pueblo, Indians could go their own ways, women marrying women, men marrying men, dressing as they wished, for "marriage was about teamwork and social relationship." Silko writes, "In the old Pueblo worldview, we are all a mixture of male and female, and this sexual identity is changing constantly. Sexual inhibition did not begin until the Christian missionaries arrived."

When the masculine shadow fears that the feminine will overwhelm it, the anima is stifled. It winds up stunted and passive, like the woman in Frank's dream. The anima's passion cannot be given free rein for fear of what it will do. The anima will out, however. Its gift to posterity is its positive appearance in Frank's books. Those close to him have lived with its waspish, negative side. As Rose said, "He did not treat even a bride the way a woman is supposed to be treated." The only way he felt safe with a woman was if she was a whore to be discarded or a mother, the madonna. Strangely enough this whore-madonna complex threads its way through *The Lizard Woman*, where it is overtly personified in Arvilla, the protagonist's half-Indian lover and a "percentage girl." In addition, near the beginning Frank writes, "But she was a woman and Marston never forgave her that." We hear other echoes in this book of the resentment this young writer felt toward the array of feminine relatives swamping his masculinity before he left home. Moreover, Marston sees Arvilla momentarily as his wife, "a shadowy accompanying form, for the instant without appeal." Earlier he'd had a similar wifely vision of her that psychically foresaw Frank's desired version of marriage at the end of his own life. "It was simply as if he had already drained her of all new raptures and were basking in the dying glow of a passionless heat which was to hold him secure for all time."

In other words, coming full circle he was once again to find security with the mother, the madonna, this time in his desired state of Burnt Out Bliss. For what it was worth, at the very end of his life this was part of my contribution to him. Ann Merrill contributed solely to this mother role. Rose and I contributed also to the "percentage girl" aspect. Frank had to be referring to the sexual when he said he'd almost cut himself off "from the wellsprings of life" before I came along, for Ann had been simply mothering him between his relationships with Rose and me. Rose had put him in touch again with those "wellsprings" after the joylessness of being without Janey. But my work with him on a less limited, more well-rounded relationship was my main contribution, in my opinion; it helped him to develop in real life—not simply fiction—his anima, that feminine energy within a male that seeks to balance itself with his masculinity.

C. G. Jung, the originator of this term, experienced much the same difficulty in acknowledging his anima. During an interview with Esther Harding in 1922 he admitted to being afraid of women. He might well have been Frank Waters when he said, "A man must not let his masculinity be overwhelmed." In this view, to possess equal parts of femininity and masculinity is to be "overwhelmed" since the anima possesses exceptional power. Jung wrote, "In the Middle Ages, when a man discovered an anima, he got the thing arrested, and the judge had her burned as a witch."

David Tresen, in analyzing Jung's struggle, connected masculine distrust of the anima to fear of dependency and fear of delving into the unconscious. Insensitive treatment of females is characteristic of those lacking a fully developed anima. Jung had this problem, for he was raised in a traditional patriarchal society.

Frank originally saw in his wives the projected Salome/whore ("percentage girl") fragment of his anima. Because our marriage lasted longer than his others, in my case he ultimately experienced the projected mother aspect of his anima, with which he felt most comfortable. We clashed primarily when he consciously failed to give credit to the Sophia/wisdom aspect of his own anima and to my unfolding Sophia self; this he also refused to acknowledge in his three previous wives. They didn't have a clue as to what was really going on, or how complicated it was, so they bailed out and kept blaming themselves afterward.

In *The Ravaged Bridegroom,* Marion Woodman reminds women that we have our work cut out for us: "The fact remains, however, that the masculine bound to an obsolete patriarchal tradition experiences the emergence of the feminine as a threat. To disarm the masculine of its patriarchal fear of the feminine is thus crucial to releasing the creative dynamics of partnership." She goes on to caution, "To be psychologically free is to be confident in our own inner world, responsible for our own strengths and weaknesses, consciously loving ourselves and, therefore, able to love others."

On March 5, 1990, Frank wrote David Jongeward about the draining conflict of "ignoring the past, or of assimilating all its mistakes and faults without their burden of guilt." His last big dream included in *Frank Waters: Man and Mystic* indicates that he was working on the latter right up to the end but having some trouble with the "burden of guilt." In real life, he was also battling skin cancer.

The Wise Man

Under a vow of silence I have been spending two productive weeks alone in a monastery much like a Benedictine monastery I had stayed in for three days over thirty years ago in Colorado. I have been walking around alone, doing a lot of praying and being silent. I begin to realize, as I recall all my life, that I have selfishly allowed other people like my mother, sister, wives, friends to sacrifice themselves for myself. I see my overwhelming selfishness and what others have done to sacrifice so much for me.

I see that the coming out of all these realizations and memories repressed in my unconscious is the psychological aspect, while the physical manifestations of my selfishness are the skin cancers popping out all over my face. They are as deeply embedded in my flesh as this selfishness has been in my unconscious.

I meet once a day with an abbot whom I like. The sound of his voice still is vivid. He is middle-aged, between fifty and sixty. He wears a good suit and has a benign kindly face with a friendly smile. He does not wear glasses. This day at our meeting, I tell him of my realization. He agrees with me about my skin cancers representing my buried selfishness. And he warmly invites me to live in this monastery for the rest of my life. He is sure that if I enter the monastery and go into a period of begging forgiveness and give up all worldly life for the rest of my days, this worry and guilt will leave; and my skin cancers will clear up. He tries hard to persuade me to remain here forever.

"No," I tell him after thinking over this tempting offer, which at first half persuades me to stay. "I can't give up at this late stage when I'm ready to die. That would be a supreme last act of selfishness. I am going to live out my atonement for this guilt on the worldly stage where I have been acting. I can't just shuck it all and renounce my worldly life and forget it."

I like the abbot, but I think his solution to leave the world is wrong. We shake hands in friendly fashion. I tell him that I will leave in the morning and walk into town, toward community and interconnectedness.

The Lizard Woman is the story of Arvilla and Marston's grueling journey across the desert to a hideout where one of her boyfriends is holed up with gold ore that Marston is to assay. The hideout is located in the Land of the Lizard Woman, surrounded by a circular rocky formation resembling a lizard eating its own tail; it has a female face. Here Marston has a cosmic vision of the greater whole.

Years later Frank realized he had unknowingly tapped into a famous symbol of primordial unity from mankind's collective unconscious: the uroborus, a circle formed by a serpent biting its own tail. It represents "the wholeness and fullness of all space and time." It is nature's universal, cyclic return to the beginning. Referring to the Christian myth of the Garden of Eden, Frank postulated that in gaining rational thinking from the tree of knowledge man lost his intuitive awareness of cosmic unity and harmony. In his new foreword he wrote, "Yet this primordial wholeness is still retained in what Jung calls our 'collective unconscious,' its symbol of the *uroborus* emerging into consciousness through dreams, visions, and imaginary fantasies. Excessively rationalistic and materialistic, we have stifled the intuitive truth of how closely we are linked to all nature, the earth, waters and the stars above. The *uroborus*, to whomever it occurs as it did to me, offers the promise of universal unity that still lies within us waiting to be regained."

Lizard Woman is in me, part of my soul, just as she is part of everyone. She is watching over me, as I watched over Frank and helped him to see the female and the intuitive more clearly at the end of his full circle of life. At *La Vieja Loca* I bought a string of black, brown, silver, and lavender beads to hold my reading glasses. Attached was a silver lizard.

After Linda Ann and I had been in our car accident and were waiting on El Salto Road for the police, my lizard fell off. I searched for it, to no avail. A week later Linda Ann was helping a neighbor pack in preparation for a move to California. There on his kitchen counter she saw my silver lizard, its tiny circle attachment still intact.

"I know who that lizard belongs to!" she exclaimed. "*Where* did you find it?"

"My friend Cathy found it while hiking up El Salto Road," Grant replied.

"See? I *knew* Frank was with us that day," Linda Ann told me later over the phone.

The accident had been a "miracle" for her, she said. Her insurance settlement paid her rent for several months. I didn't see her for two more days, then called.

"Did you remember to get my lizard from Grant before he left?" I asked. "I want to make sure I get it back."

"Don't worry. I brought it home and put it in a jar and screwed the lid on *tight* so your lizard won't get away again!"

Now silver Lizard Woman is with me once more. At last she has found a lush space to replace her horrid dry home. When I told this story of the charm's return, a friend said, "Why, she is a hug from Frank."

22
Avanu

*"See that woman—Telesfor's wife?" Mrs. Concha points with
her chin. "She's the last Snake Woman."*

After a late morning start to Tucson one fall, Frank and I
stopped under a shady cottonwood near Española to eat our lunch.
As we started to leave, the motor of Frank's Ford burst into flames.
"Oh no!" I thought to myself. "Frank will *kill* me if his kachinas and
his portrait by Fechin go up in flames too!"

Every year I brought a few of our favorite treasures back and
forth to keep a sense of continuity between the two houses. Frank
"wouldn't do that if he were me," but he enjoyed the result.

Grabbing two full thermos bottles, I poured first orange juice,
then coffee over the motor's insides. The rest of the fire I smothered with Morgan's dog sheet that usually protected the back seat.

"I've never had anyone save a burning engine before," a mechanic said later. "Usually people panic and jump clear, letting the
whole car burn up."

It didn't seem necessary to tell him I'd saved it in panic. The
valuable Fechin portrait we had with us of Frank as a young man is
my favorite. We had duplicated it as our main Frank Waters
Foundation poster. Perhaps the motor was saved because we also

carried with us our sacred rattlesnake kachina. Kachinas are non-corporeal beings, Indians believe, that act as guides and go-be-tweens carrying messages from humans to the spirit world, and lessons and wisdom in return. Sometimes they are represented by humans, other times they appear in doll form. Made of cottonwood root painted black, our foot-high snake kachina wears brown boots, a kilt, arm and wrist bands, and feathers on his head. Crossed on his chest are two light-brown straps decorated with shells. In his hands and white mouth he holds a black-and-brown rattlesnake, as purified dancers do during the Hopi Snake Dance ceremonial to bring rain. Because it is such a sacred, powerful dance, snake kachinas seldom are carved or sold.

We also were carrying a rare black bowl from San Ildefonso Pueblo that had been signed by the famous potter Maria Martinez and her husband, Julian. Coiled around its shiny surface is Avanu, the feathered or horned serpent with lightning streaking from its mouth and rain clouds hanging above its undulating back. Avanu the great serpent who brings rain and water. It is one culture's Divine Serpent of the Beautiful Lake. It is another's Quetzalcoatl, the Toltec's Divine Serpent of Feathers and Flowers, who was also god of learning and the priesthood when assimilated by the Aztecs. In other times and places, such as China, it was a powerful rain dragon. It too carried messages between Mother Earth and spirit beings.

Universally symbolic, the snake generally represents transformation, sexual energy, and the female. It also signifies healing. Asklepios, the god of physicians, was connected with the snake; we therefore find twined snakes on the caduceus, symbol of medicine.

Snakes today are considered good luck and rainmakers at Taos Pueblo. They say the original Snake Woman was an Indian maiden who rejected all her suitors. She went instead to sit in a meadow beside the river, where she talked to her beloved Snake. Eventually she bore his child. Her father insisted that the disgraced girl marry a certain Indian man. Filled with grief, she ran off to tell her Snake. Rather than lose her to another, her lover bit her. The poison quickly ran through her body, and she died in his embrace.

In a sense, all of us who gain extra strength and harmony from honoring the snake are Snake Women.

I never get over my amazement at the meaningful coincidences that occur when one is deeply submerged in the right brain. While proofreading this chapter at the carwash, I sit on their only piece of furniture, a purple bench decorated with a white-and-purple Avanu. After writing the first draft of this section I buy Leslie Silko's newest book of essays about her favorite places to live: Laguna Pueblo and the Tucson Mountains, where she lives part time less than three miles from our home. On the book's cover is a giant serpent filled with skulls. Of our reptiles in the Tucson Mountains, she writes, "I had seen a number of large rattlesnakes that had seemed extremely gentle and tame—probably because no one had been killing them and they had forgotten how bad people were. . . . I had been able to approach and talk to the rattlesnakes that I encountered in the Tucson Mountains, and they had not coiled or rattled, and a couple of the snakes had even seemed curious about me."

A giant rattlesnake had blessed our Tucson home when I moved in during the fall of 1977. Tightly coiled at dusk on warm bricks beneath our bedroom window, it chanted in deep, steady benediction, "Whhhhhuushsh. Whhhhhuushsh." Thinking it was a broken water line, I ran indoors to get my flashlight. "Whhhhuuuushsh!" it continued to bless us. By the time I'd returned a second time with my camera, it had vanished.

"I know that feller was a big old granddaddy if it sounded like that. Regular rattlesnakes rattle like a mechanical wind-up toy," said Robert Dolan when I stopped by to meet my neighbors. "The best thing to do with all them is blow their ornery heads off. That's what we do. We've ate their meat too. Real sweet and tender it is."

Frank and I were to have only six rattlers at our home in twenty years. Dolan's place is crawling with them. You'd think they would hide out on our property, where they are appreciated. Sometimes I suspect rattlers are either stupid or suicidal, but I'm partial to them anyway.

My old hiking buddy Pete Cowgill taught me how to handle rattlesnakes, to respect them, and to talk to them. I talk to them more like a counselor than Pete did. To a rattler sunning in the middle of a road in the Tucson Mountains, he'd say as we walked up to it, "Get out of the road, you damned fool, or you'll be killed."

Next he would pick up a stick a little more than half as long as the snake's body. As the roused snake undulated across the pavement, Pete would slip his stick under its middle, then hold his catch dangling helplessly aloft with half its body on each side of the stick. Its striking distance had been halved, and it did not rattle.

Staring it in the eyes, Pete would growl, "Now we'll put you down over here in the grass safely out of harm's way, old man. See that you stay out of trouble, you hear? Or you'll wind up a rattlesnake *pancake.*"

In *Kinship with All Life,* Allen Boone details the approach to rattlers used by Grace Wiley at her Zoo for Happiness, home of many deadly snakes. Like me, Wiley believed a snake is at heart a "fine gentleman," not a troublemaker. He strikes only when he senses evil intent, is frightened, or is hurt. During public demonstrations, Wiley stood in a room furnished with just a table. In her hands she held two sticks, each about a yard long. One had a mesh tip to control striking snakes, the other a padded tip for use as a petting stick.

An angry snake set loose on the table would thrash about looking for something to strike. Nothing moved. Wiley silently talked to it, mentally complimenting and flattering it. Then quietly she began uttering these words of praise aloud while talking across to it, not down as to a lower being. She reassured it and explained that it had simply come to a new home where it would always be appreciated, loved, and cared for.

By this time the striking snake had calmed down. It allowed itself to be petted, first with Wiley's stick, then with her bare hands as it arched "its long back in catlike undulations, in order better to feel the affection-filled ministrations."

Boone writes of the hate and fear generally prevalent when white man meets rattler. He calls it a "thought-vendetta." He believes that most Indians, on the other hand, have had a live-and-let-live attitude toward rattlers, a sort of gentlemen's agreement not to harm each other. Boone views rattlesnakes as "experts of the first magnitude in dealing with thought emanations . . . able to detect and correctly appraise the particular kind of thinking" moving toward them. He emphasizes to humans "that one's thinking, in all its nakedness, always precedes him and accurately proclaims his real nature and intention."

Boone feels that favorable contact with beings of nature is the universe expressing its eternal mind in rhythms of harmonious kinship rather than in ordinary verbal communication. Repeatedly he has observed "the Divinity within all life which innately relates each of us to every other living thing, and every living thing to us, in true kinship."

A typical hunter, the principal of the school where I taught wanted nothing to do with rattlesnakes, though like Frank he was part Indian. "One place where we go hunting swarms with rattlers. I give them as wide a berth as possible. They're one thing I am afraid of. Talking to them is the *last* thing you'll catch me doing. I'm surprised Pete Cowgill doesn't hate them too," he said.

Pete was not a hunter.

At least I did convert Frank to talking with rattlesnakes. Contrary to what he later would tell people, it had not been his habit before living with me. My grandmother had talked with non-humans, which made it easier for me.

At no time were Boone's kinship views more on the mark than when a six-foot rattler four inches in diameter got stuck in our chicken-wire fence protecting a stand of evergreens from jackrabbits. Still halfway inside the enclosure, he had edged the front half of his body outside the fence through a small hole halfway up. He bulged grotesquely in the middle. Knowing that Frank was on his way home from the store, I talked soothingly to our visitor to familiarize him with my tone of voice and intent. I detailed my plan for his release and reminded him of our reciprocal responsibility: "Live and let live." Since he was too weak to argue, we proceeded with my plan after Frank's return. He was not wildly enthusiastic. I reminded him that snakes are said not to bother Indians, according to legend.

Frank stood to my right with poised rake in case our prisoner started to strike. With long hedge clippers I began cutting down through the wire toward the middle of the rattlesnake's back, all the while speaking in reassuring tones of our good intent. In the main, I controlled fearful or negative thoughts in case they might be catching. Still, a slight tremor of my hands made the task seem endless.

Luckily, this one-way conversation must have sounded like the Song of Sirens to our visitor. He hung transfixed, never making a movement or sound. At last my clippers sliced through the final strand of wire resting against the rattler's dusky diamond back. Sweating, I jumped aside as he silently heaved himself in flashing coils back inside the fence, opposite the way we'd expected. He lay there for nearly an hour regaining his cool at the base of an evergreen. Then, without making a sound, as during his entire ordeal, he was gone.

The same thing happened when a javelina, a wild pig with tusks, held up his face to me to have a jumping cholla cactus removed from his snout. And when Steve Marquez's two horses held up their muzzles to have me remove porcupine quills. Animals *know*. They know about my dream one night, that dream in which a voice said, "Your way is with animals."

Talking to animals is the secret. As with plants, it can be inward silent talking. But talk you must. Sincere compliments help. Natural, ordinary conversation is best. Repetition soothes. It doesn't have to be a chant or prayer or song; however, you can't go wrong with them either. Like me, Grandfather Coyote sang,

> Serpent on the rock, stretched in the sun,
> Crawl into your hole
> And tell the rain to come:
> My heart is drying in my belly.

We badly need rain in Taos and Tucson this spring. Today I shall see how this song works. Tone of voice is all important; it is one of the main things those of nature pick up. Conversation with these beings loses something on the printed page since it is not sparkling repartee that counts. But if you need help in getting started, here are a couple of homespun examples.

A rattlesnake the same color as the sand in the wash at Picture Rocks lay in the path of a hike I took with my former biology teacher. "Isn't she gorgeous?" I said, looking down at her brown-on-beige diamonds. Without rattling, the snake began inching in graceful coils toward our left, slowly drawing out each dazzling ripple as if seeking compliments. "You certainly are as handsome a snake as I've seen this year," I said in case she was a he. "I really do believe you rattlesnakes are the most special creatures out here. No one can help but admire your grace and beauty." This was the first time while hiking that I'd unexpectedly come upon a snake that wasn't rattling or didn't start rattling. Previously, I had talked to snakes only on our property. The professor was as impressed as I was that it worked. We were both surprised at the snake's vanity.

The other crucial ingredient needed in talking to such creatures is *common sense*. It alarmed me when Bill Edelen wrote in his nationally distributed newsletter that Frank and I talked to snakes, "recognizing their legitimate presence in the scheme of things, whereas other people in their area try to kill them." I had visions of his readers starting friendly chats with stray rattlesnakes, then trying to pick them up by their tails and pat them. To repeat, besides empathy and a little know-how, one needs *common sense* in dealing with these special beings.

Our close friend Marcia Gaiter had no common sense to speak of. She lived in the right brain and died in the right brain. By the time she realized that she needed medical help, it was too late. Yet her sensitive paintings endure. When we scattered her ashes in the Tucson Mountains in back of her studio, Frank cried and said, "I miss Marcia." Once she painted a Saint Francis *santo* to help him get over a sick spell. Another time she started painting him good-luck eyes in a circle; of its own accord, the painting turned into a mandala full of coyote eyes.

We liked to eat at a little-known Mexican place called the Mosaic on Grant and Silverbell Roads in Tucson. The last time we ever saw Edward Abbey was in there. Same tastes. At the Mosaic over dinner one night our artist friend told us she'd stumbled across a rattler coiled behind Mary Saler's back door across the patio from Marcia's studio apartment, where I used to live before marrying Frank. Another rattlesnake was holed up for the summer behind an old dresser on Mary's back porch.

"No one at Mary's ranch knows how to get rid of these two rattlers," Marcia said. "They're just little things, *babies* really. At first I thought the one near her door was a fake, someone's idea of a joke."

"We'll stop by on our way home. It's only a mile out of our way," I said. "I can move them."

"I wouldn't do that if I were you," said Dr. No.

On the way there, I began sending empathetic thoughts of good intent to the two intruders. Frank stayed in the car. At my request Marcia brought out a small plastic garbage can with a lid. Mary turned on a light to illuminate the five-foot square of concrete she called a back porch. Her door opened on its north side; another apartment opened on the west, with a dresser standing to the left. To the south was a foot-high, blue-tiled wall behind which I stationed myself, holding a long, stout stick. Mary stood safely behind her screen door. Her tenant watched from his doorway. Marcia foolishly hopped about at the porch's east entrance within striking distance of the two resident rattlers after I'd yanked the dresser out from the wall.

"Good grief, Marcia!" I exclaimed softly as their angry whirring began. "These are no *babies*. Uncoiled, this bigger one has to be over four feet long. Look how many rattles they each have."

"Oh really?" she said, dancing from foot to foot on her long, stork-like legs, catching the heel of her best shoe in a throw rug. "They seemed littler from a distance."

"For goodness' sake, get out of there!" I hissed, praying that her left brain would kick in for once. "You have to stay more than a striking length away from them. Get *off* the porch."

"I want to help you."

"You're not helping when you scare them. Poor rattlers. You're afraid with all these crazy people watching and dancing war dances around your new home, aren't you? I don't blame you. All we're going to do is move you to a more convenient home where you'll be comfortable and quiet, away from nutty people. Don't worry about a thing. We're not going to hurt you one single bit. We are not going to hurt you. We are going to help you find a new home on the desert. Help you. It's really your old home, so you will love it. So peaceful. Peaceful. Peaceful. You'll be comfortable, very comfortable. Very comfortable. Comfortable. Comfortable."

Continuing to speak softly, soothingly, hypnotically, I caught the larger one in midstrike with my stick under the middle of a coil near the center of its body but closer to the head. The bigger they are, the more one has to compensate for head weight. It complicates finding the weight center. They fall off if not centered. Their furious rattling is an incentive to quick learning. Had I been alone, they might not have rattled.

"Get the top off that can, Marcia. And use the broom to hold the other one under the doorway. *Don't* let it head toward the garden."

Swiftly I popped Papa Rattler into the garbage can and slammed down its lid just as he began to lift his fanged mouth and spit, "Hey! Whoa. What's going on here, woman?"

Off we hurried across the rear unused driveway to a rocky spot out in the desert, a spot two years later sprinkled white with Marcia's ashes.

"See, here's the good new home I promised you," I breathed, dumping him out on the ground. "Mama will be here with you in no time at all. Wait around. I can tell you're happier out here already."

Papa rattled away as if he were not really sure about the advantages of this sudden change. It was dark, but we could tell he was waiting around all right.

Back at the porch Marcia was still hopping about in the midst of her Saint Vitus's dance. She had stuck to her post, however, and was beginning to get the hang of talking to Mama Rattler, in a babbling sort of way. Mama was a little thinner than Papa and more the nervous type. Her madly undulating body was difficult to hook in the weight center. I stepped up my soothing talk and positive thinking; and after one aborted trip to the garbage can, from which she flung herself in a tizzy, I finally plopped her in and slapped down the lid, shutting off her indignant protestations. Conveniently, her mate was still rattling off at the tail out on the desert. Letting her out nearby, I wished them well. Silence descended over the warm, rocky land.

"See, I told you this would be a happier, more peaceful home. Isn't it a relief? Remember. Our motto is, 'Live and let live.' Right?"

Afterward, I was momentarily shaken at thoughts of the rattlers' unexpected size, Marcia's vulnerability, the darkness, and all the excitement. It is best to perform such services quietly and alone, or with just one trusted assistant, if necessary. The three essentials are inner and outer positive *communication, common sense,* and *respect.* Come to think of it, it's a lot like marriage.

Ever after this episode Marcia acted like a lion tamer. She wrote all her friends and relatives about it. But she never mentioned the exquisite rattlesnake portrait she painted. Nor could she know that these snakes had come to bless her sacred resting ground, making way for transformation. Her rattlesnake portrait stands watch over my own healing and transformation.

Mary Saler's ranch is a power spot. I collected innumerable pottery shards from Pottery Hill rising above it in back when I lived there from 1970 to 1977, first in the studio facing west, then in the guest house. In front, standing on an abandoned shuffleboard, one can see as the Ancient Ones did the crescent curve of the Tucson valley from Sombrero Peak on the north to "A" Mountain on the south. In 1977 Frank and I almost bought Mary's second, larger guest house in front of the shuffleboard. I didn't want to give up this beloved power spot, and while I was sunning one day my intuition told me that we must buy at once. Frank agreed. After a minor falling out with Mary, we bought a larger, more sturdy house just ten minutes away, still in the powerful but not yet fashionable Tucson Mountains.

With astounding synchronicity, writer Barbara Kingsolver bought Mary's guest house instead of us; she wrote several well-received books there. We form a power pyramid in the Tucson Mountains: Kingsolver's place at the southern base, Leslie Silko's at the apex, ours at the northern base. Perhaps we have been led there to help the rattlesnakes and all our brothers. Across the street from us are sixty untouched acres left by a lawyer to a Midwestern college as a perpetual greenbelt. Financial problems led the college to sell this land. I learned in April 1996 that a developer improbably named Don Diamond is trying to break our zoning code and develop this haven.

Six months ago, when I first returned to Tucson without Frank, one small rattler received me. Esther, who had continued to clean for our renter, had found it a couple of months earlier indoors behind my plants at the dining-room sliding door. Deathly afraid of snakes, she had called 911; firemen came to remove it. By then it had slithered out the open door and hidden under an outdoor pot, where I found it still waiting months later. It seemed to be offering its condolences, reminding me that we are all diminished by Frank's death. I had to move it three times that day. It kept returning "home."

It could have been trying to warn me about the human Diamondback too. When I return in May again, a whole convention of rattlesnakes may be waiting to let me know about Don Diamond, who is thousands of times more threatening to me than any reptilian diamondback. Perhaps the pyramid of power will be able to put a hex on him. We must do something to protect "this wild, innocent and defenseless beauty," as Abbey hymned our desert.

"Where did all these rain clouds suddenly come from today?" asks my friend Michelle, peering through our living-room window in Taos. I smile and say nothing about singing a serpent rain song this morning. It is a long story. And she's from back East. I wouldn't want her to think I am merely superstitious. She wouldn't understand that tapping into *all* these energies is part of my grief healing, as well as curative for our parched land.

Frank writes in *Masked Gods*, "Whatever can be achieved within the psyche of individual man can be duplicated in the universe without. . . . The mystic rain falls. It fills the underground lakes and reservoirs of the land as it recharges the psychic nerve centers of the body. The streams run full, the springs spout, the whole stream of life is renewed . . . we too shall learn that the internal and external must coincide, without separation, without limit, in obeisance to the mysterious laws which control both."

23
Waiting for Robert Redford

I keep waiting for Robert Redford to show up here. Of course, he has never been formally invited, but one horse whisperer ought to be able to read the mind of another horse-snake-dog whisperer. My husband was put out with him for making *The Milagro Beanfield War*, written by Taoseño John Nichols, instead of *The Man Who Killed the Deer*. Frank said Hollywood would have botched it anyway; his book could never be made into a movie.

For some years I have been closely watching Redford's work. Contrary to Frank's belief, I'm convinced that by the millennium Redford will be able to do full justice to the subtleties of *Deer*, the story of an introverted Taos Indian trying to survive in his mid–twentieth century pueblo world. Publisher Marcia Keegan and several others have recommended to Redford that he film Frank's novel.

After Marcia intervened, she said to Frank, "Now it's your turn to carry the ball. Call Redford and talk to him. He knows about *Deer*. And he's in Taos right now visiting John Nichols."

Imperiously, Frank replied, "He knows where to find me."

True, Nichols calls *Milagro* an "albatross." Although it's his most talked-about book, John considers it neither his own best book nor Redford's best movie. Having a failed deer hanging around one's neck would be worse than an albatross. Redford may be wise in keeping his distance so far.

A *Smithsonian* article about the real horse whisperer, Buck Brannaman, mentions one of my favorite books discussed here: *Kinship with All Life*. It has influenced Brannaman too in his relationships with animals. Buck taught Redford his animal approach for the movie *The Horse Whisperer*. We're tuning in on the same wavelength.

If need be, in Taos we can further the handsome actor-director's education with deer whispering. I feel the time growing nearer when waiting for Robert Redford will result in another Foundation studio paid for by sale of *Deer* book rights to the movies, and in movie marquees lighting up hearts of Frank Waters fans the world over.

On June 3, the anniversary of Frank's death, we placed long-stemmed yellow roses upon his granite deer altar. Across the miles their honeyed incense wafted my words to Robert Redford.

"You know where to find him."

For it is not difficult to find him here at his marker; in our hearts; in his books; wherever the spirit is true and pure, gentle, loving, giving . . . and forgiving.

24

Green Woman

Across the field
that old oak glows, luminescent.
Its atoms spin trails of light
nourished by your fiery life.
Snow melts your marrow and ash
into blood.
The oak receives
this communion
and flashes your presence to me
Across white empty space.
                    —Jenna Paulden

It is a two-way street. When we reach up, their energy
reaches down. Sometimes we do not recognize these encounters.
The silver lizard was one, along with the peacock feather in the
desert, and the synchronicity of "We Will Meet Again" on that
Penitente gravestone. The meaningful coincidence of having Dr.
Waxman from Mora seated beside me to stay some of my tears on
the plane to St. Louis was another. Yesterday I again visited the
Penitente cemetery, and Jenna surprised me with her poem containing the above lines, and more. Saki Karavas has died alone,

tragically, the last of Frank's close friends. At the oak tree this afternoon Frank's spirit energy leaves me a shiny orange-and-black flicker feather—our second favorite bird after magpies—once again to stay my grief, knowing that in his place I will grieve for Saki. Despite his playboy front, Saki was a generous and loving man.

Jenna Paulden writes that Frank's presence has been flashed to her. It works the other way too. Seated on an aspen stump beside the sleeping oak today, I can tell Frank has received "this communion," my presence flashing to him "across white empty space." The flicker feather is his acknowledgment and his reminder: "Up again, Old Heart. Courage and courage. . . ." On the difficult Damn First of his birthday anniversary one and a half months after his death, he left me a magpie feather.

Today's date of May 4 brings to me the realization that it is time to move out of within to upward and outward. Reach up so their energy can reach down; then we can touch. Reach outward to touch the eternal in life, like trees, water, and mountains. From them one gains true perspective. For each of ten months the third day has been a reliving of Frank's death on June 3 and another Damn First. In May, memory of this anniversary for the first time comes to me one day late, on the fourth day of the calendar month. Four is an Indian number of completion.

When you are lost, go back to the beginning. Trees have been important in my life since birth. An early baby picture shows a barefoot nymph peeking out from behind one of her grandparents' great elm trees. Even then I hugged and spoke to trees, acquiring the latter habit from my grandmother. In Oswego, Illinois, the mighty oaks in Gerry's Woods were a favorite refuge for us children, and we hid at home in a cherry tree branching up to the window of a back bedroom shared by Joan and me. Later on at my grandmother's house, outside my bedroom window a lilac bush two stories high shaped my budding senses. Everywhere in Illinois trees formed cathedral arches above our quiet streets.

In Canada during our autumn stays, trees most often were my only outdoor companions. At night I pressed the palms of my hands against them in Elmhurst, Illinois, to clear my mind after long hours of studying for a bachelor's degree while being a mom and coping with a difficult husband. In Taos at age thirty-nine I had my first treehouse in Ann Pratt's plum tree outside my apartment.

Arroyo Seco's trees spoke to me most clearly in 1969 and 1995 on this property. Aspen Son and I married. With me, Egyptian-eyed aspen shed engraven tears at his death. Since then, up Taos Ski Valley Road I have found the perfect Hugging Tree leaning toward the stream and those in pain, reminding one that what goes up does indeed come down toward good intent. "Cling to a large trunk and the branches will sway down to shield you," B. Wongar writes.

In a dream I am Green Woman, a Libra Medusa, vibrant green leaves swirling about my head instead of snakes, one with beauty and balance. I am the microcosm mirrored in the macrocosm of our collective unconscious seeking again to link reason and natural instinct. Through the greening of myself by my wooded surroundings, others will be greened.

Numerous photographs in William Anderson's book *Green Man* demonstrate how this archetype of our oneness with the earth springs out from the architecture of the ages. Most often Green Man is depicted as a leaf mask forming a man's head, or as a male head disgorging vegetation from its mouth. He is tucked into spires, corbels, and archways of cathedrals, featured on ornate tombstones and antique gateways. Sometimes he is a she, except in the blind eyes of the patriarchal world. Anderson traces omnipresent Green Man from Roman and Celtic antiquity through the Dark Ages and Gothic period to the present. He regards this composite of leaves, growth, and head as a symbol of humanity and nature united. Others have referred to Green Man as "an alternative to the tree-sacrificed Christ-God." Through the ages he has also been called "Leaf Man," "Green George," "Jack of the Green," and "May King." In Taos the "Goddess and Green Man" festival is said to symbolize the integration of masculine and feminine energies in ourselves and in our culture.

Anderson states, "When an image of great power such as the Green Man returns as he does now in a new aspect after a long absence, the purpose of its return is not only to revive forgotten memories but to present fresh truths and emotions necessary to fulfilling the potentialities of the future."

He is right when he predicts that once this archetype comes into awareness, you will find her or him "speaking to you wherever you go." As my meditation begins each morning, I sit looking out at the magnificent cottonwood shading our front yard. In its shaggy trunk appears that familiar Green Man of nature and myth named Merlin, he of pointed hat and shaggy beard with long lines of suffering for mankind etched into his face; he who guided King Arthur, as well as others, then disappeared into the forest, where some say his cry is heard to this day. When the chartreuse light slants at a different angle, my tree-trunk Green Man is Gurdjieff, wearing his furry Russian hat and radiating wisdom. Either guide will do. Dwain Freeman, an artist who shows at the Art Lab in Arroyo Seco, carves similar faces into tree roots; his best is an archetypal, miniature Saint Nicholas.

My vision refocuses on a tall young evergreen touching the cottonwood in our front yard. Though shaded by enormous old boughs, the upstart stretches tenaciously skyward, thriving, growing, expanding on its own. The monumental cottonwood is dying nobly. They remind me of us.

In the right light, a younger cottonwood nearby reveals a Spanish *señorita* tucked into its rough bark. She wears a high comb in her glistening hair. Flirtatiously, she covers the tip of her chin with a rose as full as a half-open fan. She is every inch the Green Woman of emotion and instinct. She is Old Spain, New Spain, the Martinez Land Grant under our feet. She is Life. Closing my eyes, I see her stamping her heels in a fiery flamenco. *"Viva la vida!"* she cries, like Frida Kahlo. *"Olé."*

Anderson's book examines the long history in literature of trees that speak. Much like our aspen here, the oracle in Zeus's sacred oaks of Dodona spoke through their rustling leaves and creaking boughs. King David listened to rustling mulberry leaves to hear the voice of God. In India, legendary trees foretold the approaching doom of Alexander the Great. Among other Western authors, Virgil, Dante, Spenser, and Tolkien utilized this motif of the talking tree, an aspect of the collective unconscious. *Listen*, they all teach, when the tree speaks.

Taos Indians called our property *"La Isla"* when streams of water moated it about like an island. Then too it was lush with chokecherries and wild iris, plum thickets, and giant cottonwoods. Green is its chief color, green the symbol of hope and illumination. Its rainbowed greens embrace secret sharers. Color vibrates at a higher frequency around Taos; Tucson lawns, for instance, are not the electric green of ours here. Surrounding us here are apple green, dandelion wine green, forest and cat's-eye green, shamrock, sagebrush, fern green, watercress, and wild-rose green.

Conservationist John Muir would have made a good writer-in-residence here. His father tried to teach him that nature was unredeemably wild and godless. But Muir came to equate nature with the radiance of God. He wrote, "The door to the universe is through a forest wilderness."

La Isla is my door to the universe. Its soothing green used to be mirrored indoors by green shag carpeting bought from Kay Gardner for $100 around 1979. It provided warmth and beauty, if not style. The view from our bedroom was one long sweep of green across the living room to the lawn outdoors, the cottonwoods, and Secret Garden in front, and over to the piñons and sagebrush on the reservation. The Jongewards had been cold during winter with the bare wood floors, an oxblood floor, and one made of flagstone. Frank had said, "You talked me into renting this house to Jongewards. Now *you* will have to stop that child from dancing on our valuable Indian rugs."

"Stopping a five-year-old from dancing is like asking the wind to stop blowing," I'd said with a laugh.

Thus, Kay's carpeting soon came to green our living room and guest room. Later it greened Mrs. Quintana's home when we finally bought brand-new carpeting and spread Indian rugs on top of it while we were here. After Kay's tragic death at the crossroads in Pilar south of here, it pleased me to have her still about in green memory. Years later her friends continue to keep her *camposanto*, her roadside cross at the place of death, bedecked with colorful plastic flowers. It is a reminder as one travels down the canyon to Santa Fe to say a prayer for an old friend and good times shared. "Where have all the flowers gone?" one sometimes wonders—until spring reminds us that they green and glow eternally. The Australian protagonist of one of Frank's favorite books, *Karan*, becomes a tree instead of "dying." Frank said, "*That's* the way to do it!" And it is easiest to find Frank today in trees and greenery, which heal the scars.

Carolyn Jongeward and I made green drapes for the guest room here and covered as many throw pillows as possible with olive-green slubbed-silk drapes destroyed in Tucson by ground squirrels. They came down the chimney, and our peculiar summer renter there grew too fond of them as pets to remove them. He was a lonely man, but *definitely* peculiar. Those were the green days, our "salad days." Against all reason, one expects them never to end. At least I still have some of those green throw pillows to remind me. And our outdoor greenery continues to renew itself ever more verdantly.

"Be kind to trees and they will bloom into flower for you," writes Wonger in *Karan*. "Remember, trees are relatives of man, after all."

When I told Frank about the conference center with bed-and-breakfast rooms that George and Kitty Otero had built in Mabel Luhan's former meadow, it reminded him of one of Mabel's "favorite little stories" about her religious trees.

"That 'meadow,' as you call it, used to be Mabel's apple orchard. And once a year in the fall the sisters from Holy Cross were allowed to spend the day there having a picnic and picking all the apples they wanted for the coming winter. It was quite an amusing sight to see all those black-clad figures clambering up higher and higher into the trees, their flapping habits snagging on jutting limbs. One time a sister had climbed almost to the top of the apple tree when the limb supporting her began to crack.

"Clawing frantically upward, she called, 'Save me, Mabel! Save me. I'm falling!'

"Kicking and clawing, this black-shrouded figure gradually sank lower and lower through snapping branches, still crying, 'Help me, Mabel. I'm fall-ing. Saaave me, Mabel!'

"Mabel always had to laugh when she told that story," Frank concluded. Apparently it had a happy ending.

A twelfth century Benedictine nun important to me personally, and to the world, is Hildegard of Bingen. She thought up the word *viriditas,* meaning greening power, and viewed humanity as "showered with greening refreshment, the vitality to bear fruit." In her meditations were many images of humans as vines and living branches. She saw Christ as "Greenness Incarnate." Connecting greening power with creativity, she wrote, "The word is all verdant greening, all creativity." Hildegard may have been our first Green Woman who wrote and created on a large scale. She is said to be "the first medieval woman to reflect and write at length on women," a woman activist centuries before her time. She foresaw Jung's idea of the anima and animus when she wrote, "Man cannot be called man without woman. Neither can woman be called woman without man."

Hildegard of Bingen wrote nine books, seventy poems, hundreds of letters to influential persons, and an opera that is part of seventy-seven songs she composed. In addition she preached, taught, established monasteries, and had her visions or illuminations painted as a series of mandalas. Matthew Fox suggests that we are moving "from an egological to an ecological consciousness" and nominates Hildegard as patron saint of our ecological awakening. He states, "Hildegard is deeply ecological in her spirituality." Fox quotes Laurens van der Post to the effect that we cannot find balance "unless we honor the wilderness and the natural persons within ourselves."

Hildegard cautioned individuals to nurture the self as a favorite plant or tree. This means avoiding aridity and dryness, keeping oneself fresh, green, and moist. To an abbot she wrote, "Pay careful attention lest with all the fluctuations of your thoughts the greening power which you have from God dries up in you." To another churchman she stated, "When a person loses the freshness of God's power, he is transformed into the dryness of carelessness. He lacks the juice and greenness of good works and the energies of his heart are sapped away." We need "heavenly dew," she felt, to keep our creative juices flowing instead of drying up into laziness and lack of passion for some constructive endeavor or belief in life.

Three nature symbols appearing in the mandala illuminations that were important to Hildegard as well as to Frank and me were the deer, snake, and Hopi corn kachinas; yet she lived two centuries before the kachina cult developed, and on another continent. Hildegard called the deer "the Son of God." The snake she saw as a positive symbol in the tradition of a feminine goddess symbol from matriarchal religions. She wrote that the devil had changed himself into a serpent because it was most powerful of the animal kingdom; the snake to her was therefore least demonic of all such beings. In another mandala are found figures closely resembling the Hopis' corn man and woman symbols that represent germination and awakening of new life. The Corn Mother is an echo of old Earth Mother religions celebrating the cosmic fertility of the womb. Tied in with this, possibly, is another mandala featuring the head of a red man in the center of two walls and three wings. Hildegard said the walls represented strength.

The Indian or red man so closely allied with nature had the power once to lead us to our salvation. Now that they are in danger of losing their way on the white man's path of materialism, this leadership may not be possible. Nevertheless, it can still be put to use as a prototypal model. One also is reminded by this mandala of Vine Deloria's book *God Is Red*.

One of the most powerful trees near us is the ever green Meditation Tree. On Calle Coyote, the next lane up, nestle three cypress trunks intertwined with one large, leafy branch stretching southeast from the shade toward the sun. Someone has sawed off one tree, its trunk forming by chance a seat. One's back rests against the living tree, creating a single green entity. At one's feet whispers a stream. To the left, tumbling downhill toward the western horizon, are Salomé's pastures and belled sheep, followed by our horses and pastures, the successive Quintana pastures, and the Torres pastures heavy with Charolais cattle and buffalo. Fields stack upon fields, green upon green layer, until the distant blue desert merges into cobalt sky.

Meadowlarks tranquilize the troubled spirit along with meditation focused first upon circling chakra colors: red down the spine and around in front to orange of the lower stomach, gold at the solar plexus, green heart, blue throat, turquoise or indigo third eye, lavender crown, all transforming at last into a golden shield of light surrounding and radiating through the body. A lingering image remains of a pyramid-shaped evergreen slowly being nurtured in the green landscape of the heart.

Wallace Stegner's belief that "no place, not even a wild place, is a place until it has the human attention that at its highest reach we call poetry" gives me pause to differ. Surely the meditation tree was a nameless special bit of heaven on earth before I stumbled upon it. For all we know, that tree could be a human ancestor of this land. Linda Ann sensed this in her winter poem when she saw sage and piñon bent low with snow as the Old Ones, the ancestors. This tree was a place, an entity, a being, before it received human attention, just as is the huge cottonwood lying across the *acequia madre* near the back of our property. Mushroom and fungus long ago recognized it and snuggled up to it; still they honor its fallen might. Its human attention called poetry came late upon the scene when in

Boulder, Colorado, someone in the audience left me this hurried impression after viewing a slide of the old giant:

Old tree fallen over
  the ditch
decorated with lichens
One arm raised
  in strange greeting
wrinkled skin lending
secure footing
  for dogs
people and
Spirits homeward
  bound.

—ST
2/10/96

At this Boulder conference, the speech of retired professor Joe Gordon set forth his conviction that the sense of place in Frank's writing is really a "landscape of the heart," for his works reveal an emotional, soul-deep relationship with his homeland. Elaborates Professor Charles Wilkinson, a homeland is a mixture of "landscape, smells, sounds, history, neighbors, and friends." Both professors omit the important detail that Frank's landscape is *green*, a green landscape impelling perennial growth at higher levels if properly nurtured. Leaving Arroyo Seco most years when green turned to white, as he had left Colorado for California as a young man, Frank literally sought greener pastures of the heart throughout the West for much of his life. Still, fecund Arroyo Seco remained his fixed center. "Fecund" for Frank was almost as important a word as "fey."

So many trees on our land, and close by, are special. Frank used to think that when a certain old apple tree died across the road on the reservation, he would die. It still lives. And he is now one with the old oak tree, a symbol of renewal and protection. "When old, trees grow even kinder, opening part of their trunk to let birds, animals, or men hide in the hollow," states Wongar.

Then there are the Josephine Tree, the Bear Tree, and the Abe Tree. Like Josephine herself, the Josephine Tree is gnarled and old and dying. Yet a few apples valiantly appear each summer as its roots cling to the nourishing stream bank next to our wooden bridge in front. As a child this was a place of contemplation, learning, and protest for Josephine Cordova, who owned this land before us. She remembers her mother, Maria of the Snows, setting up a small table and chair for her under the apple tree, where she read by the hour. When she suspected it might be time to work indoors, little Josephine would shinny up the stubby, rough trunk and hide behind a dense screen of green leafy branches.

"I never could figure out how my mother always knew exactly where to find me," laments Josephine.

Frank wrote in *Mountain Dialogues* and in our first Foundation newsletter:

> There is no accounting for the mysterious magnetism that draws and holds us to that one locality we know as our heart's home, whose karmic propensities or simple vibratory quality may coincide with our own. Thus have I often wondered how I happened to choose this slope of the Sangre de Cristo Mountains for my own home. . . . [The] house was a deserted adobe whose roof was falling and whose foundations needed bolstering. . . . [Yet] I always stopped a moment to admire [it] set back in a green lawn, surrounded by towering cottonwoods growing along the small stream flowing between the house and road. . . . The land in back was overgrown with chokecherry and wild plum thickets, and wild rose bushes. . . . But the first time I saw it on a walk up into the mountains, something about it claimed me.

The Bear Tree is our corner cottonwood behind the car barn, a tree next to the one that mashed my Honda. I was carrying out a basketful of papers to burn one morning when mother bear and three cubs materialized in front of me. Hurrying back inside, I hustled along Frank and his walker, and we soon joined our guests outdoors. By this time Mother Bear was nudging her cubs up the cottonwood while muttering mild threats after them that sounded like "Git! Git!" She got two of them up, closely followed by herself, and the threesome stared down at us as if we were aliens from outer space.

Maybe she recognized me as the same weirdo who had held aloft Morgan at the back of our property in 1989 and exclaimed to a similar mother bear with one cub, "See! I have a baby too! I understand exactly how you feel. They are *such* a responsibility." Mama had shaken her head in disbelief and disappeared. Briefly she'd returned to snatch up Junior, who was still stuffing himself with berries. My talking had about the same effect this time. Mother and her two good little bears quickly descended and lit out for Quintana's apple orchard as her slow-witted third child began ascending the cottonwood at last. Soon bored with staring down at us, in a short time it too descended and bumbled off in the wrong direction through the underbrush.

It could be that bears feel like cowardly lions when they can't frighten people. Or it just might be that they have one-track minds and want their *apples*. Our orchard is growing scrawny with age, but it's still Apple Heaven to some beings, along with all the other neighborhood orchards.

Although I intuit and plan that like Mabel we too shall have a small conference center in our apple orchard some day, it's more pleasing to me the way it is in my lifetime. In its heyday Frank used to encourage people to come over and pick apples from its abundant offering in the fall. They are small apples, firm and red, with a cool, sharp taste. One fall when he had a bumper crop, he invited Clara and Albert over from the Pueblo. "Help yourselves," he told them ahead of time, for they had been helpful to him in finishing up this house. He pictured them picking a few bags full, as most persons did.

To his amazement, they drove a large, expandable *wagon* pulled by horses past the stable to the orchard and filled the whole thing!

"Clara and he had been through some hard times," Frank said, "and she was a shrewd woman. She wasn't about to miss out on anything free. She probably traded the apples—for a piece of meat—for things they needed—for whatever she could get."

As our old apple trees die off, they continue to live on as firewood. In fact, they live most intensely as fire. In addition, our planet's "dead" wood continues giving to us through all our paper products, building materials, and numerous synthetic products. Crosses originally were made of wood; many still are. French-Canadian woodsmen thought the crucifixion cross was made from aspen wood; they said as a result aspens have been trembling ever since. Think of the music connected with wood through woodwinds, violins, guitars, harps, drums, and other instruments. When a piñon log burns, fire darts out from holes in it, as if the fire is playing a flute. It sings its own song of songs. A few years ago a man gave Frank his prized handmade wooden flute with a red cardinal perched on one tip. Gazing at this treasure reminds one that birdsong is another gift connected with trees, especially these spring mornings when a hallelujah chorus greets the early riser and a full-throated "Messiah" continues all day long.

A couple of years ago while meditating in Frank's chair, I heard a russet-colored bird sing her mate back to life with a heart song. He had crashed into our picture window and lay on the ground inert. She flew down near him and sang the most exquisite song I have ever heard, trilling over and over again as if it were an aria. This heart song lasted for at least twenty minutes, during which time I stayed back from the window so as not to frighten her away. She sang him back to life. When her song stopped at last, I looked out. They were both gone.

She gave me confidence. And it worked for me one time, though less melodically. It would have worked on June 3, 1995, if only I had arrived home from the grocery store and beauty parlor a few minutes earlier. And if Frank's caretaker hadn't fallen asleep. My version of a heart song is related in these journal entries beginning February 13, 1993:

Around 1:00 P.M. I returned from a Jungian workshop, unaware that Frank had accidentally disconnected himself from his oxygen. After telling him to get out of bed for lunch, I went into the kitchen to feed the dogs. Frank called feebly. He wanted to sit up and use the urinal, as he felt too weak to walk into the bathroom. As he started to use it, he seemed to be straining. I looked up at his face and saw he was having convulsions. His eyes rolled back into his head as he arched backward, choking. Then he STOPPED BREATHING. I know he died for a moment or so.

I pulled his tongue out of his throat, yanked out his false teeth and shook him. "BREATHE!" I yelled. "BREATHE, Frank! BREATHE." I put every ounce of my breath and will into him; I was afraid I didn't remember CPR well enough to try it.

At last he *did* breathe!!!

I ran to call 911, then dashed back to Frank and reconnected his oxygen. He had another series of convulsions. I soothed him with soft pats and words, since he was still breathing.

Luckily, Dr. Farr was in the emergency room, just about to leave. When we got there, he thought Frank's color was awful, although it was *comparatively* good. At home his face had been whitish blue. He'd gotten a clean bill of health the previous day. One day later he had pneumonia and a fibrillating heart. For the next twelve days he remained in the hospital. During this interim I spent ten-hour days running interference for him, which these days is essential for survival in most such institutions. Sometimes I feel as if Frank's illnesses are consuming *me*. But remembering the foregoing scene keeps me grateful. His return was a true gift from the Troops, and much appreciated.

When he was safely out of the woods, I kidded with Dr. Farr in front of Frank, "At least I know now that Frank can hear me from the Other Side and will obey from there. That's more than he does here!"

In the hospital one day when Frank was feeling nervous, I suggested, "Maybe you don't know how to meditate properly. Maybe you should consider another way."

"I think of a great massed power or energy coming in, one greater than any human source," he said.

"That's part of it. It's interesting to think about the chakras and color too. Green is the color around the heart, which is near the upper stomach and your ulcer. Imaging green or a green tree in that area is powerful, like the evergreen branches Indians hold to symbolize everlasting life while dancing."

"I like that tree idea," Frank said. "It reminds me again of that book where the man turned into a tree. That's the easiest transition I've ever heard of, or read about."

"Well, green is for *living* too. It's especially for living! In your symbol dictionary Cirlot says the green tree stands for 'inexhaustible life.' Think GREEN."

In Cirlot's book, the tree is said to be the center of the world. And it is the center of our world here in Arroyo Seco. My personal symbol of spring this year is our first green tree, towering at least three stories high next to Abe's Bar & Grill. Perfectly symmetrical, it seems to be some type of willow. Since no one can identify it for sure, I call it an "Abe Tree." In front of the old church a block away looms an evergreen that is even taller, taller than the church's high-peaked roof and almost as wide as its adobe walls. This grand Old One is truly a symbol of renewal and life everlasting.

The Chinese called the bamboo, cherry tree, and pine "the three friends," for they were said to remain ever green—although here our cherry trees do not. Here in Arroyo Seco the piñon, juniper, and pine are truly our "three friends." In Indian ceremonials the "four friends" most often used have been these three and the spruce. It is no wonder that in this area D. H. Lawrence used to write seated outdoors while leaning against an evergreen tree. I often lean against our aspens and feel their Greening Power rush out from roots, trunks, eyes, branches, and leaves. To me, above all else trees symbolize creativity.

Yet we are sapping creativity, damaging our souls, demolishing our Greening Power by murdering our trees. Read Charles Little's book *The Dying of the Trees*, or any of a hundred others, to learn about what acid rain and Ultraviolet B radiation are doing to trees.

Aspens have been called the world's largest living organisms. Covering 106 acres in Utah, one stand of genetically identical quaking aspen has been cloned naturally from a single aspen; forty-seven thousand aspen stems are growing from one unbroken, interconnected mass of root. Thousands of these cloned root systems grow in the Rocky Mountain region, including Taos at its southern end. Our single aspen root system that was just seven stems beside the driveway on the west in 1947 has circled our home, run underneath it and over to Salomé's yard, where it is popping up all over the place, virtually humming with Green Power. What most people don't realize is that the so-called "Taos hum" is throbbing Green Power!

Part of this power is its tranquilizing effect, both literally and figuratively. In a book she did about aspens with author Ann Zwinger, Barbara Sparks includes some startling photographs of aspens bared of bark by elk. It is thought that like related willow twigs, aspen may contain salicylic acid, a major ingredient of aspirin. Healing energy flows from the earth into plants and trees, out to us, through sun and air, and back to earth in a cosmic uroborus of wholeness. It is up to us *right now* to save our Greening Power, to utilize it properly, and to preserve it for the future.

As Wallace Stegner wrote in his *Wilderness Letter*, an inspiration for the Frank Waters Foundation and its stewardship objectives, "Save a piece of country like that intact, and it does not matter in the slightest that only a few people every year will go into it. This is precisely its value. . . . We simply need that wild country available to us, even if we never do more than drive to its edge and look in."

25
No Agua, No Vida

It is strange to experience "focused creative discipline." It sounds so organized, but it's really like a horse held with a loose rein. Heading back to the barn, or your writing goal, it tends to run away with you. For this chapter head I'd planned to steal the perfect title, "House of Waters," which David Jongeward had used in his chapter about living here at our place during seven winters. Instead, "No Water, No Life" galloped into the title from a headline in the current *Taos News*. Our water shortage prompted a subtitle there, warning that we're "going to be hurting." Actually, we are hurting already. Sixteen thousand acres are burning out of control in the ancient Indian ruins and pine forests around Los Alamos, and it is only spring. One house fire in Taos took seventy thousand gallons of water to fight.

Fields are dry in Arroyo Seco; there will not be enough Mother Ditch water to keep all of them green and lush this summer. That means a shortage of hay for animals next winter as well as a shortage of other crops. Fire is a frightening hazard, in both residential and forest areas.

Since we are just a mile down El Salto Road from the main slope of the mountains, our runoff crises are generally less dire than those of neighbors closer to town. Downhill from us, in front of

Celestino's and Bolivar's homes, the stream in front flattens out. Bolivar is the hardest hit. He says even with a motor, it is hard to draw up enough water for his front yard and for the orchard in front of his sister's place next to him.

One year I discovered that Bolivar without permission had installed underwater a thick yellow hose resembling a fire hose. It stretched across half the front of our property bounded by the local stream. Angrily, I spent an entire morning dragging the monster serpent back over to Celestino's property, where my energy gave out. That evening after work Bolivar came charging over like a bull. He is of medium height with massive shoulders and a large head that seems to rise straight out of this mountain of shoulders and long arms.

When my horse Ginger tore her leg on a barbed-wire fence in our back pasture, Bolivar had come over each evening and each morning before dawn to give her a shot, for which I had no stomach. To me these mornings were memorable, permeated with the sweet smell of hay and the first gentle sounds of day: horses nickering, cows murmuring sleepily, buffalo snoring, a rooster crowing, birds cheeping, sheep bells beginning to clink and clank. I admired Bolivar's skill with animals and his tenacious way of living and succeeding in this tough land.

I've often wondered since our encounter over the water situation how I got the nerve to stand up to him. During our shouting match we tramped up and down and around the Sacred Aspen Grove like *two* mad bulls. At one point Bolivar's wife showed up, dissolved into tears, and faded away. Perhaps I was striking a blow for all fading-away wives. Or maybe it was the memory of Janey shouting at Mrs. Quintana about her loose pig. Most likely it was simply a matter of what water issues do to people in these parts. A female neighbor said later, "Let the *men* fight it out. Don't you get involved."

Frank, who personally avoided confrontation with neighbors at all cost, stayed in the house the whole time and "never heard a thing," though it was summertime and all the doors and windows were open. Afterward he said I had done "the right thing."

Bolivar and I quickly worked our way past the water issue and got down to the basics of a grudge he had secretly nursed for a long time; it stemmed from the negative remarks about his parents that Frank had allegedly written. We went 'round and 'round about this and about Frank supposedly writing that the Quintanas were "dumb Mexicans," which was news to me and later to my husband.

"If he even wrote any of that in the first place, why blame me? *I* didn't write it. That's the main point."

"He *wrote* that."

"*I* didn't write it! And he didn't ever say or think you were 'dumb Mexicans.' He liked your parents a lot. What he wrote about your parents, that one part, he didn't think was an insult. But I argued with him not to take a chance."

"He *wrote* that one part."

"*I* didn't write it. Besides, your own cousin is still going around saying the *same thing*. In front of me. I thought maybe Frank was making up that part. But your *own* cousin is *still* saying that!"

"Don't tell me this. Let's go over there. Right now! We'll see what cousin has anything like that to say. Let's go!"

"Don't blame me. Why don't you tell all this to *Frank* and take *him* over there?"

Bolivar blinked his eyes in confusion. "Because I respect him . . . I . . . I respect my elders. I always have. I have been taught to respect my elders."

As Vargas Llosa observed, "What's certain is that literature does not solve problems—instead it creates them—and rather than happy, it makes people more apt to be unhappy." Luckily I kept this thought to myself.

"You have a mosquito on your forehead," I said.

Bolivar crushed it with a fierce blow.

"You admit the Indians own the other half of the stream," he continued. "Next time I'm putting my hose on *that* side of the stream."

"Go ahead. I'll tell the Indians."

"The Indians hate Frank."

"Some do. Some don't."

"*All* the Indians hate him. The Indians all hate Frank! They won't pay any attention to you."

"You just try it and see."

"We *welcomed* Frank and Janey, his *first* wife. We were friendly to them. Neighbors."

I guess he'd forgotten the loose pig incident. And he was off on his wife count, but that happened sometimes even to Frank. Two passing hippies tried hard to ignore us shouting at each other on the bridge while Morgan yapped at their heels.

"You have *always* been good neighbors, like helping me twice a day with Ginger's shots. We couldn't have *survived* this long without your neighborliness. Frank never has looked down on you. He has repeatedly written that your simpler way of life attuned to nature is best for everyone. You don't *need* all that water. We should each take just what we *need.* That way there's enough for all," I tried to reason.

"What do you know? You've only lived here two years. You're just a rich woman from Tucson."

"Listen!" I said, boiling over at this infamy. "I've lived in Taos since 1968. 1968! Even if it doesn't seem long to you, it's longer than most people along this road have lived here. I am not rich. I'm *poor.* And I've worked *hard* all my life as a schoolteacher."

"Oh, yes. A schoolteacher. And we're just 'dumb Mexicans.' Frank wrote that."

"He DID NOT."

"Oh yes, and you came up with this Foundation idea. I read. I'm not a 'dumb Mexican.' I can figure out what's going on. Materialism. That's all it is that counts. Money! You're going to build these ugly giant buildings all over the place. All for *money.*"

"We may build a *few* teeny, tiny houses. Small. *Not* big. Where you can't see them. We won't get any money for creative people living here. And at least our little studios will look better than those *ugly trailers* all over the back of your land, right up against our property."

I regret saying this. My hang-up about mobile homes isn't their fault. I understand the financial aspect, and his daughter's place has won contests for being beautifully landscaped.

Surprisingly, Bolivar acted slightly more subdued at this remark. "My children are going to build real houses some day. They want to build. But this way they get started in something like a house with only one payment. That's all they can afford now. I started in a trailer. Now I have a house bigger than *yours*. They will too someday."

"Listen, Bolivar. You're not an *autocrat*. You're not *king* of this place!"

"This used to be *our* land. It was my *tía's*. My grandmother's sister's! Now you want everything *private*," Bolivar roared on, breaking three sticks at once across his knees. "Now our children can't come here anymore to catch fish."

"I want to *watch* our fish. I have a favorite fish family. I don't want them all to disappear like they did last year when those kids netted them. Fermin, the *acequia* commissioner, says I should tell the Game and Fish guys about them taking all the fish. But I haven't. I don't care if your grandkids want to *wade* here, as they did when they were little, and try to catch fish with their *hands*."

"You're a NEWCOMER. A NEWCOMER. And you always will be!"

After laying his terrible curse upon me, Bolivar charged off toward home. It was dark by then. We both sounded hoarse.

To calm myself, I tried to think of him as a little boy. He had once confided, "An old man named Felix Valencia used to live in a little house where your barn is now. When I was no more than nine, Felix told me, 'If you take a black cat and baste it in salted water and roast it on top of a chimney, you can speak to the Devil!'

"Let me tell you, I was plenty scared," Bolivar said. "I took off running full blast! And I didn't come back here for a long time."

He must have thought he was speaking to the Devil for sure when he came across me on this same property.

The only other run-in I've had was with Bolivar's nephew, Arnold, and his friend Ramon after they'd left a mess in our driveway and stream while rebuilding our bridge. First I had to rake up and carry away two wheelbarrow loads of rotted wood, nails, and debris. Then I retrieved the old lumber they had dumped into the swollen, diamond-clear stream, recently cleaned after heavy spring runoffs had threatened to flood the neighborhood. Ignoring my cleanup request, Ramon and Arnold had bucked off down El Salto Road in their dented pickup with Ramon shouting back, "You're a Hot One to work for, man!"

Stepping into our ice-cold rushing stream, I felt very much the "Hot One." Someone else's mess to clean up, on top of paying $728 for a rattletrap cracked wooden bridge and getting gypped out of three twelve-foot pine boards. As usual, Frank had remained invisible during this encounter.

Feet protected by sturdy-soled sneakers, I reached for a smooth five-foot sapling uprooted by raging water that had set our neighbors to sandbagging these stream banks back in May. Stomping upstream with my sapling cane, I felt like the Ancient of the Ancients. My anger cooled quickly, very quickly. And the years melted away. My mind skipped back to those happy days when my two young sons were learning to catch crawdaddies; back even farther to wading with cows, fat bloodsuckers, and Frances Gerry in Gerry's creek meandering through their woods in Oswego. My hands turned to ice cubes as I hauled out chunks of ant-riddled wood and fresh-sawn lumber. At the same time my feet and ankles began to feel good for the first time in months. Not really numb but painless. They felt young and happy again, as I did. I had been limping about barely able to stand on pronating feet with ankles swollen from tendonitis.

"Just the normal wear and tear that comes with age," a costly Tucson specialist had said the previous month. "Try soaking your feet in Epsom salts diluted with warm water. Takes down the swelling, if you're lucky."

For an hour I tugged and lugged, until the stream at last was free of wood, beer cans, and tiny souvenir whiskey bottles. Next morning, bright and early, I returned for more sprucing up: breaking off dead, low-hanging tree limbs, uprooting dandelion fluff and elephant-eared burdock along the eroded banks. Above me on the bank was my own Secret Garden burgeoning with wild rose bushes, cilantro, burdock, wild plum trees, ancient cottonwoods, and aspen. Robins and magpies and whirring hummingbird wings harmonized with the voice of the stream.

By the fourth day of this psychological and physiological treatment my feet felt fully mobile, firmly grounded. I could stand on a chair again, walk with scarcely a limp, take fifty steps in medium-heeled shoes. Not since Mother's Day had I been able to wear heels. Thrilled with this cure, I tried to share it with others, only to be met with skepticism and sarcasm.

Mary Taylor said, "I can see your sign out in front already: 'Barbara Blavatsky's Magical Mountain Spring Water Cure—Two Bits.'"

And a male visitor, wearing a $90 pair of shoes that stiffened as quickly as his numbed feet, exclaimed with all the lofty hauteur of a Yale alumnus, "At least I had the sense to get right back out. Forty-five degrees is my idea of torture, not a cure."

"Cold running water like this is extremely therapeutic," I murmured, secure in the knowledge that it had blessed me. "If the water cure is good enough for a pope and royalty, it should be good enough for all of us."

The story of the Kneipp Water Cure was not for the likes of these Doubting Thomases. Confirming that I'd stumbled upon one of the most miraculous of ancient cures, my new German friend Elka Lockridge had filled me in about the great water healer Father Sebastian Kneipp. In 1893 Pope Leo XIII sent for him to treat the pope's illness with Kneipp's noted water cure. For his healing services to mankind, Pope Leo subsequently bestowed upon Father Kneipp the title of monsignor. All others with similar requests for this famous water cure had to travel to Kneipp's office themselves, no matter what their titles. These included the Prince of Wales, Baron Rothschild, and German and Austrian royalty. Archdukes Joseph and Ferdinand of Austria were photographed standing barefoot in the snow beside Father Kneipp as they "hardened their constitutions." Upon recovering from Bright's disease in 1892, Archduke Joseph donated money for a large public park in the German town of Woerishofen, where Kneipp lived and practiced.

Born in Bavaria on May 21, 1821, Sebastian became a weaver like his impoverished father. At age twenty-one the young man set out on his own, hoping to study for the priesthood. With the help of a perceptive clergyman and much concentrated schooling, Kneipp was ordained a priest in 1852. Three years later he became chaplain and father confessor at Woerishofen. The intense effort to reach his goal brought on a physical breakdown that may have been tuberculosis. Kneipp was sent home to his family to die.

Bedridden and bored, he relieved the monotony of waiting for death by reading. After studying several thick volumes on natural healing, he came at last to a slim text called *The Art of Healing with Water*. From then on Kneipp immersed himself daily in a frigid nearby stream, no matter what the weather. He cured an ailing friend as well as himself, and together they spread his healing technique: drinking water and bathing combined with proper breathing, food, herbs, and sunshine.

Kneipp's ideas were similar to those of Vincent Priessnitz, who fifty years earlier had been too far ahead of his time when he founded hydrotherapy. Instead of being honored by the pope and royalty, Priessnitz had been convicted of witchcraft for taking patients back to nature to be healed by streams, forests, sunny fields, herbs, and natural foods.

After many years of successful cures and acclaim, Kneipp died in 1897. Schools teaching his method sprang up in Germany, particularly around Woerishofen. At least one, attended by Elka, offers professional accreditation. Father Kneipp expressed the golden rule of this teaching in his preface to the fiftieth edition of *My Water Cure*: "Learn ye to know water, its applications and its effects, and it will bring you help where help is possible!"

Another man who knew water well and used it to advantage was Viktor Schauberger, a Bavarian who worked most of his life uncovering the secrets of natural energy. His family had descended from ancient Bavarian aristocracy and men interested in forestry; their motto was "Faithful to the Quiet Forests," and their crest displayed wild roses garlanding a tree trunk. From his great-great-grandfather on down through Viktor, the Schauberger men were forest wardens. His mother too was a nature lover. She taught him, "If occasionally life is really hard, and you don't know where to turn, go to a stream and listen to its music. Then everything will be alright again." His own guiding principle was, "First understand Nature, then copy it."

Schauberger discovered that water is strongest, or most full of energy, when it is coldest, shaded by trees, and flowing naturally along its own course. He was able to put his ideas to work when Prince Adolf von Schaumburg-Lippe, the local prince who owned most of Schauberg's forestry district, announced a competition to initiate a procedure that would profitably transport mature timber from the prince's obscure forests to market. A competition committee turned down Viktor's brilliant idea without the prince ever hearing about it.

After a fateful meeting with Viktor, the prince's wife brought his plan to her husband's attention. Schauberger invented a curving chute that caused the lumber to move in the natural zigzag rhythm of a snake. He replenished the main stream of water periodically with fresh cold water from subsidiary streams along the way, and he ran the lumber through on clear, moonlit nights, when water is coldest. Winning this competition made Schauberger's reputation. He became head warden for all the prince's forest and hunting territories, then state consultant for timber flotation installations, and a builder of log flumes throughout Europe in the 1920s and '30s. In 1951 Viktor and his son Walter, an engineer, founded an environmental protection organization in Austria called the Green Front. It was based on the premises that the forest is a power center creating energy, and it is the "cradle of living water," which is the "earth's blood."

Our Arroyo Seco stream is part of such a power center. It's as cold as I can stand it at forty-five degrees—*full* of energy. It is shaded by great old trees and meanders in its own natural zigzag pattern, like a snake. Its peopled rock faces and native inhabitants entertain me too. On the fifth day of relaxation and curing I hit the jackpot: an entire family of speckled trout! At first just one fish makes its presence known. When Junior brushes against my white shoe submerged in water, I suspect it is a piece of wood. Twice more he nudges my foot insistently.

The stream is lower this day. Salomé has illegally diverted part of it to water his front yard. I will "let the men settle it." Celestino calls Salomé "beaver" in Spanish. *"Castor,"* Celestino says with a laugh, looking at his wife for affirmation. Clorinda always laughs at Celestino's jokes, even when no one else realizes they are jokes except for the crinkles around the corners of his eyes. My feet and ankles are soaking in a deeper hole than ordinary to compensate for the Beaver's inroads on our water supply. I am not fully aware that this is Home Sweet Home until Junior, about six inches long, stares directly up at me. Shyly, he flirts his fins like fans.

"Maybe he's a snake," I decide, mesmerized by his unblinking eyes. "I'd better make sure."

As my twig gently pokes about, Junior flashes off. Back and forth, up and down, showing off, he leaps with laughter straight up out of the glittering water. He definitely is a trout, an extroverted one at that. As he disappears, I probe in widening circles. "Where *are* you?" I whisper.

To my delight, from under a shadowed ledge Mama Trout suddenly peers, lean and long and much more freckled than Junior. Her dorsal fin is firm and high-rounded, threaded with white. Nearly ten inches long, she remains properly sedate as I bend close to study her dusky beauty. She does not fancy my reading glasses, however, when I don them for an even closer look. Off she whisks to perform her daily chores, no doubt whispering an echoing, "Where *are* you, Junior?"

Content with my two new acquaintances, I begin to dry my feet while standing on the grassy bank. With a start I drop my orange towel after glancing down at the sheltering rock ledge below.

Regally poised beneath it like a king on his throne lies Father Fish, over one foot long, thick and gloriously speckled. He emanates a superb aloofness that keeps me on the bank and spares him my reading-glasses-scrutiny. After all, he makes clear, I am intruding upon his native habitat. Mother and Junior frisk up and around him, reminding him, "The family that plays together, stays together." Glittering with royal splendor, he flashes off after them. Together they bound up the waterfall and away.

Viktor Schauberger discovered that a naturally flowing water-course like our stream builds up energy flowing in the opposite direction of the stream: "It is this energy that is used by the trout. In a suitably formed waterfall this energy flow can be distinguished as a channel of light within the streaming water. The trout seeks out this energy flow, and is sucked upwards as if in a whirlwind."

Trout like our frigid stream's positive energy, which is characteristic of water approaching 4°C. This cold temperature increases spiral and reverse flow and makes water alive and healthy; new healthy water builds when oxygen is bound by hydrogen in a process Schauberger termed "emulsion." In H_2O warmer than 4°C, oxygen binds hydrogen and the water begins to degenerate, allowing pathogenic bacteria to form.

When I return in the evening, Salomé has finished his beavering for the day, the upper sluice gates are open, and the stream is roaring. The swollen waterfall pounds the trout ledge, and I can see nothing of Home Sweet Home in the white, frothing turmoil of water. It makes one realize that much can be said for the ebbs of life, the quieter times, the so-called waning time when nature opens up to the vigilant and faithful.

In retrospect it is apparent that I unwittingly molded Mother Fish in my own image, always caretaking and whisking off to perform the daily chores, doing *all* the chores as Frank battled the numerous ills of his nineties. According to Bernie Siegel's findings described in *Love, Medicine and Miracles*, much of my feet and ankles problem is psychological. Indeed, I often did feel as if Frank were "walking the feet off me," working the feet off me with all the running of errands, transacting of business, and caregiving. One of Siegel's patients who suffered from cancer of the throat had been repeatedly squeezed about the throat as a child and told to "shut up!" Another with breast cancer said she "needed to get something off her chest." And a third with a diseased backbone observed that he had always been considered "spineless." All of us caregivers, in particular, will do well to remember these examples and to seek therapeutic counteraction *in time.*

My water healing is speeded by replacing insidious negative psychological messages with positive ones. Seated in a comfortable chair facing the huge cottonwood in our front yard, during morning meditations indoors I repeatedly affirm, "My legs, feet, and ankles are as straight and strong as that cottonwood trunk; they are healed and whole." Sitting in a folding chair in the stream while resting from walking up and down, I repeat my affirmation and open myself to continuous cosmic healing.

"Parallel processing" is another facet of the healing process. If a part of me continues nonstop all day long to repeat these messages, healing occurs much faster. In his book *The Holographic Universe* Michael Talbot tells of a woman named Cassandra afflicted with multiple personality disorder. Cassandra coined the term "parallel processing." She attributed her rapid healing ability and the slowing of her aging to a subpersonality named Celese "whose sole function is to spend twenty-four hours a day meditating and imaging the body's well-being. According to Cassandra, it is this full-time attention to her health by the subpersonality that gives her an edge over normal people."

Similarly, in *Fools Crow: Wisdom of Power* Tom Mails refers to the use by Pueblo Indians of feather prayer sticks called *pahos*—like those in our home—to perform what could be called "parallel processing." Mails writes of Indian customs he has observed, "The *pahos* continue to pray for them while they are occupied with daily tasks."

I have my clients image their different personality aspects, such as the female self, or anima, identified in Jungian psychology; the male self, or animus; and the Free Child self. The Healer Within is another self we must come to know, it seems to me, if we are effectively to utilize this helpful concept of "parallel processing." Personifying one's personality aspects, even naming them as Cassandra did, helps to make them more real, usable, and controllable; communication and affirmative action become possible with awareness. If I can image my negative animus, for example, I can more easily order it to "go fly a kite" when it stands in the way of my achieving or doing. It says, "You can't do that. You can't write a book." I say, "Get lost, George!" And keep on writing.

It can be effective to identify the Healer Within as a specific mental picture of a person or legendary being. For me he is Merlin, the Green Man, prophet, magician, and mentor in Arthurian legends. For some years I have owned a pewter statue one and a half inches high of a wizard named Merlin. Bearded, he wears a peaked hat and holds a crystal ball in his right hand; in his left he brandishes a gnarled walking stick like my water stick. As mentioned, I also see his beard, face, and pointed hat engraven in the trunk of our inspirational cottonwood in the front yard. It therefore seems natural and appropriate for my Healer Within to be personified as Merlin—the Merlin Within. Seeing him daily in the tree trunk and on my desk makes it easier to repeat my affirmations to myself and to him, just to make sure he doesn't forget his endless task of "parallel processing." It is also appropriate that this personification is masculine, for he functions as doer, and he gives me male company during my grieving while I'm not yet enthusiastic about getting involved again in human male dynamics.

Fools Crow, the Teton Sioux medicine man, personified key elements of his healing into concrete objects somewhat like my pewter statue or my turquoise bear fetish, only simpler. His personifications of healing most often were made of sticks ornamented with personal possessions. They too enhanced the power of positive thinking and doing. In interviews for Mails's book, the old holy man maintained that people first must heal themselves. "Then this understanding can be sent out from them to the rest of creation," Fools Crow said. In this way we can help to heal the entire planet.

The trouble is that often we don't bother with the *first* step, much less the second. "People do not do what is for their own best good," the wise medicine man added.

Fools Crow gazed deep into advanced souls—the Frank Waters type—and observed, "Spiritual people do not suffer as much from anxiety as other people do, and they do not worry as much about being chiefs or pleasing others just to get ahead in life. Instead, the things they do are personally rewarding. They feel good about themselves, and they naturally take care of themselves as they ought to."

I came from the sea. I can live outside the sea only because I carry within me an internal ocean. I return in primordial memory to the sea as I soak here in the Arroyo Seco River. The stream's music is one of our primordial sounds, like "om." Here my mind distinctly hears what Malvina Hoffman called the "choir of invisible forces." This day the primordial voice of the stream is that of a mighty Thunderer. Our meek little stream has grown into a Zeus, a veritable Odin. When the Thunderer speaks, I hang on his every word. His words send me soaring to the Sacred Mountain peak and beyond to the Source, then plunging back into the depths of our foaming waterfall, the other Source. I boost one foot onto Footprint Rock, where the ancestors have stood, then hoist myself astride our "river" as I balance one leg upon Buddha Head Boulder, the other upon Sleepy Head Rock. Buddha Head, looking like a mischievous E.T., laughs and spits water up at my face.

"Have you no respect, sir, for the Colossus of Rhodes?"

"I am colosssal in my own way," it squeaks and spits. "We each are colossssal in our own way. Sssometimes we just don't ssee it, that'sss all. Yet it'ss here for us to ssee, right in our own front yardsss."

We laugh, and the stream goes on its merry way hissing, shishing, shushing, sloshing, slashing, splashing, gurgling, gargling, gossiping, humming, hymning, whispering, roaring, declaiming.

Mostly it laughs at me, for when I'm not the Colossus of Rhodes, I am Captain Bligh or Captain Hook—something ferocious—or Captain of My Ship. Then again I am eternal youth, Peter Pan. When she catches me in this pose, Pam Trachta says I actually look twenty years younger. "I can fly. I can fly. I can fly!"

Oh, how the rocks gurgle with laughter. Even Serenity Pool sloshes its sides when I sing out boldly with my hands on my hips, "Second turn to the right, and straight on till morning!" They don't realize I've found my path: Straight On Till Morning.

As Joseph Campbell writes, "If you follow your bliss, you put yourself on a kind of track, which has been there all the while waiting for you, and the life that you ought to be living is the one you are living."

Our rivers, streams, and lakes here are sacred as well as primordial. Our neighbors rose from them, according to legend. Father Sun made them, and they came up in clans out of the lake at Mount Blanca just two hours north of here. Sun bade them, "Meet at the Canyon of the Red Willows." So came the Feather People, who settled on the south side of Taos beside Ranchos de Taos Creek, where petroglyphs remain to this good day. Then came the Shell People. After them arrived the Water People, who first were fish.

They swam up the Rio Grande and Taos Rivers to Ranchos Creek, where the Feather and Shell clans lived together. When they came to greet the newcomers, they saw all the fish standing up there in the water.

The two clans said, "Those are some of our people. Hurry! Bring two maidens and some bean plants with which to strike these fish."

After the girls struck the fish with bean plants, they became people. To this good day that creek is known by some as the Place of the Fish Standing Up People. I know; I used to live there in the little Hispanic community of Los Cordovas in old Ciria Montoya's home, a hacienda that has partially crumbled along with a *torreon*, or high tower to protect the Spanish from marauding Indians. It is still a power spot. Ciria lived to be 101 years old, protected she thought by the patron saint of farmers, San Ysidro, who prayed while his guardian angel plowed, and by San Antonio, whose face she turned to the wall whenever anything disappeared and didn't reappear. When she was ninety-five, a doctor removed a needle from the palm of her hand. For over half a century she had unknowingly carried it in her hand as a souvenir of washing rugs by hand in the creek of the Fish Standing Up People.

A darker archetype associated with rivers, streams, and lakes is La Llorona, mentioned before here. In most tales she weeps near a body of water where her child or children were drowned by her or her wealthy lover as he was about to abandon her. This archetype springing from the collective unconscious appears in some form in every culture. She is part of our unconscious. She shows us what not to do. Susan Smith may have been influenced by the negative side of this embedded archetype to dispose of her children as she did. Certainly the remainder of her life will be as tragic as has been the fabled afterlife of La Llorona. At a recent grief workshop this tale was to have been discussed, but the speaker never arrived. Instead guitarist Lorenzo Gonzales sang of La Llorona's different forms: the "Dark One"; the "Lady of Celestial Blue"; a green chile woman, "spicy but delicious"; the one who "is not even a shadow" now; the one for whom wind-tossed flowers cry in the cemetery— "I don't know what's wrong with the flowers. . . ." Any grieving person can identify with those words: "I don't know what's wrong with the flowers." Then one spring day dandelions start to blaze. When the flowers go right again, it's time to hold a Flower Ceremony.

The perfect place to celebrate is beside a body of water. Instead of attending Holy Trinity this morning, I listen to its soothing sacred bell while attending Serenity Stream Church. After last night's rain the air is pungent with the dusky smell of wet wood. The acrid odor of wild cilantro stimulates my senses. I chew a sprig of it as sacrificial wafer and wine. Red-breasted robins choir their morning hymn to nature while magpies scold a sermon. Suitably proper in vests of white, long black tails aglow with iridescence, they preen and squawk and chase pagan Trickster out of church as I toss purple garlands of wild iris to water sprites burbling with laughter.

Earlier at Casa Fresen Linda Ann had asked Stan, a Buddhist, "Are you on your way to or from church?"

Stan replied, "I *am* in church."

Amen, brother. Buffalo Head Rock under the waterfall at the edge of Serenity Pool today resembles a great cosmic fish, a fabulous Leviathan carrying the waters of the world upon its back. According to Cirlot, the fish is "a symbol of profound life, of the spiritual world that lies under the world of appearances . . . the life-force surging up." It reminds me to work through my grief, rather than let it stagnate, and to change that energy into a positive, higher, life-giving force. I must reinvent my Frank energy. Water is also a fine place to transmute grief into feelings of joy, love, and appreciation for departed ones.

Water helps me to see the cosmic holographic structure of my universe. Surrounding me is a grand kiva containing fire, rocks, water, tree beings, mountain beings, air, stars, sun and moon, sea creatures, animals, relatives and friends, and the Troops with their wisdom people such as Merlin, Fools Crow and his uncle Black Elk, Chief Joseph, and Hildegard of Bingen. Intermingled with all, touching and guiding all, is the Source—the superimplicate order. As in a holographic photograph, when I slant my life one way, certain of these entities stand out to assist me. Slant it another way and others come forth.

My holographic universe is similar to Aldo Leopold's "round river," a smaller cosmic vision in which "the current is the stream of energy which flows out of the soil into plants, thence into animals, thence back into the soil in a never ending circuit of life."

Water is creative in that it helps to focus clear vision. Even a shower or bath can clear cobwebs from the mind and replace them with vision. Frank saw the vision for his basic structure of *The Man Who Killed the Deer* in a washbasin, for instance. In the last analysis, you are the creator of creativity, assisted by cosmic gifts such as water.

Jung said, "When spirit becomes heavy, it turns to water. . . . Therefore the way of the soul . . . leads to water." He built his sanctuary tower beside the water and played in water and sand to renew himself.

In *Women Who Run with the Wolves*, Estés has an entire metaphorical chapter about water nourishing creativity. And she repeatedly advocates going to water—even for five minutes a month—to renew and reenergize the neglected dynamic parts of ourselves.

An extra bonus of water contact is bringing a family or a couple together again, counteracting the drifting tendency. Some of my happiest, most sustaining memories are of picnics beside streams, rivers, lakes, and oceans. They started when I was a child, continued through my first marriage, and extended through my relationship with Frank and beyond. Today the sight of a picnic basket temporarily overwhelms me with sadness, another unexpected Damn First. Ten days before Frank died we went on our last picnic together at Gates Pass near Tucson. Ron Kampfe, a picnic hater before we came into his life, wrote of this happy gathering:

> One week before you rolled out of bed in Seco and kissed the good earth good-bye, we picnicked. You, Barbara, L. D. and Laverne Clark, Charlene and I broke sourdough, chicken bones, and the neck off a fine wine bottle. There was some blood shared with all that breaking going on.
>
> We had luck. We found a clean table where you could roll up nicely in your oxygen-tanked wheelchair. There were bees instead of flies.
>
> We were all happy with ourselves together. The sun was full of itself, too, as it set far to the flat-out west in a sherbet way: lemon, orange, strawberry.
>
> Your voice rose above our table talk, "Look! A woman with hair of fire!" Our eyes blazed in wonder. She was not being consumed, but she was on fire all the same.
>
> She said, "It's the henna, the sun, the wind, my split ends." She knew we all had seen her in a special light; that she had been

seen by someone special, that she had been in your eyes, Frank. She was the Virgin of Guadalupe, said a friend.

Our last Taos picnic together seems so ordinary. One seldom recognizes Lasts. The approach to our Lucky Seven picnic area—the seventh up Taos Ski Valley Road—is a steep gravel road curving sharply down into a sanctuary domed with tall pines and skirted by Arroyo Hondo River chanting paeans of praise to all Water Worshipers. Its joyous song joins our laughter and soothes the strained rough edges from too much partying with too many people last night. Tal Luther's face then was white and drawn. Today he sits relaxed and talkative, his face flooded a healthy pink color. Marilyn's red hair and shy smile glisten with reflected brilliance from the stream tumbling at our feet. Frank as ever is Puff the Magic Dragon, dragging in audible puffs of oxygen on each inhalation of breath, his face at peace with the woodland glowing about him.

We eat well, Inés and Alex Blackburn's deviled eggs and chicken strips blending with my chicken salad, pasta, olives, and couscous salad, mostly from Casa Fresen; Marilyn's fruit salad, a vivid still life of sliced peaches, strawberries, bing cherries, and green grapes; and leftover key lime pie topped with real whipped cream and sparked with Johannesburg Riesling or "Passionfruit Delight."

The six of us sit in a semicircle of folding chairs facing the river and talk eagerly of books and persons and plans for the future. Navy-blue clouds up the canyon warn us to make the most of our short time together even as shafts of sunlight light up the forest primeval and halo our heads as if we have stepped back in time into the green trysting glade of Hester Prynne and Reverend Dimmesdale.

For me, a picnic without wading is not a picnic. Changing from silver sandals into an old pair of walking shoes, I plunge into the shallow icy water singing my name, luring me ever farther from the shore into a raging current that tugs at the ruffled hem of my blue denim skirt, seeking to wrest my feet from under me. Grabbing an aspen branch bronzed by water, I dig in, defying mischievous water sprites, and pick my way across treacherous gold, ruby, and azure rocks until I reach a sandy cove sparkling with flecks of gold. Treasure! It has to be the real thing! Prospectors long ago struck gold not far above us at the old mining camp at Twining. Yet somehow my gold treasure eludes me time after time, grain by grain, sifting through my fingers like the sands of time running out for all of us.

To help save the Rio Grande River, two months after Frank's death an ecologically minded group holds a water rite beside the river near Pilar along Old Taos Road where we also used to picnic. Two messenger eagles circle overhead. I cry and cannot speak when asked.

I remember Ann Merrill and me swimming here in our underwear, as Frank watched from the bank. When she went back, I floated on forever into the glorious sunset. This fleeting moment on the Rio Grande lives on in Ann's poem, written later in our pasture.

The horse is running along
the fence, whinnying
for her hurt friend.
Reminds me of Frank
running on the river bank
when Barbara swims.

26
Home of the Mountain Spirit

Oh Sacred Mountain,
Give me your eye
To look at the world
With God.

All winter the Place of the Red Willows has been scarlet with low willow wands. With little vegetation to detract from their beauty, along the roadside in Arroyo Seco they have glowed brick red, henna, burnt orange, lavender, or silvery mauve. Competition is setting in now. Cottonwoods have changed from pearl-gray to pewter, tall willow trees from antique gold to marigold to molten red-gold. Apricot trees glow with pale pink blooms; aspens are afloat with gray caterpillar strands changing to silver catkins. Fragile jonquils quiver palely aloof from forsythia flinging citrus yellow to the sun. Dandelions beam probing sunlight into the new dark corner of my heart, a place of brooding over Saki's passing, which seems a final piece of Frank—and of an era—dissolved into nothingness. Saki's death is yet another *camposanto*, another flowered cross along a stationed trail of grief.

It came to me outdoors while looking down at the ground after his impressive funeral that Saki Karavas lives on in the bright smiling yellow of spring's first dandelions rather than as a tree. In Greek Orthodox belief Saki died during Bright Week, their most special time of the year. Bright Week celebrates the Resurrection; thus, Saki had the great honor of being resurrected symbolically with Christ. Saki's transition also included a bronze casket, masses of flowers, Spanish and Greek music, a magnificent feast for his friends, and an imposing headstone. He had told me, first in Greek, then in English, "Show me the graves of your ancestors and I know who you are." Noula, his mother, frequently reminded him of this old Greek saying; Noula, who dressed like a fairy princess all her life.

They have the most singular burial plot in Sierra Vista Cemetery, the Karavas family and one visitor. It's a full house. Noula, who was born on magical Ithaca, has the largest monument, of course. Behind her are her husband, his brother, and an aunt, also born on Ithaca. To the left of Noula's marker is the smaller headstone of Evelyn Gaspard, first wife of a noted Taos artist about whom Frank wrote a book. Saki lies eternally beside his mother, to the east. Three bare trees and two small evergreens watch over them.

Kasantzakis says to you, Saki, "This earthen womb knows unerringly the worth of each of her children."

As symbolically fitting as Bright Week and glowing dandelions is Saki's icon memorial card: on one side a golden Noula madonna clutches her perennial child; on the other a poem reminds us of our happy times with Saki, our laughing times, the bright and sunny days, the "afterglow of smiles" he leaves behind.

Despite Bright Week and the perfection of Saki's farewell tribute, the next day I feel dull and depressed. After ten months, with spring in the air, this reaction has not been anticipated. For the first time ever, on the drive home from a full day of errands in Santa Fe, the rugged pink adobe landscape looks as bleak as I feel.

Desperately I turn to an old Tewa chant that I adapted in the '70s to bring me back here forever. Staring across the Tucson valley at a gigantic rock formation resembling the head of an Indian chieftain wearing a warbonnet and engraven by nature into the Catalina Mountains, I had repeated this chant day after day, year after year. It ended with a stanza beseeching the universe to bring me back to Frank and to Taos Sacred Mountain. On this doleful Saturday I chant instead to Taos Sacred Mountain:

My home over there
My home over there
Now I remember it
And when I see that mountain far away
Why then I weep, alas,
What can I do?
What can I do? Alas, what can I do?
My home over there
My home over there
Now I remember it
And I beg you
Please bring me back to light and joy
Bring zest for life
Back into my heart
I beg you please
Bring necessary
Help for the Foundation
Send me help to ease these burdens ·
Keep me safe and happy here
One with Sacred Taos Mountain
My home over here
My home over here.

Indians say, "If the mountains speak to you, you will always come back to them." It helps a great deal for us to speak to them as well, particularly in the form of a repetitious chant. Perhaps a chant calls forth energy of the universe and nature while lulling individual reason and ego to sleep. The universe communicates through us when we set aside reason and ego for as long as possible. But we also have the privilege of initiating dialogue. In short, we must learn to think like mountains, as Aldo Leopold expressed it, for they reflect the peak within ourselves, the greater Self.

As Judy Romero-Oak once wrote in the *Taos News*, the artist measures the Mountain's perspective with his thumb; the priest worships the One who made the Mother Mountain; the philosopher measures the perspective of life by the Mountain.

If you cannot communicate with mountains, sooner or later you will leave them. Legend has it that the tears of an Indian maiden pining for her lost lover seeped into the heart of Taos Sacred Mountain. They crystallized into a jewel that attracts good-hearted persons and repels those with war in their hearts. Other legends claim that the magnetic Mother Spirit of this mountain drew the Feather People up Taos Canyon and the Water People up the Rio Grande River. After climbing the gorge walls they became people. In the heart of Taos Mountain lies the *sipapu* called Blue Lake, the place of emergence for Taos Indians. "It is our church," they say.

The dual peaks of Taos Mountain and El Cuchillo del Media above us have been compared to Mount Gerizim and Mount Ebal, the Old Testament mountains of blessing and cursing. Romero-Oak related this version of one of the darker legends connected with the duality of El Cuchillo: "The Indians tell of a jealous wife who followed her husband and his lover to the top of the mountain and fought with the other woman. They both rolled over the edge of the cliff and were torn to pieces. They left their white clothes hanging on the sharp roots and it became known later as 'El Salto,' the falling-off place. Often in the spring a waterfall freezes and looks like shiny white garments hanging over it."

One hour after my arrival home from Santa Fe on Saturday two Texans bring the Foundation a check for $7,500 to reinstate a movie option deal that had gone sour a week before Frank's death. Why should this startle me when the option had to do with Frank's first book, *The Lizard Woman*, a symbol of the uroborus? The next day, Sunday, a tall, dark, handsome man in his sixties unexpectedly takes me to a fund-raising breakfast on the reservation and to a preliminary showing of the dynamite movie *Caught*, where I meet Edward James Olmos, who says he is interested in playing the crazy gold-miner role in *The Lizard Woman*. At breakfast I had given my escort, Dan Budnik, a copy of *The Lizard Woman*. He passes it on directly to Olmos. My chant has been heard.

Dan, a close friend of both Frank and Saki, is in town for the funeral. I can hear those two departed ones laughing their heavenly heads off at coming through for me, in no way that could have been expected. Dan always will be like a brother to me—not my type—but the two good-bye kisses he bestows upon my cheek in front of a long line of theatergoers will have Taos gossiping for months. Saki throve on gossip, and Frank did not disdain it. I suspect that gossip and intrigue are as much honey and nectar to our gods today as they were to the Olympians in ancient Greece. And I know that Saki will be a sought-after local ghost, a graying Greek Charles Boyer wearing a silk cravat, dancing a celestial tango.

They do attend to serious business, these hovering spirits. The following day, Monday, at the blinking light six miles down the road Peter Wood sees a stranger named Mike Romero hauling boulders. Mike has a Bobcat, Peter learns. By noon Mike has Frank's monument boulder and granite meditation chair in proper position after a winter of lying askew where they had been abandoned by a hotheaded fellow named Cahn who had left in a huff after a lean, mean aspen scratched his pickup a mite. Frank had liked old man Cahn. I myself do not feel the same about his son. Sympathetic Mike Romero precipitates a shower of tears when he says of Frank, "I can tell you loved him—a *lot*." Now I know why the Easter Island face on the west end of Taos Sacred Mountain smiled at me on Saturday for the first time in weeks.

The men optioning *The Lizard Woman* said, "It's simply a matter of getting the boulder moving again."

All sorts of boulders are moving.

On this same Monday, as I turn to a book Frank edited called *Cuchama and Sacred Mountains*, he sends me a handwritten message of love, an inscription from February 1982 that I had totally forgotten: "Dear Barbara—This book, tidy as it looks, bears the marks of so much of your work—ms. corrections, galley revisions and proofreading, telephone dialogues with Chuck Adams, letters to Ohio [Press], our trip to Stanford and interlude at Las Vegas, and months of waiting—it should most properly be inscribed by you to that innocent bystander Cuchama, which has stood so impassively. Love—Frank."

Monday evening a stranger calls to say an artist has left at his store a charcoal sketch of Frank done several years ago. I pick it up this fourth day after my Mountain Chant, the fourth day of completion. The charcoal is a gaunt and ghastly Frank from another realm. I shudder at first. Then I remember that he has been through a lot, after all. And he is half smiling. Most important, he is communicating. A pressing deadline also has unexpectedly been extended for me today. I am grateful for all. This fourth day most likely will complete the magic of Saturday's chanting. I shall store away my Mountain Chant until another rainy, overwhelming day.

In his foreword to *Cuchama* Lama Anagarika Govinda wrote:

> To see the greatness of a mountain, one must be at a distance from it; to understand its form, one must move around it; to experience its moods, one must see it at sunrise and sunset, at noon and at midnight, in sun and in rain, in snow and storm, in summer and winter, and in spring and autumn. He who can see the mountain in this manner comes near to the life of the mountain, which is as intense as that of a human being. Mountains grow and decay, they breathe and pulsate with life. They attract and collect invisible energies from their surroundings.

Frank appreciated growing up close to the vibrating energy of Pikes Peak, a "spiritual font." In *The Colorado* he wrote, "Next time, by hook or crook, make sure you're born with a mountain in the front yard." With a mountain so close, he added, you don't have to travel. It's a "whole world heaped up in layers." By 1980 he was lamenting the human destruction of this sacred peak's energy and that of Cheyenne Mountain nearby. He thought the military had hopelessly gutted Cheyenne Mountain of its soul. Rather than viewing Pikes Peak as dead, he stated in a *Cuchama* footnote that it "had withdrawn to itself its benevolent influence." Of its former psychic renown he observed, "Pike's Peak in Colorado, 14,110 feet high, was one of the most notable sacred mountains in the United States. The Ute Creation Myth centered upon it, and its mythical origin parallels stories of the Flood. Its spiritual forces, like a great magnet, drew people to it for centuries. It was a mecca for Utes coming down from the Rockies, and for Arapahoes, Kiowas, and Cheyennes from the Great Plains to the east, who dropped votive offerings in the medicinal spring at its foot."

In *The Colorado* he described what it had meant to him personally:

> When you're no bigger than *that* you can hang on the grimy window curtains and watch it hour after hour. Then you know it best with all its moods and mutations, its sternness, dignity and immeasurable depth. It is like the face of an old medicine man, which only a child can understand. Other times it's just a grand spectacle of a thing—a whole show in itself. In the evening when the sun snags on the rimrock and the hollows fill up with red and lilac, damson blue and purple; when the summer storms explode against its shoulder like soap bubbles filled with father's pipe smoke, and the deer-horn lightning sprouts from the crags; or even in winter when its slopes turn slick and green as Blue Ribbon bottle glass.

Govinda in his foreword for *Cuchama* compared sacred mountains to personalities of human leaders who possess the power to influence others. Three characteristics make up such a personality, he thought: "consistency, harmony, and one-pointedness of character." A sacred mountain with these charismatic characteristics has so great a cosmic power that its psychic and magnetic vibrations draw people to it intuitively, he felt. They don't have to be told or urged to make pilgrimages to such a spot. This is a different, intriguing idea from that of our writing workshop members who theorized that humans make a spot sacred.

The main part of *Cuchama* was written by W. Y. Evans-Wentz, with whom Frank had begun corresponding in 1947. A world authority on Tibetan Buddhism, Evans-Wentz had edited and annotated ancient treatises such as *The Tibetan Book of the Dead* and *Tibet's Great Yogi Milarepa*. After reading *Masked Gods*, he was surprised at how deeply Frank had delved into esotericism and at how closely American Indian religion paralleled that of Hindus and Tibetans. Evans-Wentz became increasingly interested in a mountain named Mount Tecate, or Cuchama, located in northern Mexico outside the town of Tecate; it was said to be sacred once to Cochimís, Yumas, and other Indians. In 1953 Evans-Wentz wrote Frank that he was beginning to write a book about sacred mountains located in Tibet, India, and China but needed information on America's sacred mountains. Frank sent some material; they met in San Diego and later visited Cuchama together.

Born in 1879, Evans-Wentz had spent his early years in southern California and later earned B.A. and M.A. degrees at Stanford University. He received a doctorate in comparative religions at Oxford University and a doctorate at the University of Rennes in France with a thesis titled "The Fairy Faith in Celtic Countries," a subject he'd researched for four years. Evans-Wentz inherited a five-thousand-acre ranch about twenty-five miles south of San Diego that included Cuchama. At his death in 1965 almost half this ranch was deeded to the state of California, including the sacred mountain. The rest went to Stanford, along with Evans-Wentz's manuscripts and private papers. Years later Chuck Adams found the forgotten sacred mountains manuscript at Stanford and convinced Frank to coedit and annotate it for publication by the University of Ohio Press, which had acquired rights to Frank's preferred publishing house, Swallow Press.

Income from the ranch and other bequests were used by Stanford to set up a professorship, scholarships, and lectures on Oriental philosophies and world religions. On May 5, 1981, at

Stanford's annual W. Y. Evans-Wentz Lecture, Frank presented his talk "Symbols and Sacred Mountains: Comparable Themes in Buddhism and American Religion." He felt honored but nervous about presenting his controversial ideas at such a prestigious institution. The talk lacked the depth of his writings and in a more minor way, like Evans-Wentz's book, was a jumble of interesting concepts. The book generally lacked depth, detail, cohesiveness, and good writing. Nevertheless, we had a good time there. Frank pulled out of his wrong-side-of-the-tracks syndrome, and we secretly acted like two delighted, mischievous kids who had successfully sneaked into a circus under the rear tent flap without paying. Better yet, Frank got paid for it.

Perhaps Cuchama had decayed by the time Frank, Susie, and I drove there for a picnic in the early '90s. It didn't look like a sacred mountain, and it didn't feel like a sacred mountain. Its name means Exalted High Place; yet it is only 3,887 feet high, unforested now, sprawling horizontally, tending toward flatness. The road was badly maintained that April, and a steep washed-out arroyo stopped us near a rocky area about a mile before the ascent began. Susie was not as adventurous as Frank and I. She was already acting nervous when a police car with flashing lights drove up to the rocky promontory we had chosen as our picnic spot. I continued unpacking our picnic lunch, a chair for Frank, and his portable oxygen unit as the officer approached.

"You know all eyes are on you here, don't you?" he asked.

"Really!" I said, eyeing the barren landscape.

"Really?" Susie said, nervously fingering a long, lethal Bowie knife she had brought along as protection.

"We haven't seen a soul," Frank said.

"In the first place, this is a hiding place for those who illegally leave Mexico. Then there are the drug smugglers. These illegals are watching you. In the second place, those whose duty it is to catch the illegals are watching you *and* them. Shots have been known to be fired."

"Really!" Frank said.

305

"Really?" Susie said.

"You probably won't be shot at. We can't *guarantee* anything. Remember, many eyes are upon you right this moment. The hills around you are full of eyes, some good, some bad! Take care. This is not a good place to be. But enjoy your picnic." The officer waved and drove slowly off toward Tecate, which we could see sprawled below us behind a chain-link fence at the border.

Tucked in a boulder crevice above us I found a mattress, a milk carton, and a plastic water bottle. Frank and I enjoyed our picnic immensely. All these dangerous "eyes" added relish. But I will always remember Susie as a whirling dervish that day. Every so often she'd grab her brutal Bowie knife, brandish it before her, and whirl in a flashing 360-degree circle.

"Just checking!" she would say in all seriousness. "Nobody's getting away with anything!"

We saw no eyes, no other persons, no bullets. There may yet be more to this Exalted High Place than meets the eye. Cuchama seemed grateful to sense once again humble pilgrims of the spirit. For this, it may have protected us. And it is helpful to feel in harmony with nature when one becomes involved in potentially tense situations.

Govinda was right when he said sacred mountains are more powerful when seen and felt from a distance. I experienced this at Baboquiviri, the phallus-shaped sacred mountain in southern Arizona of the Tohono O'odham Indians, once called Papagos. It is the most challenging mountain to climb in those parts, and it is best to rappel down with an expert like Pete who knows where to place the ropes. Within Babo is a cave from which is said to have emerged the O'odham culture hero, the man in the maze on their baskets. On top I did not feel Babo's full power as I did while staying at the picturesque ranch below.

From below, Baboquiviri looked like a mammoth eagle with a great hooked beak. In my mind, hundreds of miles away I can see and feel him still. Indians say the eagle is a sacred messenger. And in Rudolfo Anaya's chapter in *Man and Mystic* he uses the eagle as a metaphor for Frank. The setting on the ranch below was peaceful and nurturing, with fan-tailed peacocks strolling through rich stands of cacti, tall saguaro, and shady mesquite trees. Yet this powerful presence above kept me awake, urging me on to the next step in my growth. I'd had fun with Pete; I had learned much from him. He is a very special man. But he was not the best man for me at this evolving stage in my life. Baboquiviri gave me the awareness and the courage to tell him so, right then and there. A Tewa Indian prayer teaches, "Within and around the mountains, your authority returns to you."

Pete subsequently visited my son and my brother to tell them I had suddenly gone off my rocker and to urge them to "reason" with me. They shook their heads in sympathy, knowing better than to waste any breath on me. Men loved Pete's outdoorsmanship. Women too. He could be sexy. The priceless gift built into reaching a panoramic stage of life is that one glimpses overviews of how the universe communicates through oneself and how it has sent just the right teachers when they were needed, the right movers and shakers. Now it was time to move on to the teachings of Taos Sacred Mountain and its mate along with those of other mountains, and of mountain men. This book mainly is made of their teachings.

The white crown of sacred Fujiyama, "the Honorable Mountain," towers over twelve thousand feet above sea level in Japan. At its summit is a shrine to the "Princess Who Maketh the Blossoms of the Trees to Flower." At its base each spring blossom azaleas and cherry trees, mirrored in five sacred lakes. Yaye Takayama, wife of Taos artist Michio Takayama, used to call Pedernal Peak "Little Fuji." Viewed from her porch in Taos, it brought her much solace in this home away from Japan for more than twenty years before her death. Out in front at the beginning of our driveway I too can see the flat-topped mesa off in the west near Abiquiu, Georgia O'Keeffe country. From here Pedernal Peak is always blue, usually three tiered shades lighter than the navy-blue rock formation nearest us but still far out on the carpeted plains past the Rio Grande gorge.

According to the story of emergence related by Navajo medicine man Hasteen Klah, Pedernal Peak was the birthplace of Changing Woman, the great Earth Mother of his people. She is the Southwest's "Princess Who Maketh the Blossoms of the Trees to Flower." Changing Woman possesses reproductive and birth power for all that exists on earth. In charge of all vegetation and female rain, she might also be called the Navajos' Green Woman. Like the earth, she renews her youth as the seasons progress from winter to summer. When ill, Navajos therefore chant to her so that they too may renew themselves. She created the people of the West from her own epidermis. She created the horse, and the black stick she placed on her son Monster Slayer's forehead became deer antlers. She helps humans overcome the results of their ignorance. She stands for peace. Her rituals attract good. And she is far-seeing, for she has binoculars made of rock crystal.

The birth of Changing Woman on sacred Pedernal Peak was auspicious. First a dark cloud hovered over the peak for four days; rain drenched the mountain, signifying that a supernatural event was occurring. Arcing from sky to mountain, a rainbow then heralded the arrival of this sacred child of Earth Spirit and Sky Spirit. Bluebirds sang out promise of peace, happiness, and success. The backboard of Changing Woman's cradle was made of straight lightning; it was rounded at the top in front with a rainbow. Red sun rays crisscrossed the infant's chest and feet. Dressed in a white cloud robe, she was covered with blue, white, and yellow clouds and laced in by sunbeams crossed with zigzag lightning. She fed and throve upon sacred white shell pollen moistened with the dew of beautiful flowers.

When Changing Woman lost her baby teeth, she threw them to the east after receiving a new set of white shell teeth from the gods. As a young woman, Changing Woman met Sun at a spring as he watered his white horse. She let sunlight enter her, and fresh spring water too. She and Sun together represented life, though she herself was primarily of the earth. Soon Changing Woman gave birth to twins: Monster Slayer, the son of Light; and Child-of-the-

Water. These two rid the world of monsters. Taking animals with her as company, Changing Woman traveled at last to the western ocean, where Sun had built for her a white shell house, a place for him to rest at the end of each day.

Still we pay homage to Changing Woman, who is our expanding selves, and to "Little Fuji," which gives us the truth of mountains. As a Japanese writer observed about Mount Fuji, "To know the real Fuji, one must look at the self in relation to Fuji rather than at the mountain itself. . . . When one's eyes are opened by forgetting the self and becoming one with Fuji, then one will know the true form of the mountain."

The same is true of writing, as well as of daily living. Forget your little self, the uncertain inadequate self, and the archetypal greater Self comes through. Set aside reason and ego, and it takes only discipline to sit down and let this Self pour through the open way; to have focused creative *discipline* is the invaluable lesson a human mountain taught me by example. A mountain is a perfect symbol for one's archetypal Self; it has the same energy and spirituality, and it puts the puny self in proper perspective. Look a mountain in the face, talk to it regularly, and it will make you larger.

You don't have to be "born with a mountain in your front yard." You can come to mountains in midlife, as I did, and you will become a changed woman. You can marry one, as I did. You will probably never be able to live without mountains again, like me. Like Changing Woman, you will be born again on the mountain with lightning for a backbone, a rainbow as your third eye, trees in your heart, sun in your womb, water at your feet. You will grow young again, no matter what your age, each season you live with a mountain's *passion*. Perhaps you will be fortunate enough someday to gravitate to the West and live in a white shell house made of adobe where the Leo sun will come to you in spirit at the end of each long day.

Scott Momaday wrote that nature defines the best in us. It *is* the best in us. Tell me how you feel about nature and I know who you are.

27
Feather

Our lives are shaped
as much by those who leave us
as by those who stay.

Strange what difficult patches the Quiltmaker gives us to complete. Darwine and I are back in the same dread emergency-room cubicle where I said good-bye to Frank's body in the hospital trimmed in Taos Blue for good luck. When the same kind doctor consults with me about her, I begin to shake. It helps that the nurse who hugs is nowhere to be seen. My storm of tears is stayed until I reach the car.

Like Frank at his death, Darwine is ninety-two and has emphysema. Unlike Frank, she suffers from increasing paranoia and senility. Moreover, she will survive this visit and thrive for some months to come. As a smart real estate saleswoman, she once had a good sense of humor. Now no one else will assume power of attorney to help her, not even her relatives, for on the surface she is an impossible woman. Her father, a writer, admired the work of Charles Darwin; thus the first name of his favorite daughter. How sad, in some respects, that she is one of the fittest of the species to survive. By contrast, she makes me appreciate Frank ever more profoundly. She uses his walker.

In her home during her more irascible moments Darwine refers to me as "the Queen Bee." When she cannot remember this exalted title in the emergency room, she calls me merely "the Butterfly." Or "a bowl of shit."

"The Butterfly" reminds me of the rampant bear in my dream. It too is a symbol of emergence and resurrection since it hibernates, then comes back to life. Besides being redemptive, it is thought to have curative powers. The bear has also been called symbolic of the "great compassionate Self," Matthew Fox writes in *Confessions*.

Like me, my friends often wonder why I bother with Darwine. Perhaps this is why. During times of grieving one begins to explore and to live more fully the "great compassionate Self," the soul. "To encounter the bear is to wake up." Paradoxically, to encounter death is to wake up, to live more inwardly, to live more keenly.

My widowed friend Irene comforts Kit upon the death of her dog, Kit's only companion: "You just have to lie there and let it roll over you like a Mack truck. But while you're lying there, be sure to look up at the stars!"

Besides relating my journey with Frank, these chapters are part of the story of my survival and awakening, my looking up at the stars. Elie Wiesel insists, "Whoever survives a test, whatever it may be, must tell the story." Survival is a celebration of mortality or immortality. It is a celebration of the enduring coyote in our beloved Trickster, in Frank, in myself, in all of us.

In looking up at the stars, I am comforted to know that Frank is in his proper place as one of the Pleiades, the Harmonious Ones. And Orion has its own special message for me. I like to look at "my" constellation from the waist down and consider its three belt stars as the top of its head. This way the smaller figure has one hand firmly planted on its hip with its legs striding forward across the sky. Ever since my sons used the expression as teenagers, indomitable Orion has seemed to encourage me, "Keep on truckin', Barbara. Keep on truckin'."

The final step in grief recovery is reinvesting the energy formerly invested in a departed one. This energy of mine has been reinvested in the Frank Waters Foundation. In his autobiography Arthur Rubenstein wrote, "The Power of Creation seems to favor human beings who accept and love life unconditionally." This is what our Foundation is about. Creating, loving life, accepting. Giving. Growing. Listening, seeing, touching, and reaching out. We are primarily reaching out to creative persons who will appreciate two-month residencies in small studios where they can write, paint, or compose in a tranquil setting rich in spirit of place. As mentioned, our motto is "Sheltering the Creative Spirit."

Two golden eagles fly in low over our first *casita* for artists and writers on the day builder Peter Wood finishes this labor of love. They dip and salute as I sit resting on the porch after waxing the wine-red cement floor of our simple cabin. The female flies to the Sacred Aspen Grove and perches above Frank's granite monument carved by Ted Egri.

Repeatedly the male eagle circles widely toward the east, flies in from the north, and dips low to my left. He lifts close above his mate, soars on around toward Frank's wooden cross under the oak tree in the upper pasture. The two of them join in tight circles above this pastoral cross fashioned by Lee Bentley, swoop past me, and come to rest above our front yard upon an arced cottonwood limb matching the curve of a crescent moon behind them.

Standing below them, I thank them for the eagle feather they have left for our retreat, and perhaps for my emergence. Frank always said feathers were lucky. It is another caress from him.

Then they fly off into the west, like Quetzalcoatl. He promised to return when needed. They may too. But this singular Blessing of the Eagles is enough.

Someone up there cares.

Bibliography

Aldington, Richard. *D. H. Lawrence: Portrait of a Genius But. . . .* New York: Collier, 1967.

Aldo, Leopold. *Round River.* Edited by Luna B. Leopold. New York: Oxford University Press, 1953.

———. *A Sand Country Almanac.* New York: Oxford University Press, 1949.

Alexandersson, Olof. *Living Water.* Rev. ed. Bath, England: Gateway Books, 1990.

Anaya, Rudolfo A. *Bless Me, Última.* Berkeley: Quinto Sol Publications, 1972.

Anderson, George K., and Karl J. Holzknecht, eds. *The Literature of England.* Chicago: Scott, Foresman, 1953.

Anderson, William. *Green Man.* London: HarperCollins Publishers, 1990.

Barrie, J. M. *Peter Pan.* New York: Henry Holt, 1987.

Berkus, Rusty. *To Heal Again.* Encino, Calif.: Red Rose Press, 1984.

Bingham, Hiram. *Lost City of the Incas.* New York: Duell, Sloan and Pearce, 1948.

Bolls, Imogene. "The Walk to the Upper Pasture." *Studies in Frank Waters* 17 (October 1995): 16–17.

Boone, J. Allen. *Kinship with All Life.* San Francisco: HarperCollins Publishers, 1976.

Brett, Dorothy. *Lawrence and Brett: A Friendship*. Philadelphia: J. B. Lippincott, 1933.

Bynner, Witter. *Journey with Genius*. New York: John Day Company, 1951.

Byrne, Janet. *A Genius for Living*. New York: HarperCollins Publishers, 1995.

Campbell, Joseph. *The Power of Myth*. New York: Doubleday, 1988.

Cather, Willa. *Death Comes for the Archbishop*. New York: Alfred A. Knopf, 1955.

Christensen, Oscar C. "Adlerian Family Counseling." Classroom lecture at University of Arizona, Tucson, 1986.

Cirlot, J. E. *A Dictionary of Symbols*. New York: Philosophical Library, 1971.

Clark, Glenn. "The Divine Plan." N.p., n.d.

Cordova, Josephine M. *No Lloro Pero Me Acuerdo*. Dallas: Taylor Publishing, 1976.

Cross, Milton, and David Ewen, eds. "Wolfgang Amadeus Mozart." Quoting Goethe in *Encyclopedia of the Great Composers and Their Music*. Vol 2. Garden City: Doubleday, 1953.

Dean, Winnie. *Jefferson: Queen of the Cypress*. Dallas: Mathis, Van Nort, 1953.

Deloria, Vine, Jr. *God Is Red*. New York: Grosset & Dunlap, 1973.

———, ed. *Frank Waters: Man and Mystic*. Athens: Ohio University Press, Swallow Press, 1993.

Elkins, Andrew. "'So Strangely Married': Peggy Pond Church's *The Ripened Fields: Fifteen Sonnets of a Marriage*." *Western American Literature*, vol. 30, no. 4 (February 1996): 353–372.

Estés, Clarissa Pinkola. "The Creative Fire." *Magical Blend*, no. 43 (July 1994): 31.

———. *Women Who Run with the Wolves*. New York: Ballantine Books, 1992.

Evans-Wentz, W. Y. *Cuchama and Sacred Mountains*. Edited by Frank Waters and Charles L. Adams. Athens: Ohio University Press, Swallow Press, 1981.

———, ed. *The Tibetan Book of the Dead*. 3d. ed. London: Oxford University Press, 1957.

———, ed. *Tibet's Great Yogi Milarepa*. London: Oxford University Press, 1928.

Fields, Rick. *The Code of the Warrior.* New York: Harper Collins Publishers, HarperPerennial, 1991.

Fletcher, Colin. *The Man Who Walked Through Time.* New York: Alfred A. Knopf, 1968.

Foster, Joseph. *D. H. Lawrence in Taos.* Albuquerque: University of New Mexico, 1972.

Fox, Matthew. *Confessions.* San Francisco: HarperCollins Publishers, 1996.

———. *Illuminations of Hildegard of Bingen.* Santa Fe: Bear & Company, 1985.

Franz, Marie-Louise von. *The Way of the Dream.* Toronto: Windrose Films, 1988.

Gillmor, Frances, and Louisa Wade Wetherill. *Traders to the Navajos.* Albuquerque: University of New Mexico Press, 1952.

Grattan, Virginia L. *Mary Colter: Builder upon the Red Earth.* Flagstaff, Ariz.: Northland Press, 1980.

Green, Martin. *The von Richthofen Sisters.* New York: Basic Books, 1974.

Hannah, Barbara. *Jung: His Life and Work.* New York: G. P. Putnam's Sons, Perigee Books, 1976.

Harding, M. Esther. *The Way of All Women.* New York: G. P. Putnam's Sons, 1970.

———.*Woman's Mysteries: Ancient and Modern.* New York: Harper & Row Publishers, Harper Colophon Books, 1971.

Heinke, Linda Ann. "Second Snowfall." *Frank Waters Foundation Newsletter,* vol. 4, no. 9 (April–July 1996): 3.

Hemingway, Ernest. *A Farewell to Arms.* New York: Charles Scribner's Sons, 1929.

Hemming, John. *The Conquest of the Incas.* New York: Harcourt Brace Jovanovich, 1970.

"Hiking in the Canyon." *The Guide: Grand Canyon National Park, South Rim,* vol. 19, no. 2 (November 12, 1995–March 2, 1996).

Hoffman, Malvina. *Heads and Tales.* New York: Charles Scribner's Sons, 1936.

Jongeward, David. *Weaver of Worlds.* Rochester, Vt.: Destiny Books, 1990.

Jung, C. G. *Memories, Dreams, Reflections.* Edited by Aniela Jaffé. New York: Random House, Vintage Books, 1961.

———, ed. *Man and His Symbols.* Garden City: Doubleday, Windfall Book, 1964.

Kampfe, R. Gray. "On Being Open: Seven Settings." *Sonora Review*, Milestones, 15th Anniversary Issue, 31 (Spring 1996): 97.

Kelley, H. H., and others. *Close Relationships*. New York: W. H. Freeman, 1983.

Klah, Hasteen. *Navajo Creation Myth: The Story of the Emergence*. Vol 1. Recorded by Mary C. Wheelwright. Santa Fe: Museum of Navajo Ceremonial Art, 1942.

Komp, Diane M. *Hope Springs from Mended Places*. San Francisco: HarperCollins Publishers, Zondervan, 1994.

Krutch, Joseph Wood. *Grand Canyon*. New York: William Sloane Associates, 1958.

Lawrence, D. H. *The Woman Who Rode Away*. In *The Complete Short Stories of D. H. Lawrence*. Vol. 2. New York: Viking, 1961.

Lawrence, Frieda. *Frieda Lawrence: The Memoirs and Correspondence*. Edited by E. W. Tedlock, Jr. New York: Alfred A. Knopf, 1964.

———. *Not I, but the Wind*. New York: Viking Press, 1934.

Leman, Kevin. *The Birth Order Book: Why You Are the Way You Are*. New York: Dell Publishing, 1985.

Lenzkes, Susan. *When Life Takes What Matters*. Grand Rapids, Mich.: Discovery House Publishers, 1993.

Lindbergh, Anne Morrow. *Gift from the Sea*. New York: Random House, Pantheon Books, 1955.

Little, Charles. *The Dying of the Trees*. New York: Viking, 1995.

Lowe, John. *Edward James: A Surrealist Life*. London: William Collins, 1991.

Luhan, Mabel. *Lorenzo in Taos*. New York: Alfred A. Knopf, 1932.

———. *Winter in Taos*. Denver: Sage Books, 1935.

Lyon, Thomas J. *Frank Waters*. New York: Twayne Publishers, 1973.

Mails, Thomas E. *Fools Crow: Wisdom of Power*. Garden City: Doubleday, 1979.

McLuhan, T. C. *The Way of the Earth*. New York: Simon & Schuster, Touchstone, 1994.

Mertz, Henriette. *The Wine Dark Sea*. Chicago: Henriette Mertz, 1964.

Meryman, Richard. "The Wyeth Family: American Visions." *National Geographic*, vol. 180, no. 1 (July 1991): 78–109.

Miller, Arthur. *After the Fall*. New York: Viking Press, 1964.

Milton, John R., ed. *Conversations with Frank Waters.* Chicago: Swallow Press, Sage Books, 1971.

Momaday, N. Scott. *The Man Made of Words.* New York: St. Martin's Press, 1997.

Morrill, Claire. *A Taos Mosaic.* Albuquerque: University of New Mexico Press. 1973

Noble, David. "A New 'American Classic.'" *Santa Fe Reporter,* June 21–27, 1995.

Paulden, Jenna. "Sacred Oak." *Frank Waters Foundation Newsletter,* vol. 4, no. 9 (April–July 1996): 6.

Passenger Department of the Santa Fe, ed. *The Grand Canyon of Arizona.* Chicago: Passenger Department of the Santa Fe, 1906.

Peterson, Roger Tory. *A Field Guide to Western Birds.* 2d. ed. Boston: Houghton Mifflin, 1941.

Priestley, J. B. *Midnight on the Desert.* New York: Harper & Brothers Publishers, 1937.

Rinpoche, Soygal. *The Tibetan Book of Living and Dying.* Edited by Patrick Gaffney and Andrew Harvey. San Francisco: HarperCollins Publishers, 1992.

Romero-Oak, Judy. "A Jewel That Attracts Those of Good Heart." *Taos News. Summer Visitors' Guide,* 1987.

Rubenstein, Arthur. *My Young Days.* New York: Alfred A. Knopf, 1973.

Ruderman, Judith. *D. H. Lawrence and the Devouring Mother: The Search for a Patriarchal Ideal of Leadership.* Durham: Duke University Press, 1984.

Sagar, Keith, ed. *D. H. Lawrence and New Mexico.* Salt Lake City: Gibbs M. Smith, Peregrine Smith, 1982.

———. *The Life of D. H. Lawrence.* London: Eyre Methuen, 1980.

Salter, Christopher L. "New Views of Space: The Los Angeleno Use of Landscape as Therapy." *South Dakota Review,* vol. 18, nos. 1–2 (spring-summer 1981).

Sanford, John A. *The Invisible Partners.* New York: Paulist Press, 1980.

Schele, Linda, and Peter Mathews. *The Code of Kings.* New York: Scribner, 1998.

Siegel, Bernie S. *Love, Medicine and Miracles.* New York: Harper & Row Publishers, Perennial Library, 1988.

Silko, Leslie Marmon. *Yellow Woman and a Beauty of the Spirit.* New York: Simon & Shuster, 1996.

Simmons, Marc. *Witchcraft in the Southwest.* Lincoln: University of Nebraska Press, Bison Book, 1980.

Stegner, Wallace. *The Sound of Mountain Water.* Lincoln: University of Nebraska Press, Bison Book, 1985.

———. *Where the Bluebird Sings to the Lemonade Springs.* New York: Random House, 1992.

Stevens, Barry. *Don't Push the River.* Lafayette, Calif.: Real People Press, 1970.

Storm, Hyemeyohsts. *Seven Arrows.* New York: Harper & Row Publishers, 1972.

Talbot, Michael. *The Holographic Universe.* New York: HarperCollins Publishers, 1991.

Tanner, Terence A. *Frank Waters: A Bibliography.* Glenwood, Ill.: Meyerbooks, 1983.

Thomas, Caitlin. *Caitlin: Life with Dylan Thomas.* New York: Henry Holt, 1986.

Torres, Larry. "Interview with Waters Remembered." *Taos News,* June 15, 1995.

———. "Jose de Gracia Gonzales: A Re-discovered Treasure." *Taos News,* October 19, 1995.

———. "Presentamos el mapa historic de Arroyo Seco." *Taos News,* January 25, 1996.

Tresan, David I. "The Analyst's Anima: Its Implications for Analysis." Unpublished chapter presented at Ghost Ranch Conference for Jungian Analysts and Candidates, 1990, Abiquiu, N.M. Quoting C. G. Jung in "C. G. Jung Speaking," recorded interview, edited by McGuire and Hull.

Vargas Llosa, Mario. *The Cubs and Other Stories.* New York: Harper & Row Publishers, 1977.

Waters, Frank. *Below Grass Roots.* New York: Liveright Publishing, 1937.

———. *Book of the Hopi.* New York: Viking Press, 1963.

———. *Brave Are My People.* Athens: Ohio University Press, Swallow Press, 1998.

———. *The Colorado.* Rivers of America Series. New York: Rinehart, 1946.

———. *The Dust Within the Rock.* New York: Liveright Publishing, 1940.

———. *Fever Pitch*. New York: Horace Liveright, 1930.

———. *Flight from Fiesta*. Santa Fe: Rydal Press, 1986.

———. *Leon Gaspard*. Flagstaff, Ariz.: Northland Press, 1964.

———. *The Lizard Woman*. Reprint with a foreword by Frank Waters. Austin: Thorp Springs Press, 1984.

———. *The Man Who Killed the Deer*. Denver: University of Denver Press, 1942.

———. *Masked Gods*. 2d. ed. Denver: Sage Books, 1950.

———. *Mexico Mystique*. Chicago: Swallow Press, Sage Books, 1975.

———. *Midas of the Rockies*. 3d ed. Chicago: Swallow Press, Sage Books, 1972.

———. *Mountain Dialogues*. Athens: Ohio University Press, Sage/Swallow Press, 1981.

———. "Notes on Los Angeles." *South Dakota Review*, vol. 18, nos. 1–2 (spring–summer 1981): 14–23.

———. *Of Time and Change*. Denver: MacMurray & Beck, 1998.

———. *People of the Valley*. New York: Farrar & Rinehart, 1941.

———. *Pike's Peak*. Athens: Ohio University Press, Swallow Press, 1987.

———. *Pumpkin Seed Point*. Chicago: Swallow Press, Sage Books, 1969.

———. *To Possess the Land*. Chicago: Swallow Press, Sage Books, 1973.

———. *The Wild Earth's Nobility*. New York: Liveright Publishing, 1935.

———. *The Woman at Otowi Crossing*. Chicago: Swallow Press, Sage Books, 1966.

———. *The Yogi of Cockroach Court*. New York: Rinehart, 1947.

Wendel, Paul. *Father Kneipps Health Teachings*. Brooklyn: Dr. Paul Wendel, 1947.

Wilcox, Joan Parisi, and Elizabeth B. Jenkins. "Journey to Q'ollorit'i: Initiation into Andean Mysticism." *Shaman's Drum*, no. 40 (winter 1996): 34–49.

Wilder, Mitchell L., and Edgar Breitenbach. *Santos: The Religious Folk Art of New Mexico*. New York: Hacker Art Books, 1976.

Wilson, N. R., ed. *The Joys of Christmas*. New York: William Morrow, 1988.

Wongar, B. *Karan*. New York: Dodd, Mead, 1985.

Woodman, Marion. *The Ravaged Bridegroom*. Toronto: Inner City Books, 1990.

Zwinger, Ann. *Aspen*. Salt Lake City: Gibbs Smith, Peregrine Smith Books, 1991.